Dark before Daybreak

DARK BEFORE DAYBREAK

Earnestine Rodgers Robinson
and Todd V. Robinson

WordText Publisher

Copyright © 2018 by WordText Publisher LLC.

All rights reserved. International copyright secured. No part of this book may be reproduced or transmitted in any form or by any means including photocopying and recording without the permission in writing from the Publisher. For more information, address Robro LLC, P.O. Box 1021, Memphis, Tennessee, 38101-1021.

Printed in the United States of America

Managing Editor: Cheryle R. Jackson
Copyediting: Michelle R. McKissack
Cover and Book Design: Todd V. Robinson

ISBN: 0988655284

ISBN-13: 978-0-9886552-8-7

TRIBUTE

A special tribute is due to my husband, Charles Robinson:
For all of the love, support and inspiration that he gave to me, encouraging me to always continue in my God-ordained work.

DEDICATION

To my children, Todd, Cheryle, Craig, Michelle and Gaius:
Special thanks for all of the sacrifices and for your unyielding support and contributions.

CONTENTS

1	Coming of Age	1
2	My Hometown	5
3	Crossroads	7
4	Born with a Purpose	19
5	Going up North	29
6	Twist of Fate	45
7	Chicago	61
8	Welcome Back to the Old South	81
9	A Gift from God	93
10	Uphill Journey	103
11	Sounds of a Miracle	113
12	Vanishing Hope	123
13	Rebirth of Purpose	135
14	Battle on Many Fronts	151
15	No Rest for the Weary	165
16	Leap of Faith	179
17	The First Victory	199
18	Center Stage	221
19	A Time of Crises	231
20	Triumph in Prague	253
21	Dark before Daybreak	269
22	Secret of My Success	285

Chapter 1

Coming of Age

D aybreak is and has always been a special time for me. Whether it was the inviting embrace of the morning light starting its ascent over a distant horizon or the early illumination piercing its way through the barely visible slits of my bedroom curtains, the meaning was the same—the promise of a new day. The first light of dawn enthralls me with the hopeful arrival of something new, something good. But there is one ironic twist, an inescapable fact that I could never ignore: the morning is always its darkest before dawn.

Lying in my bed, waiting painstakingly in the dark for the first light to signal the start of morning was when time seemed to drag out endlessly, creeping along without any hint of relief. My mind, fully awake, would race ahead and attempt to accomplish every task on my list, but the darkness firmly anchored my reality to my bed. And while part of me was anxious for the darkness to pass, I often used this quiet solitude to pray and reflect.

During these moments of contemplation, I often thought about my purpose in life. My mind would invariably drift over my past, recounting the ups and downs. It was easy to separate the passage of time into convenient parcels of good days and bad days or to simply label past experiences as pleasant or unrequited. But life is never that simple and its lessons are far more complicated than the sum of its parts.

Embracing the good in the light of day is natural and rewarding; but the dark brooding times…that's a different matter. For years, I had lumped every failure and disappointment into the usual pile of difficult memories. Whenever those memories resurfaced, I would either mentally replay them till I could no longer tolerate the familiar sting or glance over them to avoid the discomfort. This was my state of affairs as my trials and tribulations in life continued to mount. Yet, interestingly, my plight of disappointments and mishaps did not breed the bitterness that may have been expected; instead, something else happened.

Somewhere along my journey I began to look past my problems, past the darkness and see my hardships with a different perspective. Maybe, the closed doors of rejection were really detours to open doors of opportunity, or the perceived failures were actually corrections that directed me to the right path of success. Then, it became clear. Every financial and cultural obstacle that I had encountered in my quest to fulfill my dream was not just a hindrance; it was a valuable commodity, a required element that was needed to propel me and strengthen my resolve. In this light, failure and success were not existential enemies of one another; they were symbiotically linked together as strands in the thread of life and success.

So, for those who doubt and want proof of this type of "coming of age," all they need to do is look at my life.

Chapter 2

My Hometown

Away from the illustrious concert stages of Carnegie Hall and Europe where I would eventually bow in triumph, there was Memphis, Tennessee, my birthplace. A river town, nestled on a small bluff above the Mississippi River and geographically wedged between the states of Mississippi and Arkansas, Memphis in 1938, at the time of my birth, was worlds away from my future. Composing classical music is not the most likely career that one would expect to come out of the Deep South. Such a career choice is unimaginable when you consider that I grew up during an era blighted with despair in the midst of segregation. Yet, it happened to me.

    Freshly scarred by the influenza pandemic and the Great Depression, Memphis was still caught in the hypnotic haze of the antebellum South. People, who were old enough to have spent most of their adult lives before I was born, talked about an existence that sounded dismal. They often spoke of seeing lines of colored men drenched in sweat, pulling bales of cotton off of riverboats and barges at the downtown harbor. Their faces were stained with the despair of the past and frozen with the emptiness of their destiny. Even the hot, humid air surrounding their bodies, lazily hanged and drifted – waiting for a breeze of change. But they knew better; after all, they were living in the heart of Dixie, and things were not changing. Memphis was surrounded by hundreds of miles of nothing but cotton fields, which, at that time, strategically crowned Memphis, the world's largest cotton producer. Cotton was king, and there was little chance of anything else for Negroes. Yes, this was Memphis, my hometown at the time when I was born.

    Lying on the outskirts of the city was a segregated community called Douglass, named after the famous statesman and former slave, Frederick Douglass. This small neighborhood was surrounded by a complex of cotton mills and rubber tree work plants which created an industrial moat that seemed to further isolate the tiny cluster of homes and unpaved streets from the outside world. It was here that my journey started and almost ended in death just as it was beginning.

Chapter 3

Crossroads

My family history is primarily an oral one. There is nothing written down. All knowledge about my past kin is the result of folklore, in which stories told by my parents and other relatives have been pieced together to form the fabric of my genealogy. My roots have never been traced back to some faraway land, nor do I claim that any part of my lineage stems from a famous person, but I do know from stories passed down that my background is a woven tapestry that is both uniquely and distinctly American. The ethnicity of my ancestors is a kaleidoscope of African, European and Native American bloodlines that have been mixed with the influence of slavery and segregation and blended into the single cultural entity of American Black. This is my legacy.

Hailing almost exclusively from the Deep South within the states of Tennessee, Mississippi and Arkansas, my family's settlement and pilgrimage from one state to another was largely determined by calamity. In the early 1900s, my paternal grandparents were sharecroppers in Mississippi, and my grandfather, called "Grandpappy" by all of his grandchildren, was a gentle man who was very devoted to his family. He was also the pastor of a small church, and most of his members worked alongside him on the same plantation. They picked cotton, a job that was not for the fainthearted. It was a laborious task that required one's back to be bent and stooped over while dragging a heavy sack. From first light to sundown, this awkward position was maintained as you moved down long planted rows where you teased cotton bolls away from the thorny clutches of a plant that sometimes left your fingers torn and bleeding; and, this was all done under the sweltering heat of the Mississippi sun.

It was a grueling life, but in those days, people like my grandparents endured the misery with little complaint. However, there is a breaking point, and on one particular day it happened with Grandpappy. While working in the cotton field, his wife, who was pregnant at the time, sat down on the ground, grimacing in pain. It was generally understood that it was never acceptable to stop working unless told to do so by the overseer, but the pain in her body had become so great that my grandmother had to stop at the end of her cotton row to rest and rub her stomach. Showing no compassion and seeing her behavior as insolent, the overseer, a white man, jumped off of his horse and began to demand that my grandmother return to work. Despite her sitting in the dirt in obvious pain, the overseer was relentless in his demand and his anger began to grow. Worrying about what was going to happen next, Grandpappy began to plead that he would do his work plus hers, but his pleas fell on deaf ears. Then, somewhere between the rage and their yelling, it happened. The overseer began to kick my grandmother, calling her lazy and demanding her to get up. Within moments of watching his crying wife and their unborn child receiving this type of cruelty, Grandpappy snapped and instinctively lashed out. The fight did not last long, but when it was finished, the white man was lying on the ground – unconscious.

No one knows how long it took for the horror to sink into the faces of those who witnessed this, but it was a universal fact that regardless of the circumstances, any black man who struck a white man in Mississippi was as good as dead. There would be no inquiry, no trial, only a lynching. Knowing this, my grandfather immediately grabbed his wife and the rest of his family and fled into the nearby woods. They stopped for nothing: no belongings, no clothes, no money; they ran for their lives. During those days, horse and buggy was the most common means of travel but that mode of transportation was too slow to make their getaway. Aided by a clandestine network of Masons, my grandparents with their young children hopped a freight train under the cover of night and escaped Mississippi.

With the sunrise, they found themselves in Arkansas, and even though they had gotten away, reprisal was a looming and constant fear. As a result, neither Grandpappy nor the rest of the family talked much about the terror of that day, and that fear did not fade with the passage of time.

Growing up, I was never allowed to set foot on Mississippi soil. Daddy never took us to Mississippi to visit relatives or even to attend a funeral of a relative. As a child, I could never remember the word "Mississippi" being mentioned without utter trepidation.

Although being partly shrouded in secrecy, the stories surrounding my grandparents on my father's side were colorful, grand events, which seemed to come to life every time someone talked about them. Unfortunately, I never got a chance to know my mother's parents. Both had passed away before I was born. But what I do remember is based entirely on stories Momma and my older siblings told me, and from these recounted tales, the one person that stood legendarily in my imagination was my maternal grandmother, Lizanne. Anyone who had ever met her always talked about her beauty. She had long black hair and an appearance that was both physically striking and quietly captivating. Walking down the street, it was hard for anyone not to notice her, but among her grandchildren, it was her inner beauty and quiet compassion that made her an alluring favorite. The way she showered all of her grandchildren with love and her surprises of fresh-baked cookies, wrapped in linen napkins, made her a hero. However, most of the other recounted tales involving her were usually filled with hardships.

In 1910, she gave birth to my mother, Euber Bolton, when life was peaceful for her, but by 1918, things had turned. The flu outbreak had grabbed the country and ravaged both her community and her home. According to my mother, there was not a household that did not experience death. It was during this time that my grandmother lost her husband and oldest daughter. Struggling and looking for a fresh start, she decided to move to Arkansas where her oldest son, Buddy, lived. Her choice to leave Memphis must have been a difficult one for she worried that access to schools for her children would not be as good in Arkansas. Also, she was leaving behind a very important commodity – land. James Bolton, her late husband and my maternal grandfather, was the son of a slave who worked on a vast plantation near Memphis. Hoboken plantation, as it was called then, was owned by Wade H. Bolton who was also a partner in one of the largest cotton and slave trading firms in the South. Upon his death, the prominent landowner, in a will, gave land to his former slaves who had been recently freed by the Civil War. The bequeathed land was choice real estate; even to this day, that very same plantation extends into the northern part of the metro Memphis area and is home to shopping centers, housing developments and schools. Despite the promise of wealth and land ownership, Lizanne left Memphis and everything else with it. She only brought her two young children, Chester and Euber, and her granddaughter, Coless (the child of her recently deceased daughter) who she was now raising as her own. Once in Arkansas, they settled in the small farming community of Gilmore and joined a local church, pastored by "Grandpappy," my paternal grandfather, who had also established roots in the same town after his escape from Mississippi.

    Grandpappy had seven children that included one daughter whom he doted over, and six sons whom he also loved but who he also commonly referred to as "ruffians." By today's standards it wouldn't sound like much, but the problem was that the boys led so-called "flashy lifestyles." They did not go to church as often as Grandpappy would have liked which meant going to church through the week and twice on Sundays. They also liked to play baseball, and that meant games on Sunday evenings, which was the main reason why they missed church. Though Grandpappy wasn't thrilled about their comings and goings, it was this very same behavior that made his sons, including my father, James Everett Rodgers, very popular, especially with the ladies. With his charisma, rugged good looks and his travels around the region as a pitcher on a team in the Negro Baseball circuit, it was only natural that women across the state would often swoon and fall for my father.

Despite all the women that Daddy met, there was one young lady back at home that had captured his attention and his heart – my mother, Euber Bolton. She was also a member at Grandpappy's church, and it was not long before my father started to openly court her. And this is where the problem started. Grandpappy did not like this one bit. Despite James being his own son, he felt that his son was not good enough for my mother, a young lady whom he esteemed as a faithful member and good Christian, and now, one of his ruffian sons was courting her. He was not standing for it. Even with his objection, he probably knew that his son would not listen to him. So, Grandpappy told my mother that if she married a "rank sinner" like his son, he would "turn her out of the church." Somewhat distraught by the dilemma, my father, who had by this time fallen in love, asked his own mother what to do. Without hesitation she said, "Marry her." Well, my father asked for my mother's hand in marriage, and Grandpappy did as he said he would do; he threw my mother out of the church but not in some physical or dramatic fashion. He simply no longer considered her a church member in good standing. But, shortly thereafter, he invited her back into the church. It was only natural since he was the one who married them in the first place – Christmas Day, 1928.

The newlyweds settled into the rural farming community of Gilmore where they had grown up. During those early years, the Great Depression made life even more difficult and challenging. Each day was faced with hard work and abbreviated rest. Each year, they planted seed, harvested crops and struggled to survive; and with the passing of time, the family grew one child at a time. Despite the challenges, my parents had fallen into the cadence of the world surrounding them, keeping the natural rhythm of the rise and fall of the sun over their cultivated fields. Everything was in harmony until the flood of 1937.

By historical accounts, the Great Flood of 1937 was described as record-breaking and epic, but from the stories told by my people, it was life altering. The beginning of the flood seemed innocuous at its onset and was simply mentioned as inches on a water gauge, but the Ohio River, which is one of the main tributaries that merges into the Mississippi River, soon became engorged with rains and melting snow from the North. With little warning, the expanding water quickly grew and developed into a monstrous being, giving birth to a flood and spewing destruction in its reach. Delivering its swollen contents downstream through its watery tentacles, levies were quickly smashed, and sandbags were washed away like sediment down a sewer. While the rising flood was relentless in its destruction, there was yet another element that was insidious in its havoc; it was the daily freezing rain which was sporadically mixed with snow and sleet that added to the misery, a misery that started in December and continued through January. With each day, the massive flood grew in its devastation as it leveled entire communities and towns in Kentucky, Arkansas, Tennessee, and nine other states. For miles, there was no sanitation, no roads, no telephone wires, and no electricity...only frigid water. People, who waited for the water to recede, soon became trapped on their roofs or had their fate sealed in a watery grave.

The situation was critical by the time my parents and their four children escaped. They had to leave their house by boat, and according to my oldest sister, Odesser, the only thing that they managed to salvage was one bed. The entire family, both immediate and extended, fled the flood in Arkansas to higher ground in Memphis, Tennessee. There in a small house on the outskirts of the city, my parents, grandparents, uncles, aunts and all their children took refuge. At night, the floor became a carpet of sleeping people as the house became packed with several families, waiting out the flood. Finally, in February, as the waters receded, people began to filter back to their homes in Arkansas, looking to salvage the fragments of their former lives, and in the midst of this upheaval, I was born on Ground Hog's day, February 2, 1938.

It was also during this time that my father came to a crossroads of choosing between the familiarity of rural living and the unforeseen potential of city life in Memphis. The recent calamity had exposed the fragility of his previous existence and, now, the financial responsibility of a growing family had brought his dilemma into sharp focus. Returning to Arkansas was the safe choice but only guaranteed the basics and staying in Memphis was a risk into a world of unknown but also with unparalleled potential. Although the immediate circumstances around him looked bleak, my father embraced hope. With a leap of faith, he decided to stay in Memphis and put down roots in the small community of Douglass, seeking a different future, one that was more promising than being a sharecropper.

Settling into Memphis was an incredible and daunting task—a large family with no money, no job, and no possessions except for the clothes on their backs. But after experiencing the trials and tribulations of sharecropping, surviving the Depression, and escaping the Flood, I think my parents viewed starting a new life in Memphis as just another hurdle that they would overcome. Daddy soon found work at the nearby rubber plant and my mother, who was an excellent cook, sold fried apple turnovers to the men at the plant. But this was not enough. His family was growing in size, and the house that they had moved into was too small. While a large family was an asset on a farm, it was an entirely different matter in the city. Despite his hard work, it was not enough. He needed a trade, a business of his own.

With the mounting responsibilities and shrinking resources, his back was pressed firmly against a wall of desperation. It was his defining moment; he had to make a decision. According to my mother, it was during that time that her "rank sinner" husband turned his life over to Christ and started to trust Him for everything. Praying for an answer to his problems, the solution presented itself out of necessity. He remodeled our house, eventually adding a second story, and sometime during this remodeling and other small construction jobs, he realized that he had an innate ability in reading blueprints and a talent with numbers. Both of my parents had attended high school (which was an unusual feat for blacks at that time), and although my father was industrious, he didn't have any previous training or apprenticeship in construction. Nevertheless, his acumen for his new trade came with ease, and he began to use money from smaller construction jobs to buy and develop plots of land. Momma said that by the time they had seven children, Daddy owned seven lots, one for each of his children. With time, the growing reputation of his skills and integrity brought him a partnership with Mr. Henley, a white man who was a contractor. Within the span of ten years, Daddy had gone from being a sharecropper to owning his company and helping to build subdivisions. His dedication did not just lie with his family but extended to the community; not only did he hire men from the neighborhood, but he also taught the construction business to others, who eventually started their own businesses, thereby strengthening the community.

During this time, Daddy was also involved in the community as a minister and assistant pastor of a neighborhood church, but he quickly became pastor of Homeland Church of God in Christ. Shortly, after becoming pastor, he became deeply concerned about the condition of the church building. Momma said that Daddy felt condemned every time that he drove up to the church in his new car, with his new house and saw the Lord's house in dire need of repairs. After a struggle, he convinced the deacons that a new building was needed, and in 1953, Daddy rebuilt the church without labor costs into a modern building that remains in use today.

Although Douglass seemed isolated from the rest of the world, it was a great place to grow up. The narrow-graveled streets encircled homes that were close in proximity to one another but housed neighbors who were even closer. During the evenings in the summertime, the adults would sit on their porches, watch their small children chase lightning bugs, and engage in conversation with anyone who walked past them. My sister, Doris, would tell the story how she sometimes dreaded walking down the street and having to greet everyone in the process. "How ya do? Good evening. How are you?" were the types of salutations that continued all the way down the street, and each individual would wait for you to speak. A house could not be passed without conversation about the weather or questions about our parents or something school-related. She said that if you mistakenly forgot something and went back home, the salutations would start all over again as you returned.

Besides the door-to-door dissemination of information, everyone knew that the neighborhood store was the main hub for exchanging news and stories. Though Daddy had built the store, he rented it to Mr. McGary in exchange for a monthly fee. However, because the store was so close to our home, my mother would often send my siblings and me for items, which we charged to our account; and, naturally, my siblings and I would always add candy and soda to the list. As a result, my mother once said, "James never got a dime from the store. We ate up the profits." But she full well knew that the real money came from the rent he collected from the apartment over the store.

Chapter 4

Born with a Purpose

When I was young, one of my favorite outings was going to Crawfordsville, Arkansas to visit my mother's only brother, Uncle Chester, and his family who lived and farmed there. During these trips, the excitement that my siblings and I felt was barely containable, but this excitement was in direct contrast to the boring terrain of what we saw when looking out the window of the car. There was nothing to see, only flat land

and a tree line in the distance that seemed to disappear into the background. In fact, the only exciting features about the region were the interesting names of the nearby towns – Marked Tree, Three Forks and Promised Land. The land itself was nothing but an expanse of cotton and soybean fields, a landscape that looked bleak with its endless monotony, but in spirit, it was much more than the sparse topography; it was the land of my people and in my mind as a child, that meant hanging out and playing with cousins.

For decades, my ancestors had cultivated their lives as farmers. It was not only a place where they planted and harvested but also where they laughed and worshipped. It was a place where they overcame struggles and shared hope. As a result, this land was the legacy of my kin, and even though my parents had moved to Memphis, our frequent visits back to Arkansas were always something we looked forward to and cherished. However, there was one part of the trip that we all dreaded – the crossing of the Mississippi River on the Harahan Bridge, a bridge that still stands today and looks even scarier now.

At that time, the Harahan Bridge was the only bridge that crossed the Mississippi River between Memphis and Arkansas, and it stretched nearly one mile. It was originally built as a railroad bridge with a single narrow lane on each side of the train tracks for car travel. Even though its frame was made of steel, the bridge looked frail as it was covered in rust, and the lanes that cars drove across were comprised only of wooden planks bolted to the steel frame. Of course, the perceived notion of the bridge being dangerous was further enhanced by an incident that happened years earlier when one of the car lanes had to be repaired after it was destroyed in a mysterious fire.

Normally, whenever we took trips in the car, there was a struggle, or should I say a fight, among my siblings as to who would get the window seats. But this was never the case during the crossings of that bridge. Even my brother, Hick, who was the most daring of the group would sit glued to his seat, watching the large iron support beams whizz by our car windows. As children, we all knew that the only thing below us was nothing but muddy water. But that was not the scary part. Every now and then you would find yourself caught on the bridge at the same time when a train was crossing it. The large locomotive and freight cars roared past us within several feet of our car, seemingly within arm's reach, bellowing out a deafening noise and gusts of wind that would cause the entire bridge to shriek and shake, forcing our car to bounce and skip along the planks. No one talked.

My mother would often tease us saying, "They don't even allow cats to walk across the bridge because they would make the whole thing shake." Her comment didn't make a whole lot of sense, but we were scared all the more. Along the entire length of the bridge, we would stare back and forth between the train and Daddy's grip on the vibrating steering wheel, and everyone knew that waiting more than a hundred feet below us was the mighty, muddy Mississippi River. That was the Harahan Bridge; and my childhood memories of it increased as I got older; and its legend was kept alive with the tales of my siblings and cousins on how they, in their imagination, faced death repeatedly during their crossings.

With a childlike excitement, my mother always looked forward to the trips to Arkansas to visit her brother. She loved the country and would, on occasion, talk about how she rode horses bareback as a little girl and how she enjoyed going fishing. My mother was an attractive woman with a small frame, small eyes and high, prominent cheekbones. She wasn't big on chitchat and was known for her one-liner answers to any situation or question; however, she thought deeply and observed much. Nature with its surroundings seemed to communicate to her keen senses as she had a poetic way of looking at the ordinary in life. I recall on one occasion she said that the trees were praising God on a hot summer day when a gentle wind came along, rustling a cool, fresh breeze causing the leaves to wave back and forth like lifted hands. Then, when the crickets would seem to sing extra loud in August, she would tell us, "They're chirping their last serenade of the season. Summer's almost gone, and fall is just around the corner." My maternal grandmother, Lizanne, said that my mother inherited those special traits from her grandfather who was Native-American and from her grandmother who was African.

Sometimes my father couldn't make the trip to Arkansas, so Uncle Chester would come to pick us up. On one fateful trip when I was just a toddler, the visit was cut short. I'm told that after drinking water from a well, I became ill, developed diarrhea and my health rapidly deteriorated. My mother abruptly ended her stay and Uncle Chester quickly returned us back to Memphis where we went straight to John Gaston Hospital. News of my mother taking me to the hospital was huge, and everyone in my extended family on both sides of the Mississippi River was talking about it. Part of the reason for the uproar was that rarely anyone in my family, or the neighborhood for that matter, went to the doctor. Any fever, cuts, or minor ailments usually were nursed and prayed for by our parents. But when a doctor was called in, that usually meant that someone was either seriously ill or near death, and word had gotten out that I was rushed to the doctor. The news created widespread alarm in everyone from relatives to neighbors to church members, and they all offered their prayers. This type of response was a common reaction; it was a call to arms.

Prayer was a universal tool used to deal with the harsh realities of life, and my situation was becoming dire.

According to my mother, the doctor at the hospital simply wrote a prescription for me and sent me home. But as she tended to me day and night, administering the medicine, life continued to fade from my body. She said that I had stopped eating and would barely open my eyes when she spoke or held me. As I lay listless in her lap, my chest panting and my lips turning blue, she broke down in tears and turned to my father, "James, take her. I can't stand watching the last breath go out of her." After handing me to Daddy, she left home in the middle of the night and went over to my Aunt Ruth's house who lived in our neighborhood. Momma said that she left walking, almost running, but expecting someone to run after her to deliver the inevitable news. Instead, my aunt, knowing her grievous situation, greeted her at the front door with a glimmer of hope.

"Eu-bah, I've been praying, and the Lord has said to me that your baby is going to live, and that He has a special purpose for her life."

I don't know the exact events that took place that night, but the next morning, when my mother went home and walked into her bedroom, she was astonished to find my limp, pale body, her baby, still faintly breathing.

"James...you mean, she's yet hanging on?"

My father sitting at the foot of the bed, answered in his usual calm demeanor. "I've been praying, and the Lord has instructed me to change doctors."

His words were always delivered with a soothing effect. Some people said that his calm demeanor was due to his clergy position of being a pastor. However, most people, who closely knew my father, said that he had always been a gentle and sincere person who seemed to season and ripen more after becoming a minister. Physically, he had a bold appearance. Standing well above six feet, his broad and thick shoulders rested on top of a muscular body that had been crafted by years of playing baseball and farming. Daddy, who was often called "Red" because of his fair complexion, had strong facial features and a gait that reflected confidence. Yet, there was one characteristic about him that everyone noted – his aura, which seemed to both command respect and placate those around him.

At the apex of my near-death experience, my mother said that she and my father sat motionless on the bed, not talking, but quietly praying until the new doctor arrived. His name was Dr. Brawner and he was colored. That's what black people were called back then. Dr. Brawner had delivered me in the same house, just over a year ago, where now I lay sick unto death. After he had finished examining me and the medicine bottle, he came to a quick conclusion, "Reverend, it's not the sickness that's killing her, it's the medicine. It's too strong for her. One more dose and she would be dead." Needless to say, the medicine was stopped, and I recovered.

I was the fifth of eleven children. My mother always said that she had three sets of children with the first child in the first group being born in 1929 and the youngest child of the last group was born in 1955. When I was a teenager, I was the oldest child living at home, so I think that made me the oldest of the second group. This hierarchy was important as your status within the pecking order was determined by the group that you were born in; my older brothers and sisters in the first group commanded orders with my younger siblings and me being on the receiving end. The oldest, James, Jr., was followed by Odesser, Dorothy Mae and Hick who was two years older than me. Everyone called James, Jr. by his nickname, "Coonie," because he was an avid hunter of rabbits and raccoons, but it was Odesser who was the "real boss." When she gave a command, it was law, and all the siblings universally respected her authority.

Growing up in a large family provided much excitement, and of course, there were lessons to be learned. One such lesson occurred when Coonie and Odesser were in the kitchen on a Sunday night while my parents were at church. In fact, it seems that most of the unexpected things usually occurred on this particular night of the week when the older siblings were left in charge to watch the younger ones. I remember on one occasion, that everyone was sitting in the kitchen while Coonie was cleaning my Daddy's rifle. Engrossed with the handling of the rifle, he repeatedly opened it, checked the gun barrel, and closed it. Then, with concentrated precision, he would slowly aim around the kitchen past the children, and with an imaginary squeeze of the trigger, he would say, "Bang!" Then, he would lean back into his chair, smiling with satisfaction, and repeat the whole process. I was mesmerized with his seemingly masterful use of the gun and the play action of his hunting skills. With each movement, I followed his gaze, tracking his aim, pretending we were on a hunt...waiting for his lips to say, "Bang." However, I did not realize that my younger siblings were also captivated by this scene until my older sister, Odesser, yelled at Coonie.

"Boy! Are you crazy? Stop pointing that gun at people!"

Coonie snapped back, "I know what I'm doing. Besides, this gun ain't loaded."

"Just the same, don't point it at anyone," Odesser exclaimed.

Even though Odesser was younger than Coonie, she had this motherly wit and an authoritative way of barking an order that made you take notice, but Coonie was reluctant to acquiesce to her demand.

"I'll prove that there're no bullets in this rifle," he said, and then pointed the gun to the floor and squeezed the trigger, "BANG!" blowing a hole in the floor. We all jumped and stared at the gun and the hole in the floor in disbelief. It was at that time that I learned from an early age – don't play with guns.

Of course, all the lessons learned were not always as shocking. Most of them usually stemmed from practical jokes or ridicule that was often masterminded by my brother Hick, the fourth oldest. He rarely targeted Coonie or Odesser but everyone else was fair and frequent game. Growing up, we had this tradition in our home at Christmastime where the kids would each decorate their own personal box that Daddy would fill with goodies on Christmas Eve. On one early and warm morning, Hick woke me up along with two of my other siblings, Doris Jean and Jonathan, who were younger than me.

"Wake up! Wake up! It's Christmas! Hurry! It's Christmas! Come and see your boxes!"

Confused and half dazed with sleep in our eyes, we quickly believed that it was Christmas and started jumping up and down with joy. Running behind my brother and screaming with excitement, we ran into the room to find boxes. As we collapsed in front of them, our happiness was soon shattered to see the boxes filled with nothing but rocks. Of course, my brother was rolling on the floor, laughing hysterically at us. I remembered feeling numb and stupid. We were so ashamed that he had fooled us, especially since we knew that it was...summertime. But we were young, half awake and half wishing that it were truly Christmas. Lesson learned that day: don't be so gullible.

Despite the occasional perils of having older siblings, I had a good childhood, and the wonderful memories of my early years are ever before me. In fact, there is one specific memory that stands out as one of my most cherished and one that could easily be considered prophetic. It happened when I was very young. I would often stand in front of the kitchen cabinet, which had a pullout metal slab. Normally, it was used to prepare food, but in my imaginary world as a child, it was a piano. I would sing and hum a tune and pretend that I was playing the piano as my fingers danced across the invisible keys. This activity was such a frequent practice of mine that it was largely ignored by my family, and when I was immersed in my piano playing, I also ignored the world around me. During one of these impromptu concerts, a stranger was at our house. It was common for people conducting business in our neighborhood to stop by and ask to use our phone. We were one of a few homes that had telephone service. As a result, insurance agents, policemen and the like would spot the telephone poles and follow the wire to our house. During one such occasion while one of those familiar strangers used our phone, I was singing and playing my pretend piano, oblivious to my surroundings, but my concentration was broken when the stranger asked me, "Do you play the piano?" Startled by his interruption, I softly responded, "No," and continued to play in my imaginary world.

Chapter 5

Going up North

It was the 1950s, and if you were black, regardless of your wealth, career or position in the community, public policy afforded you few choices. It was a way of life; and it was called segregation, which, in theory, was described as "separate but equal," but in reality, it was restricted access to everything for blacks. This meant being forced to live in a few designated areas with limited selection of resources and schools. However, this institutionalized separation, known as Jim Crow laws, had a surprising effect that was largely unnoticed. By being forced to live together in one area, the differences in education and prosperity among blacks were not points of fracture. There were no socioeconomic lines that divided them; instead, blacks in those segregated and, yet, diverse areas had unknowingly forged a unity among themselves, resulting in an endearing sense of community identity.

Within our neighborhood, there were doctors, lawyers, and teachers living side-by-side with laborers, ditch-diggers, and those who were illiterate and possessed no skills. Jim Crow had brought them together, causing them to rely on one another for support while standing collectively in the quagmire of racial discrimination, hoping for a better tomorrow. No matter what his or her salary or educational level, everyone out of necessity became your parent, brother, or sister—all taking care of one another. As a result, living in Douglass was an extraordinary experience where the neighbors shared among themselves, their joys, their accomplishments, and their misfortunes—essentially, bonding together throughout their entire lives.

During one particular harsh winter, Ms. Nettles, a single parent, came to our house to ask for heating coal. She was one of our neighbors who had recently had a child and was struggling to live on a very meager existence. Of course, my parents helped her – not out of pity but out of a sense that we were all connected. As a result, the neighbors would frequently check on her and assist her in any way that they could until she got on her feet again. This was not the exception but the norm. Similar incidents occurred routinely throughout the neighborhood and frequently involved my family and others helping out because we were in a position to do so.

Another such incident that I remember dealt with the intermittent disappearance of clothes from our backyard. Because our family was so large, laundry was an enormous task that required my mother to wash often. Hanging the laundry on the clothesline in our backyard to dry, she took great pride in displaying her wash. She loved to methodically place each item in perfect alignment with clothespins that were always perpendicular to the clothesline. The entire backyard seemed to light up as the sun captured and reflected off the whites and blazing colors. Adding to the spectacle was the wind that would cause the clothing to flap with such a ferocious energy as if it were applauding its own artistic efforts. This would draw so much attention that the neighbors would often comment how they loved to see my mother hanging wash on the line. But, from time to time, some of our clothing, especially the children's clothes and blankets, would disappear. Despite the theft, no fingers were pointed, no glaring stares or allegations were made among neighbors, and even though my sisters and brothers would start to argue as to who was responsible for the theft, our parents would quickly dismiss our conversation by stating that whoever took the clothes probably needed them. That was it; nothing else was said and everybody understood. That was the unspoken and prevailing notion in Douglass: everyone helped one another. In this manner, Douglass had truly become in every sense of the word, a community. Even to this day, when I meet someone from the old neighborhood, it is as though I am meeting a family member.

This wonderful spirit was also carried over into the neighborhood school that I attended for twelve years. Although the school system was segregated, and we had to use hand-me-down and outdated books from the white schools, our teachers were dedicated and would often go beyond the call of duty in teaching us. One such teacher was Erness Bright, who was my homeroom teacher. She also taught music appreciation and was over the choir. She was academically exceptional and had enrolled in Fisk University at the young age of fifteen; and upon graduation, she became a teacher, an occupation that was considered a top position for blacks in the 1950s. Ironically, I did not gravitate toward her because of some latent desire for music but because of who she was and her enthusiasm. She had an indescribable joy when she talked about music, and when she exposed us to composers and music that were so foreign to me, I felt like I was stepping into another world. Our classroom was constantly infused with the sounds of Handel, Beethoven and Dvorak. She talked of faraway places and elaborate operas, and although it was only a music appreciation class, she demanded that we learn the rudimentary principles of how to read music. Of course, all of this was fascinating to me, but it was the persona of Erness, not music, which sparked my interest.

    She was a petite woman, bursting with energy and only seven years my senior. Since Erness was so close in age to her students, my best friend, Mattie Pearl, and I saw Erness as our contemporary, and we admired her style. I remember the first time that I saw her outside of the classroom. I was looking in store windows in downtown Memphis when someone called out my name. Startled and turning around, initially I didn't see anyone that I recognized. All I saw were white people around me, or so I thought. Then, finally, a young woman near me, playfully spoke, "Earnestine, you don't hear me speaking to you?" There she was, my music teacher, wrapped in a beautiful pastel sundress and wearing a large-brimmed straw hat with dark sunglasses. She reached out to hug me in a warm embrace and I envisioned myself being greeted by a fashion model. Truthfully, she blended right in with the crowd because she was so fair-skinned. She could have "passed" for being white. "Passing" was a concept that some light-skinned blacks did back then to escape the hardships that being colored brought during that era. But after that experience, I admired her for much more than her style.

When I told Mattie Pearl about the downtown encounter, she screamed with excitement. It was only natural that as 15-year-old girls we were caught up with Erness, especially Mattie Pearl who had a beautiful soprano voice and sang in the choir. In fact, it was Mattie Pearl, also known as M.P, who coerced me to join the glee club with her. For Mattie Pearl, music was her first love. She made it her mission to keep me up-to-date on the hottest songs from the "Hit Parade." She would never just tell me the titles of the songs. No, that would be too mundane; she had to perform every song with dramatic flair. Sometimes, she would show up at my house on Sunday afternoons in a pretty dress and petticoat. With a melodious, "Hello," she would glide through the front door and twirl into our living room, turning in circles while watching her petticoat spin until she landed softly on our sofa with outstretched arms. Then she began to sing the latest hit song. It was wonderful to watch her, and my mother enjoyed her entrances because she reminded her of a movie star. M.P. and I were inseparable. We did our homework together, talked on the phone for endless hours and even played monopoly at our favorite teacher's house, which was Erness.

With M.P. and Erness, I was constantly surrounded by musical influences; yet, despite this, I never showed an overwhelming interest in music. That's ironic because as a child, I use to pretend to bang on the keys, and then continuing into my adult years, I had this recurring dream of my playing the piano. I would only see my hands as they flowed and danced across piano keys. There was never any sound associated with the dream, just the image of my hands and the keyboard. The meaning behind the dream never occurred to me. There was never any angst associated with it, no provocation to explore something deeper. In my mind, it was just a dream, although recurring, but nonetheless only a dream. Nothing more.

Within my small world, life in Douglass was idyllic, but the other side of reality was only a few blocks away. Beyond the insular border of our community, the color of my skin automatically labeled everyone like me as a second-class citizen. However, Daddy always told us that we were made in the image of God and that qualified us as first class, equal to all and second to none, no matter how we were perceived or treated. But change was coming that would alter the status quo and forever change my neighborhood, my family and my life. Foreshadowing of this change was very subtle in the beginning and mostly ignored by me. The principal of our school would ofttimes call an impromptu assembly where he would announce among other things, "Young people, you've got to be ready when the doors for black people are opened." M.P. and I would often look at one another and remark, "He called an assembly for this?" Then, there was my father, who at breakfast one morning, read to us from the paper about the recent Supreme Court decision in Brown vs. Board of Education. He looked stunned and finally commented, "Well, it's all over with now." He knew that the old Jim Crow ways were fading away.

Despite this political and cultural upheaval that loomed on the horizon, as a stereotypical teenager, I was self-absorbed in my own life. It was difficult for me to focus beyond the current state of my daily activities. But something was happening. Slowly, we started to peel back the absurdities of everyday life and each in our own way began to inspect and question what was acceptable.

Walking in downtown Memphis, it was commonplace to

see signs marked as "colored" or "white only." Bathrooms, public facilities, entrances and lunch counters, they all had labels and restrictions. We could only go to the zoo on Thursdays, watch movies from the balcony or ride the bus in the back. I remembered one occasion when the back door of the bus jammed against a post making it difficult for me to get off. So, I rushed to the front to exit and was told by the bus driver that I could not leave out the front door. I ignored him and left anyway. Later, when I was asked how I felt when I did that, I said, "Free." Even though segregation was as commonplace as green grass and blue skies, my siblings and I thought that it was all rather silly, but all the same, it was wearing thin with my generation. On another occasion, my sister, Odesser, drank from the "colored" water fountain. Then, she walked over to the "white only" fountain, and after taking a couple of sips, she threw her head back, mimicking pensive thought. Finally, she turned toward us, "Their water tastes the same to me!" We all immediately burst into laughter.

But segregation was no laughing matter. It was serious and a profitable business for whites. After all, this was Memphis, a crown jewel of the South where cotton was king, and the cotton trade was a legacy that was deeply rooted on the backs of generations of slaves and watered with their blood and tears, a legacy that was now governed by Jim Crow. Some of these laws were written and some of them were unspoken ordinances, but no matter what their form, these laws had a singular purpose of attempting to strip blacks of their dignity, keeping them subservient and giving the allusion that they were unworthy of hope.

Employment was another area that was strangled by Jim Crow. The lack of jobs and opportunity in the black community did not oscillate with the rise and fall of the economy. It was always bleak; opportunity for blacks did not exist within the financial section of the local paper. A steady job for blacks in the private sector usually consisted of manual labor or custodial work, and then, there was a "good job" like working as an elevator operator, a post that was commonly regarded as an enviable position within the black community. This highly-regarded status was largely due to two factors: it was indoors away from the harsh elements, usually located inside nice office buildings or retail stores, and it did not require any strenuous physical labor. Consequently, employment as an elevator operator was highly desirable but rarely available. Therefore, it was by coincidence that I landed a job, working the elevator at Robinson's clothing store.

My cousin, who actually held the position, was taking a vacation and wanted me to work in her place. I liked my "supposedly" prestigious position of operating an elevator but was told that I must never sit although a stool was provided. I did not realize the effect that this had on me until years later when I worked on my first job in Chicago as a medical photographer. As I mounted pictures, I always stood. Finally, one day, my boss asked me, "Why are you standing?" I was embarrassed to tell him why. I simply said, "Thank you" when he invited me to sit. Operating an elevator was pretty mundane. So, I tried to add some excitement by making a grand announcement, "Second Floor: coats, suits, dresses, watch your step." It's funny looking back at it now, since the store was very modest in appearance. First of all, the store only had two floors, and its interior was basic with plain concrete flooring, all white painted walls, and one elevator. I think my dramatic flair of floor announcements made the manager feel like he was running a big operation. In fact, the manager was so impressed with me that when my cousin returned, I quickly found myself being given a new position where I folded clothes and helped with the window dressing. Unfortunately, my advancement was also noticed by others who did not like the idea of a colored girl working in the store as a window dresser. A secretary from a different department approached me one day and gave me an order, "Earnestine, make sure the elevator is mopped every day."

Surprised and looking down at the polished floor, I calmly replied, "Sure. I'll tell the custodian…"

"No, I want you to do it," she snapped back, abruptly cutting me off.

I knew immediately what this was all about, but I did not respond.

Then, she said, "Say, yes Ma'am when you speak to me."

"Alright," I responded.

"Can't you say, Yes, Ma'am?"

"Yes," I replied with a defiant look.

Now, I am a daughter of the South, and I know the code. There is no logical reason why a secretary would order me to mop a floor except for one objective…to abase me. When I got home, I immediately relayed this story to my father. Not concealing his disgust, he was very quick and stern in his reply, "Steen, don't go back there." I was a little startled by his strong reaction. Maybe, his emotional response stemmed from years of sharecropping or maybe something else, but he was adamant when he told me not to go back to that job. Even though I never returned to that store to work, I was nonetheless disappointed. After all, I was good at what I did, and I enjoyed having customers ask me for advice or suggestions with their outfits, but in the end, the only thing that mattered was the color of my skin.

During my formative years, separation based on race was the norm. It was so ubiquitous in my world that it was hard to envision anything else. However, just as my ancestors and the slaves did before us, whenever we did talk of things being different and better, we usually talked about "going up North." Dreaming of traveling to the northern section of the United States always seemed to soothe any feelings of repression that blacks may have felt as a result of their marginal existence in the South. It was more than just a destination. "Going up North" represented a dream of a new beginning of equality and prosperity. Therefore, when I was offered the chance to attend either a "New Homemakers of America" student convention in Virginia or an American Junior Red Cross camping trip to Wisconsin, my immediate response was, "I want to go up North."

While in high school, I was a volunteer and president of a local American Junior Red Cross chapter that represented the five black high schools in Memphis. Along with spending my time during the summer months doing general duties at the American Red Cross main office, as president I was also responsible for supervising the preparation of care boxes that were sent to soldiers of the Korean War. Sometimes, the work was long, but I enjoyed the fellowship and camaraderie of the students from the other black schools. Besides, I liked imagining our packages being shipped to the other side of the world and the expressions on the soldiers' faces as they opened a box from Memphis.

During one particular long day, Virginia Broom, who was our Red Cross supervisor, called me into her office and asked me to sit down. The whole formal approach made me nervous, and I began searching her face for clues of what I thought would be my impending demise. Ms. Broom, who was white, was very considerate and passionate about helping others. She began to tell me how impressed she was with my work and diligence, but I started mentally preparing myself for the disappointment, waiting to hear, "We like you and your work, but..." However, she told me something that my ears could not comprehend.

"Earnestine, you have been selected to attend the midwestern summer camp of the American Junior Red Cross."

I couldn't believe it. Part of me was frozen in disbelief, and the other part was ecstatic, jumping up and down with joy. "I was going up North!" All of my life, up until I was sixteen, I had only traveled in western Tennessee and Arkansas. But in the summer of 1954, I boarded a train headed for Lake Geneva, Wisconsin. Since this was the first time that I had traveled by myself, I became nervous as the train slowly pulled away from the station, watching my family on the platform disappear from view. However, my apprehension soon began to melt away as my eyes focused on the changing terrain. Looking out the window, my thoughts raced along with the click-clack sound of the train tracks, and I viewed the scenery as it metamorphosed from the familiarity of the South and into a landscape awash with new images. Every time the conductor called out the name of a new town, "Fulton! Centralia! Champaign!" my heart quickened as I scanned my surroundings. The air was becoming more crisp, leaving behind the humid haze; even the grass seemed greener. I was being pulled away from the South and slipping into a new world.

Upon my arrival in Wisconsin, it was clear that I was no longer in the South. Of course, there were grass and trees and buildings, and the clouds still floated above me in the sky, but there were hardly any black people. I stood in awe as boys and girls scrambled to gather their belongings and load buses used to transport us to the campsite. In a sea of white teenagers and adult chaperones, there I was. Lining up for the bus, there was no "white only" line; and once on the bus, no one seemed aware or even cared that I was sitting at the front of the bus. I was truly "up North." The campsite was situated in the Wisconsin Dells, a famous tourist destination along the banks of the Wisconsin River, and I was mesmerized as we drove past rolling hills of green carpet, through clumps of dense forest and over streams that were lined with sandstone formations which seemed to be standing guard awaiting our arrival.

The campsite was like nothing that I had ever seen. It consisted of large tents, and the foundation of each tent was a wooden floor that was elevated above the ground. Once I stepped inside, I was greeted by a roomy and clean interior with a cot, desk and wardrobe stand, occupying each corner, but my biggest surprise was that my three roommates who were busily unpacking – were white. My body immediately felt like it had congealed into a frozen block of ice as the stark contrast of my reality hit me like an arctic blast. Up until two days ago, I had been forced to live my entire life in segregation. I had never gone to the zoo on the same day with white people, eaten at a lunch counter with white people or even sat in the same area with white people during a movie. Now I was living in the same room with three white girls. Regaining my composure, I slowly looked around, and instinctively, I cautiously waited for something or someone to come bursting into the tent to stop me and redirect me to the "other" section. Then, as one of the girls approached me, I thought to myself — "Here it comes, get ready."

"Hi. I'm Hazel."

I was stunned. She was smiling at me; in fact, she was very friendly. Before I could respond, Hazel stretched out her hand toward me. With a lump starting to form in my throat, I shook her hand and softly spoke, "Hi, I'm Earnestine."

"This is Dorothy and Caroline," said Hazel pointing to the other two girls. "We're all from Michigan and came here last year. So, if you have any questions, just let us know. We could probably tell you everything. Anyway, where are you from?"

When I told them that I was from Memphis, they immediately began to ask me questions about the South. They had never met anyone from the South, and they wanted to know how hot it got in Memphis and how long was my trip. And that was that. Within a few minutes, I felt like we were just a group of four teenage girls. No cautious or disapproving looks, no black vs. white, no "colored not allowed" signs, no prejudice—just four normal chatty teenagers with no regard for the color of our skin. As I sat there lost in reflection and marveling about all that had happened, Hazel who was clearly the most outspoken of the group, asked me, "Is your hair naturally curly?" It was clear from the expression on her face that she was not being malicious, and it was also evident from her question that she probably had not met many black people, and now that she was living with one, she had a million questions. I chuckled and said, "No. Is your hair naturally curly?" She nodded politely, yes, and although she was not totally satisfied with my answer, she resisted the urge to ask any additional questions…at that time.

Everyone at the camp was from the Midwest except for two of us, me and another black girl who had come from the South. Initially, I thought it was an odd coincidence, but later, I found out that it was by design. The southern conference of the American Junior Red Cross did not allow colored people to attend their summer camps. However, Ms. Broom, my supervisor, who was so embarrassed by the segregation rule, had redirected my appointment to the midwestern conference. Of course, she did not dwell on this, but I was always grateful to Ms. Broom. It was one of the first lessons and reminders of what my parents often told me, "When one door is closed to you, God will always open another."

After ten days at camp, I boarded the train and headed back south, but I could not resist the opportunity of getting off the train in Chicago. Officially, I told my parents that I wanted to visit my aunt and uncle; unofficially, I wanted to see the magnificent city that had only existed within the pages of magazines and my imagination. As the train moved through the city and pulled into Union Station, I was shocked by the vastness of it all: skyscrapers that seemed to reach far into the heavens and miles upon miles of buildings that stretched out before me in an endless, man-made forest without trees. Stepping outside of Union Station, oceans of people, both black and white, flowed past me without any awareness of their surroundings. For the next several days, my relatives gave me a grand tour of Chicago complete with colorful stories that added to my list of remarkable tales.

As I boarded the train on my return to Memphis, I was bursting at the seams with excitement, eager to share my adventures with my family. Even though my enthusiasm did not change with the passing hours of the trip, something else did. The names of Northern towns were now being replaced with Southern ones. The air was slowly becoming thicker and heavier and the once diverse collection of travelers in my car had changed and become monochromatic – it was now "colored only." I was returning back to the old South. Reaching my destination, the train slowly crept into Central Station, screeching to a jarring halt. Gone were the skyscrapers, the rolling Wisconsin hills, and the resemblance of equality. The excitement of my past adventure had now become a souvenir of memories cast in my mind, but in my heart, there was something else. Walking off the train onto the platform, the familiar atmosphere of segregation hung around me, but I looked beyond it; there was something far more important. Then, it happened. I finally spotted the smiling faces of my family, and joy erupted within me as I was wrapped up in their warm embrace. I was back home, and it felt good. That was the summer of 1954.

Chapter 6

Twist of Fate

Despite being awarded a four-year merit scholarship to an historically black college in my hometown, I turned it down because I wanted to experience something in a new environment, and the idea of going away to college and living in the dormitory represented a way to venture out and explore. With my acceptance to Fisk University in Nashville, Tennessee, home of the renowned Fisk Jubilee Singers, my long-awaited dream was now a reality. However, there was an unmistakable part of me that was hesitant about the move and being pulled away from the warmth and security of my family and neighborhood. The apprehension, which had unexpectedly started to swell in me, quickly dissipated with the sights and sounds of the college campus as I arrived in the fall of 1956.

Even though I only had to travel a couple hundred miles from Memphis to attend Fisk, I romanticized about the distance of my new independence. Looking out onto a new world from my dorm window, I watched the fall leaves as they floated, swirling in their descent. The air had a hint of coolness that felt refreshing whenever I took in a deep breath. Autumn was my favorite season, and although only a few of the trees had started to turn, my view of the campus was awash with a palate of brilliant images and dazzling colors. My surroundings captivated me. Every time I passed the "Fisk University" sign in the Oval, a grassy knoll that served as the nucleus of the school, I thought of the distinguished alumni and luminaries that graced this campus: W. E. B. Du Bois, Ida B. Wells, James Weldon Johnson and Aaron Douglass who founded the art department at Fisk and was a champion of the Harlem Renaissance period. But my euphoria was abruptly interrupted by an upperclassman, trying to capture my attention.

"Hey, freshman! Freshman!" she cried out.

It was at that time when I suddenly remembered that I was wearing a silly beanie on my head, a tradition during the first week of school, which signaled to the upperclassmen who of the students was a freshman.

I responded with the required salutation, "Your slightest wish is my command, most noble Fiskite," and bowed with contrived humbleness.

"You see that fellow over there in the blue shirt," pointing across the lawn. "That's my boyfriend. Go give him these clothes hangers."

After accomplishing my assigned freshman duty, I made my way to my dorm room in Jubilee Hall, being careful to avoid other upperclassmen. I tolerated the "freshman ritual," however trivial and innocent the tasks, but by the end of the first week, my patience was wearing thin. There were other more pressing matters. Besides making the usual adjustment to residential college life, there was the plight of college placement exams. It was required of all freshmen during the first week to take a series of exams, which were responsible for two things: assessing your level of knowledge for placement in courses and increasing the already heightened anxiety of every freshman.

One day after finishing my exams, Rhoda Miller, a fellow classmate also in her first year, rushed into the dining hall and approached me. She was out of breath from running.

"Earnestine! Our names are on the campus bulletin board."

Shocked by the news, I shouted, "What?"

"Yeah, we have to report to the head of the English department," she said.

Immediately, I thought, "I just got here. What could be going wrong already?"

My trepidation stemmed from the idea of walking into an unknown situation and not due to any academic concerns. In high school, other classmates used to comment on how I was always so serious about "completing my lesson," but despite this characterization, I never considered myself a bookworm or being exceptional even though I was valedictorian of my graduating class. Nevertheless, I was now worried about why I had been singled out on a bulletin board posting. Once we reached the English department, we found out that we had both scored very high on the English placement exam. It was required of us to write an essay from predetermined titles. We learned that members of the department were so impressed with our essays that they offered us the opportunity to skip the freshman writing courses. Rhoda, who had already declared herself an English major, wrote an essay on "The Great Fire" while I chose to write on "The Disadvantages of Being a Millionaire." Even though at that time I was idealistic and a bit naive about life, the topic intrigued me; as I got older, my opinion on that subject changed. When I think of all the positive things that can be done with a million dollars, I am amused at my viewpoint back then. Now, I would say that although the pitfalls are there, the advantages far outweigh the disadvantages. No matter the philosophical implications, it was my writing style that had caught the professors' attention, and despite my early success in college literature and repetitive advice to pursue a career in writing, I was focused on the field of mathematics.

College had proven to be quite exciting and enjoyable for me despite the fact that I repeatedly sprained my ankle during my first semester. The first time, the sprain quickly healed but the second one was more severe. The simple task of walking around campus became an arduous and embarrassing chore of limping from one place to another on crutches. In both cases, the injuries were the result of my pursuit of a romantic notion that I was good at volleyball. Growing up, I had heard all the stories of my father playing baseball, and my oldest sister, Odesser, was an exceptional athlete in both baseball and track. However, I knew that my slender frame did not possess the speed or the power for either sport, but I figured that I was taller than most girls my age, making volleyball a natural choice. I also felt that I had the mental toughness for sports since I had grown up between two boys.

Unfortunately, my interest in volleyball was short-lived; the beginning of the end happened during one physical education class. I remembered standing at the net and sizing up the competition. On the serve, the ball was a line drive directly to me. Instinctively, I jumped to spike the ball in a quick return; as I successfully hit it back over the net, the ball zoomed past the outstretched hands of my opponents. Unfortunately, it was the last thing that I remembered. When I landed on my feet, I felt a sharp pain in my right ankle, which seemed to shoot through my body. At that moment, the image of the net fell away as I collapsed to the floor, and the faces of my classmates disappeared into a fog of pain. The only thing greater than my agony was the humiliation of the accident unfolding in front of everyone. Since I could barely stand, I was carried out on a stretcher past a crowd of peering eyes and pointing fingers. I knew that this sprain was much worse than the first one just six weeks earlier.

Within the span of only a couple of months, I had injured my ankle twice during my first semester, and somehow, it seemed that fate had always allowed my father in his travels across the state to see me on crutches on both occasions. In addition to Memphis, my father pastored a church in Knoxville in East Tennessee. So, he routinely stopped to visit me at Fisk in Nashville, which was right in the middle of the state. With my first injury, I tried to mask and minimize my limping during his visit. He simply glanced at my ankle and dismissed it within his private thoughts. But the second time was a different matter. He stared at me in complete shock when he watched me hobble into the dorm lobby in a cast and on crutches. With each step closer to him, I could sense that the wrinkles on his forehead and between his eyes were deepening with dismay.

I kept thinking, "How am I going to explain this?" Then,

I thought that I would appeal to his love for sports and his past as a baseball player, so I started my pitch. "Daddy, I..." But my words choked when I looked into his face and saw an expression of hurt and deep concern; finally, after a long pause, he spoke.

"Steen, by now, you ought to realize that this game is not for you." His words were calm, brief and resolute; and he was right. I had no defense. Thus, my unrealistic aspirations for sports ended.

My father was always thoughtful and direct in his praise and criticism. When he spoke to you, it was as if no one else existed in the room. His advice was like a soothing antidote – an asset for a clergyman. Daddy was also superintendent of the East Tennessee jurisdiction of the Church of God in Christ, which meant overseeing all of the churches in that region. His duties required him to routinely travel a highway where the destination was ten hours in one direction. He relished having company on such long trips, and he especially enjoyed having his family ride with him. If I were traveling by myself with him, I would read aloud all the signs along the road and chatted for hours—a ritual he enjoyed because it was both entertaining and it kept him from getting drowsy. During those trips he rarely talked about work; instead, he focused his attention on me, asking about school and my friends, and laughing at my funny stories. He would engage in my endless banter as if it were the most important conversation on the planet. I enjoyed our special time together and cherished those trips. As a result, I was very excited to see him when he picked me up for Christmas break of 1956.

The highway between Nashville and Memphis was a two-lane road that twisted around hills, past crops and large reaches of countryside that were only populated by brief glimpses of cows and rural towns. The drive was long and well-crafted for extended conversations. During a break from my endless chatter, I glanced at my father and noticed that he was deep in thought and detached from the passing landscape.

"Daughter," he usually began the dialogue in this manner whenever he initiated one of his parent-child conversations that involved either comments, questions or sharing one of his life experiences. His calm voice paused, gaining my attention. "Have you decided what you're going to do?"

"Well, next semester, I'll be finished with my required classes. After that, I'll probably declare my major in math."

He probed further, "That's good, but have you given any thought about what you want to do after you graduate?"

I responded, "I think I'll probably be a math teacher, but there's plenty of time to think about it."

"Daughter, if you pray and ask God, He will direct you in your purpose in life." Then he paused for a moment and continued, "When you graduate from college, help the next one go to college, and then if he can help the next one, you all can go to college."

I was confused. Daddy was talking like he was not going to be around, and his tone was something that I had never experienced from him. It felt uncomfortable and I could not think of anything to say. So, I just stared blankly at the asphalt rushing under the car; the volume of my thoughts was so loud that I could barely hear the car's engine.

Finally, changing the subject, my father then asked me, "Did you receive the stationery that I left for you at your Uncle Abner's house?"

"Oh...yes," I replied gleefully, relieved to get the conversation back to something lighthearted.

"Good, you need to write your mother more, and call less," he said with a slight smile. This was his half-jokingly way of reminding me of those expensive long-distance charges with my frequent calls home.

Once we reached home, I was immediately greeted at the front door by my younger brothers and sisters, who were clearly excited to see me and caught up in the holiday spirit. Inside, the aroma of fresh-baked cakes and sweet potato pies was intoxicating. Walking into my home was like stepping out of the cold rain and being wrapped up in a warm blanket that sparkled with festive ribbon. It was my home in full Christmas splendor.

For the next several days, there was a steady stream of neighbors, friends, church members and relatives flowing through our house. Heavy traffic through our front door was always routine in our home, but during the holiday season the toll seemed to increase by tenfold. They came with laughter and joy, they came with gifts, and on this particular holiday they came to hear my college tales. As part of our family tradition, my father would always buy bushels of apples, oranges and pecans along with boxes of peppermint candy. Anyone visiting our home usually ended up either nibbling on pie, eating fruit or cracking pecans. There seemed to be a nutcracker or an empty plate of crumbs in every room. Eating pecans was my favorite. There was something especially soothing about the sound of cracking pecans, then picking the nut out of the shell and popping it in my mouth along with a piece of peppermint. It still is a favorite Christmas treat of mine.

Everyone who came to our home that holiday wanted to hear my stories, and since I was the first one in my family to go to college, a simple summary would not suffice. They wanted a detailed account of everything: what I wore, what I ate, whom I met and where I lived. No detail was insignificant as I told my stories over and over. Each day became a pageantry of visitation and storytelling, a pattern that was interrupted only by another favorite holiday tradition – helping my mother with baking which took nearly a week to complete. Momma loved to cook, and she was excellent at it. Everyone tried to duplicate her recipes, especially her sweet potato pie, which she readily shared with anyone who asked. However, no one could mimic her keen sense of smell and taste or her ability to accurately measure a pinch, dash or smidgen. As a result, very few came close to her culinary excellence.

Cooking with my mother was similar to my time spent with my father during car trips. Momma was not a big talker; to say that she was a quiet person was an understatement, but she was expressive in her own unique way. Most of the time she simply conveyed her message with a single phrase or two, but the time we shared in the kitchen was different. It was intimate. We talked, shared stories and laughed with little regard for time. In fact, some of the most revealing feelings about my mother's childhood would often be unearthed during those moments. Even though we spent long hours together in the kitchen with the object of preparing food, I actually never cooked anything during those sessions. Momma did not trust anyone "to experiment," as she called it, with her meals or holiday dishes. However, as her apprentice, I was allowed to watch, ask questions and do ancillary supportive tasks such as sifting the flour or grating coconut. You could ask questions, but the act of actually putting ingredients in the mixing bowl was strictly forbidden. That line was never to be crossed.

As we sat in the kitchen, it seemed that the entire neighborhood would drift in, sit down and tell us their stories as well. Sometimes during these lively conversations, my mother's eyes would meet mine and for a brief moment, we would share a communication, no words, just an understanding that only occurred between the two of us. Then, as quickly as the shared moment occurred, it would quickly fade as we smiled in unison. It was during these unspoken, intimate moments that I felt especially close to my mother, a connection that extended beyond the obvious genetic bond of mother and daughter and could not be encapsulated by mere words.

The few months away at college had only increased my appreciation for the love of my family. The magic of Christmas was palpable, and its energy bounced and danced each time a visitor crossed our threshold, or when a child rehearsed a scripture for the church program or when a freshly baked cake was being pulled from the oven. The joy was everywhere, and it seemed like this particular Christmas was my best ever.

Unfortunately, the images and emotions of that holiday were soon shattered. Just days after Christmas, my father became acutely ill, and the joy of that season turned into nostalgic remnants. Walking into my parents' bedroom on the 31st of December, I found my father lying in bed, slowly rubbing his abdomen in obvious pain. That scene is permanently etched in my memory because prior to that moment, I had never seen my father sick, not even with a common cold. For all of my life, he was a man who had worked from sunup to sundown doing back-wrenching tasks without incident, a man whose physical stature and character embroiled formidable strength, a man who was now lying almost motionless before me. Perplexed by his appearance and his faintly audible moan, I could barely hear his request for rubbing liniment for his abdomen. But the salve did not abate his misery, and by the next morning, my father was transported by ambulance to John Gaston Hospital.

The city hospital was bustling with activity and scores of people at every step. Yet, despite all the human noise, the atmosphere was bland. Maybe it was the slate green paint or aseptic vapors, but the mood was cold and foreign. I stood in a corner near my father's bed, hoping that my current reality was nothing more than a nightmare, which would abruptly end upon my waking up. Instead, I stood there fully conscious and witnessed a never-ending river of concerned visitors, a flood of worried faces that was only sporadically interrupted by a nurse or doctor. He was diagnosed with appendicitis, but the faces and terse words of the medical staff hinted at something more ominous.

By the next morning, a young doctor came bouncing into our room with fresh energy. "Reverend, we thought we were going to lose you last night," grabbing his stethoscope. His words grabbed me as being a bit too nonchalant. From his young appearance and carefree demeanor, it was apparent that he was either a new doctor or still in training. He was followed by another doctor, much older, who walked with a sober gait. His words were slow and deliberate and laced with several sighs. After examining my father and glancing at my mother, the older physician drew in a deep breath.

"We need to operate and take out the appendix before it ruptures. But we are having problems with his blood pressure. We're trying to control it, but it's too high. Unfortunately, we can't operate with it being so high. It makes the surgery too risky, but we're trying everything we can to lower it." He paused for a moment. "But time is critical." He took another long stare at my father's abdomen, deep in thought, and then looked at my mother, "If you need anything, let us know."

Momma sat by Daddy's bed as she had done since she was a young bride at 18 years old. Her face was frozen, stoic like stone, and her words were painfully few. And now after nearly 30 years of marriage, it was as if life was being siphoned out of her. With each passing hour, family and church members stopped by to pray, but Daddy seemed to drift further and further away from us. From my corner of the room, I watched every scene unfold, hoping and waiting for Daddy to spring from the bed. One day while my mother had stepped out into the hallway, I was sitting alone with my father when I noticed him staring intently at something, but nothing was there. I watched him for several moments. Finally, he spoke.

"Steen, there are two angels here. Quick, pull the curtains so we can have them."

Not seeing anything, I obediently pulled the curtains around his bed. Then, he slowly raised his right arm and pointed upward to the left.

"That angel will doom you," and then moving his hand slightly to the right and continuing to point upwards, he smiled slightly. "But that angel will raise you up."

I didn't know what that meant, but fear took hold of me, as I stood motionless in disbelief and shock. Not because of what he saw but his words. These were not the words of a person, soon to be released with a clean bill of health. His tone and projection were celestial, a clear disconnect from this world; and my worry deepened, finding it harder to keep believing that he was going to make it.

Over the next several days, Daddy's condition teetered and swayed on a tightrope of hope and despair. Each morning his blood pressure would improve, and he was prepped for surgery; but by the afternoon, his blood pressure would climb back up and, the surgery was postponed. With each cancellation, his return trip from the operating room found him progressively weaker. This devastating cycle continued day after day, seemingly without any endpoint. Finally, after much coercion, I was persuaded to return to college after the new semester had already started, with a medical excuse, explaining the grave prognosis of my father. Somehow, I managed to drift through the routine of attending classes until I received the call. Just one week after returning to campus, and a mere two and a half weeks after Daddy fell ill, I was told that my father was dead. He was only 49 years old. I went numb; no sound, no images, no air, just nothing. There was nothing surrounding me, only the emptiness inside me.

The next thing that I remember was riding in the car with Mrs. Ferguson, the dorm director. She had made my travel plans, drove me to the airport, and probably packed my bags since I don't have any recollection of luggage. Boarding the airplane was odd; I had never flown on an airplane. The entire sequence of events was about as foreign to me as the realization that my father would never again pick me up from school. As I struggled with the concept, I was also perplexed that none of the white passengers objected as I sat in the front of the plane. Maybe segregation was on vacation that day. Anyway, it didn't seem to matter, and I didn't care. Adding to the list of oddities of that day was something that occurred as I arrived in Memphis. A chauffeur greeted and escorted me to a limousine, which I was not expecting. Initially, I hesitated to go with him, but being emotionally exhausted and having no alternative plans for transportation home, I asked no questions, slid into the backseat and fell into a stuporous gaze until I reached Douglass. Once we pulled up in front of my house, the chauffeur accepted a very nominal fee, tipped his hat politely, and quietly drove away without mentioning who he was or who had arranged for his services.

After watching the limousine disappear from focus, I turned and saw a little boy across the street, staring at me in sadness. He raised his hand to wave but stopped as our eyes met. We understood in that moment what we were feeling. The neighborhood children often marked the time to go in the house for dinner by the time of day that Daddy came home from work. He was just that reliable to everyone. Now, the little boy and I both knew that things would never be the same.

    Not exactly sure what would meet me on the other side of the front door, I mentally prepared myself and tried to imagine the joy that I felt just a few weeks ago when I had arrived at that very same door for Christmas break, but my attempts were futile. As I walked inside the house, grief hit me like the opening of a furnace door and the heat of sadness engulfed me, burning my innermost being. All the smiles of everyone inside had been replaced with solemn faces. No longer was there laughter but only hushed mumbling, and in place of the sweet aroma of baked pies was an undeniable gloom that hung in the air. The worst was my mother. From her face, it was obvious that she was not eating. Her eyes were sunken, and cheeks hollowed. She barely lifted her head when I walked into the room. My brothers and sisters looked lost and displaced as refugees in their own home. Sadness was all around me; I almost choked as I tried to swallow the enormity of it. It was my first taste of that emotion. Everything was a blur, and everyone seemed disconnected, lost. The once familiar hustle and bustle of our home was gone, and we all struggled to find our way. Thank God for Sister Lilly Mae Garret, Daddy's secretary at church who handled all of the funeral arrangements and the program. I do not know how Momma would have made it without her.

    After the burial, I returned to college and tried to assimilate into the routine. I often thought that I would fulfill my father's dream by graduating and helping the next sibling go to college. Now I knew why he had that talk with me when he picked me up for the holidays; I guess he knew that he would not be around much longer. Unfortunately, the struggle to regain my footing was sabotaged by certain relatives who felt school was now a waste of time. They were relentless in their pursuit to persuade me to drop out of school even though they knew of the limited choices for a black female with no work experience or degree. According to them, the money spent for college would be better used for other purposes. Even though I had applied for and received a scholarship to continue my studies, the pressure for me to quit continued to mount, and after one year of hearing all the complaints, I decided to leave Fisk and move to Chicago, looking for work.

Just like milestones that mark crucial points in life, my father's passing was my personal marker. For years after that fateful day, I divided my life into before and after. Before I lost my innocence and before my planned future was taken from me, I knew what I wanted to do with my life, and then there was afterwards. At that moment, "afterwards" felt like an empty promise filled with cold despair. The once calm and organized life that I had known was now gone. The change was too abrupt and cruel; I did not have the time to prepare for the harsh reality of it, and for the first time, I asked myself the question, "What am I going to do with my life?"

Chapter 7

Chicago

It had been four years since my first visit to Chicago. Four years ago, I was happy, gleeful. My life had a mapped out promising future. But that was four years ago when Daddy was still living. Now, my second arrival into Chicago was entirely different. One year after the death of Daddy, the emptiness that I felt after he passed lingered with me. It was awful like something had been hollowed out of me. I could only imagine what it must have been like for my mother. My father had been the guiding force of the family, and with his passing we had all been derailed and were struggling to get back on track in life. Thereafter, every decision seemed to be linked to or was a consequence of his death, and after leaving Fisk, I often wondered if I had made the right decision in moving to Chicago. Staying home in Memphis to be close to my mother and my younger sisters and brothers would have been ideal, but because of segregation, I knew that I would have never found adequate work. As a result, Chicago was the perfect place to start my life over. Employment opportunities were plentiful, and the hustle and bustle of the big city would help to assuage my unhappy state of being.

I moved in with my father's uncle, Willie, and his wife, Eva. Looking back on my visit with them during the summer of 1954, I realized that it was a precursor. Little did I know that four years later, I would be living with them. I was so grateful; they treated me like I was their daughter. I remember coming home one evening, disheartened because my application for a store charge account had been denied. When Uncle Willie found out what happened, he told me, "Earnestine, take my Litton credit card and get whatever you want, pay me back any way that you want."

Staying with them provided comfort. They were warm and loving which reminded me of home, but their dwelling was a different experience. They owned and lived in a three-story building, residing on the first floor and renting the top floors. The lives of the people living upstairs were both fascinating and foreign to me, but my uncle and aunt were more like what I was used to. Their house always smelled of cooking which was the result of Aunt Eva. She was a small, feisty, seventy-six-year-old woman who always wore her hair in a bun with a hat on top and whose looks and energy betrayed her age. On Sunday mornings, she would cook both breakfast and dinner at the same time, then afterwards hop the back-porch fence, which was about two feet high, to avoid taking the longer route of walking down the steps to the gate. Then, she headed on her way to do missionary work at the jail, all before getting to the 10 o'clock morning church service.

Uncle Willie was an impeccable dresser and had been a hard and industrious worker his entire life. After fifty years of marriage, they had learned to perfectly cope and adapt to each other's patterns, moods and idiosyncrasies. Being from Mississippi, they migrated as a couple to the North looking for better opportunities, and true to their southern background, they had a large family. But unlike my family in Memphis, their children were all older, mostly with their own established families. As a result, only one son and daughter lived in the building. Their son would occasionally tease me like an older sibling, and their daughter, who lived upstairs, had taken it upon herself to adopt me as her little sister; I liked them both. Despite my difficult transition and the coldness of Chicago, I had fallen into another household that was both loving and caring.

Finding employment in Chicago was easy as I quickly landed a job in the medical photography department at Children's Memorial Hospital and started sending money home to my mother. The hospital also offered to pay half my tuition for classes at Northwestern University, so I seized the opportunity to continue my education, something I thought my father would have wanted. Although my heart was not fully in it, surprisingly, the familiarity of the classroom and taking mathematics did provide some comfort, a consolation that things were starting to flow in a more natural rhythm. I thought that maybe I was starting to return to some semblance of normalcy, but then Chicago had its first big snowstorm of the season. I had never seen anything like it. In Memphis when we got snow, everything came to a grinding halt. As a child, a forecast of snow was treated like a festive occasion. Everyone in the neighborhood talked constantly about it, and if any snow did actually fall that measured over an inch, schools were closed. It was like a gift from heaven. All the children would stay outside and play in the snow as long as our bodies could tolerate it, making homemade sleds and collecting fresh snow from on top of cars to make ice cream. Schools remained closed until the temperature would eventually rise, melting the snow, and ending our holiday. Therefore, it was out of habit that with the first snowstorm in Chicago I decided to miss classes and wait for the snow to melt. However, I soon realized that the snow wasn't going anywhere; in fact, it was increasing by the day. By the time of this realization, I had already missed the first week of classes of the second semester, which can seem like a lifetime with college courses. I remembered calling the professor of my analytical geometry and calculus class to explain my absence and ask for permission to attend the class. Even though I had registered for the course, I had yet to attend a single class because of the snow. He invited me to attend but cautioned me that I had missed a lot of coursework. In my very first class session, he gave a test and, I guess, he must have graded my paper first during the break. Before the second half of the class he called me to his desk and said to me with a look of surprise, "You are no dumb girl. You only missed one problem." I smiled, but the truth was that I no longer found mathematics fulfilling, and although my grades were good, I had lost my passion for it. I thought that the loss of interest was temporary and that my love for math would be rekindled, but it was gone like my father. My restlessness and discontentment escalated as I searched to find a meaningful interest.

That was my first winter in Chicago, and it was harsh. Coming from Memphis, I was stunned by the months of relentless snow. Then, there were the temperatures that often plummeted daily below zero and the biting wind, which seemed to rip past any winter coat and sweater I had on, sending a chill down to my bones. With the arrival of March, I was equally amazed that the snow was still piled up on the side of the road. But I reminded myself that winter could only last so long and that spring was around the corner. I eagerly waited for change.

During those months, time seemed to crawl by as only pieces and fragments of life started to fall back into place. I desperately tried to get my footing and settle into a routine. I worked during the day, and at night I read and studied, occasionally breaking the pattern with visits to my sister, Dorothy Mae, and her husband who also lived in Chicago. Though I was close to my sister, she had her own family with a young child and a small apartment. I thought it was best that I stayed with Aunt Eva and Uncle Willie. Trying to focus my attention away from what I had lost, I mentally pushed myself to keep my mind active, but Aunt Eva was concerned about this pattern and constantly worried that I was spending too much time alone.

"Child, you better put a sweater on," she would often say whenever she passed my room, but on occasion she would back up to continue her conversation. "How about helping me pick some greens?"

"Okay."

Aunt Eva, like my mother, was an excellent cook and like my mother, she did her own cooking and never invited anyone to help her. So, I knew that this type of invitation into the kitchen was her way of pulling me out of my room and into a conversation where she would casually see how I was doing. Entering the kitchen, I found Aunt Eva in her usual manner of busily opening cabinets and pulling out pots in a series of quick seamless moves, an obvious sign of her comfort and familiarity. There was a large pile of fresh collard greens on the table, and she handed me an empty pot as we sat down. "Picking greens" was a simple, repetitive task of pulling the leafy part of the plant away from its stem in preparation of cooking them. Since the process required little concentration, it was the perfect activity for reflection or conversation. After peering over her glasses at me for a few moments, she grabbed a handful of greens and started her assessment.

"Now, you told me all about your job, but you haven't mentioned anything about school."

"I'm only taking a couple of classes," I responded. Actually, I drifted from math to English to statistics. No longer did I focus on graduating; I was just trying to find myself, searching for a meaningful interest in life. I wondered what my purpose was. When I finally surfaced from my deep thoughts, I looked up and saw Aunt Eva staring at me, obviously waiting for me to expand on my answer. From the expression on her face, she had taken note of my silence, and after drawing her own conclusion, she mumbled loud enough for me to hear that universal phrase, "Uh, huh" and continued with her evaluation.

"Earnestine, you really need to get out more. You're spending way too much time in that room."

"Oh, I'm okay."

"No, it's not okay. What about your friends?"

"Well, a couple of my friends did invite me to the Young Democrats Ball"

"Oh, dear!" she exclaimed, smiling with satisfaction. "You should go."

"I'm thinking about it."

The Young Democrats were having their Annual Ball,

which was considered a grand event, and I had garnered an invitation. During the weeks leading up to the ball, something started to happen. It was hardly noticeable at first, but as I turned my attention to the usual question of what to wear to the ball, a flicker of excitement lit within me. It was so subtle that I did not realize what was happening. As a teenager, I always had a fascination with fashion, but the recent loss of my father had doused that love. However, the challenge of creating a clothing masterpiece for the event had become my muse and, in the process, had rekindled a spark in my heart. By the night of the ball, my face was aglow as I glided into the room to greet my audience, showing a faint resemblance of my former self. I vividly remember that outfit; it was a black crepe sleeveless sheath with a V-cut back that was accented with black Peau de Soie shoes, clutch purse and crystal earrings. I must have described that outfit to Aunt Eva a dozen times, but this was the official unveiling. Upon seeing me, Aunt Eva clasped her hands to her chest and blurted out her favorite catch phrase, "Oh dear!" After receiving other nods of approval from my uncle and cousins, I left for the party with an unexpected level of excitement.

 The banquet hall, located in downtown Chicago, was luxuriously decorated. The entire area was filled with a golden light that emanated from several large chandeliers that seemed to warm the air. But before I could fully appreciate and marvel at its beauty, my friends, who were eager to join the ball, rushed me through the lobby and did not slow down until we had entered into a spacious ballroom, displaying a "Young Democrats" banner on the back wall.

 The ballroom was packed with guests, black and white people mingling together, as the band struggled to be heard over a din of talking and laughter. My friends were much more excited than I was as they jumped from one conversation to another. Everyone talked about politics, professors, job hunting or who was dating whom. Only a short amount of time had passed before I was introduced to the president of the Young Democrats, Ted, a young white lawyer who, in turn, introduced me to a young black man, the vice president. His name was Charles Robinson and with the usual formality, he reached out his hand to shake mine. He was tall and handsome, but it was his rich, eloquent voice that grabbed my attention. Although he was reserved, he seemed very comfortable and at ease with himself. While others around him eagerly chatted about politics and economics, he only made sparse comments. He never appeared flappable even as the conversation around him edged jokingly toward personal jabs. As he stood there unflinching, I began to think that he had completely retreated into his private world, oddly disconnecting himself from his immediate surroundings. Then, just about the time that I was making my final conclusion about him, he unexpectedly, during a heated discourse, interjected a statement with such clarity and logic that everyone momentarily paused. So, he was listening, but as quickly as he made his comment, he retreated back into his private world and said nothing else. There was something about him, but I could not figure it out. Anyway, I mentally turned away and became lost in my own thoughts until I heard someone whisper something close to me. Looking around, I noticed that the previously aloof vice president had made his way over to me. Leaning in, he asked me again, "So, where are you from?"

"Memphis." I paused, surprised that now I had become the center of his attention. "Are you from Chicago?" I asked.

"No, Columbus, Ohio." He paused for a moment and continued, "You know, I've never visited Memphis. But I would love to see the cotton fields."

"Cotton fields? There are no cotton fields in Memphis."

"Really?" he replied looking astonished.

I looked at him, trying to see if he really didn't know or if he was trying to paint me into some stereotype. I wasn't sure what his motive was. So, I asked him, "Have you ever visited the South?"

"No," he replied.

"Do you have any relatives in the South?" I asked.

"Not that I know of."

"That's unusual. I've never met a black person who didn't have relatives from the South...Maybe, some of your ancestors ended up in Ohio through the Underground Railroad," I half joked, but by the look on his face, he took me seriously.

"I don't know. My father died when I was very young, so I don't know much about his side of the family. But I'm told that my ancestors on my mother's side migrated to America from..."

"Migrated!" interrupting him, I was astonished.

"Yeah, they were indentured servants from Great Britain."

"You're kidding! Servants from England, not American slaves?" I exploded as if I had made some incredible discovery. No wonder he didn't think the Underground Railroad was a joke.

Unfortunately, for Charles, he was starting to become self-conscious as he shifted his weight, but I was determined to reveal "that something" which my intuition had alerted me to during our introduction. It was becoming evident that our only similarity began and ended with our race; beyond that, I was starting to realize that he was different from any other black person that I had ever met. I was intrigued and wanted to know more about him. But he was reserved; so, I had a challenge.

"How many black people live in Columbus?" I asked.

"Oh, quite a few."

"A few, huh? How many blacks graduated in your high school class?"

"Nine," he responded.

"Nine! Oh, my goodness. I can't believe it."

"Why?" Charles asked.

"My entire school was solid black," I responded.

"Oh, really," he said, trying to mask his puzzlement.

Now I was stunned. What part of America did this guy come from, and then I remembered my trip to Wisconsin. I started to understand and replied, "You know, segregation."

"Oh, yeah," he remarked.

At that very moment, we simultaneously recognized one undeniable fact; we were from two totally different worlds. Despite being linked by race, everything else about us was polar opposite, a fact that became more obvious as we talked further. He was born and raised in the North with a small family and educated at a predominantly white high school and Ohio State, and I stood at the other end of the spectrum with my large family and Southern heritage. Yet, our paths had crossed, and we now felt drawn to one other. We danced and talked the rest of the evening, letting the crowd around us melt into a backdrop of insignificance.

Even though we talked for hours and I really enjoyed the conversation, I did not think anything of it beyond a single encounter. In such a large city, it was only a chance meeting, and we would probably never get another chance to speak with one another, especially since he did not ask for my number. However, a week later while at work, I was surprised when I got a call from Charles. He had remembered that I worked at Children's Memorial Hospital. Of course, his call caught me off guard, and I became a bit nervous when he invited me to a party given by his fraternity. Then, he delivered an abrupt jolt that stopped my excitement in its tracks. He said that the young lady he had planned to invite was out of town and asked if I would go with him instead. My mind erupted, "What!" Was I a second choice?" There was a dead silence on the phone. The idea of being a backup date had soured his invitation, but within the pause I could sense his awkwardness, and then I reflected on his audacity. I thought, maybe he invented that story just in case I said, "No." Anyway, I decided not to let my pride get the best of me and accepted his invitation because I really enjoyed the evening with him on our first encounter. The fraternity party was our first real date; it was August 1959, and the following month he gave me his fraternity pen and asked me to marry him. I was stunned. In the black community, certainly among the college Greek organizations, being "penned" was a special tradition, which meant that I was spoken for and an engagement ring would soon follow. I said, "Yes."

Charles was a man of contrasts. Very early on, I learned that he was not a big talker, but he encouraged me to talk. He was both introverted and outgoing. It was a bit ironic that I had been living in Chicago for over a year and despite being extroverted, I had seen very little of the city. However, that changed when I met Charles. Again, our polar opposites seemed to complement one another. He loved to explore and had been exposed to so much. I think he delighted in my naiveté and introducing me to so many new experiences. Over the next several months, we got to know one another as I discovered the city around me. We were like tourists exploring Chicago and all of its landmarks, which also included a tour of houses designed by the famous architect, Frank Lloyd Wright. Since Charles was an accountant and very much interested in finance, he gave me a tour of the Chicago Stock Exchange and even taught me how to read the stock page. Once when I asked what his middle initial, "E" stood for, he jokingly told me that it was for "exchequer." Of course, I had no idea what that was, but I knew it wasn't his name. He told me later that it was just a fancy term for treasury, and that his real middle name was Edward.

One evening when he stopped by to pick me up, Charles took me by surprise when he sat down at my aunt's piano and began playing beautiful music.

"How long have you been playing the piano?" I asked.

"Since I was a child, my folks pushed me to take lessons. At one time, my instructors wanted me to be a classical pianist, but I didn't want to," he responded with a matter of fact attitude.

"Why not?" I asked.

"I didn't like it." Then, he turned and asked me, "Do you play?"

"No, but for years I have been having this recurring dream that I am playing the piano. I don't know why I keep having this dream because I have absolutely no interest in playing."

"There must be some reason why you keep having this dream."

"I don't know, but I have no interest in music at all," being emphatic with my response. Afterwards, I told him that my two sisters took piano lessons, but when I was offered to take lessons, I turned it down. Piano lessons were not my cup of tea, but I did enjoy listening to others play. After my explanation, he hesitated for a moment before he continued playing and ended with a work by Rachmaninoff.

One thing was certain, Charles was definitely from a different world, one that had been hidden from me in the segregated South, but with him a new and exciting world had been opened up to me. Going to plays, attending art exhibits, and being invited to fashions shows at the top-notch stores, it was all brand new, and with all of this, something magical had happened. I was beginning to feel like my old self again, enjoying life and happier than I had been since the passing of my father. Describing Charles to one of my sisters in a letter, I wrote, "...he is highly intelligent, well-read, exciting, a gentleman and is crazy about me." She wrote back, "You better marry him," and on June 25, 1960, we were married at the beautiful Crerar Memorial Presbyterian Church on the south side of Chicago.

"Young, gifted and black" is a phrase that perhaps more than any other, aptly describes Charles and his relative ease of landing choice jobs during the early years of our marriage. Shortly after we were married, Charles was hired by Mercury Records as an account executive. Prior to that, he worked in finance at Provident Hospital, the largest black hospital in the country, at that time, and at a local stock brokerage firm. With his talent for numbers and his love for finance, he was beginning to develop a name for himself within the local business circles, but it was his skin color that made him a target for companies looking to add some diversity to their management ranks. After all, America was in the beginning of an era of cultural awareness, and it was not good business for companies to depict an air of exclusivity. As a result, Charles was courted by several businesses until Mercury Records finally invited him to be one of their account executives. Being drafted into the executive ranks of the corporate world meant that our presence was routinely requested at a number of functions that came with the mandatory "RSVP" stamp and were normally meant to be attended by upper level senior executives and not newly hired junior personnel like

Charles. But there we were on cultural display as the "token" black couple mixing and mingling with a sea of "old money" and "blue-bloods." The only other black people at most of these events were usually the musical artists or servants who stared at us with both bewilderment and a slight sense of unspoken accomplishment. Of course, Charles paid little to no attention to much of this; after all, he had spent his entire life being one of very few blacks at just about everything. I, on the other hand, was more self-conscious, clearly a by-product of my segregated past and limited exposure. Yet, I was able to camouflage my apprehension enough that the executives and their wives were comfortable in engaging me in banter that included everything from offering me advice on maid service to summer vacations. It was all truly mind-boggling.

My entrance into this affluent society first occurred when I attended a dinner party at the home of the then-vice-president of Mercury Records, Mr. Steinberg, who lived in Highland Park, Illinois. It was and still is an affluent suburb along the North Shore of Chicago which, among other things, serves as the summer home of the Chicago Symphony Orchestra. The Steinberg residence was extravagant by every stretch of the imagination, and Mrs. Steinberg was a gracious host as she gave me a tour of her home. At every turn, there was a dazzling array of servants beckoning to nods from her as we journeyed through the maze of hallways. Each corridor spawned into a collection of uniquely designed rooms filled with exquisite furniture that looked perfect and untouched. But it was the master bedroom that swept me off of my feet; the massive size of it seemed more than adequate to fit another small house into it. With my first step into the bedroom, my foot sank into the deep, plush off-white carpeting, giving me the allusion that I was walking on snow. As I slowly tipped around the room, my eyes marveled at the opulence, and all that I could say was, "Wow!"

Dinner was a masterpiece, a display of both culinary excellence of what was served and a theatrical exhibit of how it was served. The meal was a seven-course experience that was laden with exotic poultry, seafood and steaks that stacked inches high off the plate and was garnished with vibrantly-colored vegetables and intoxicating aromas. Everything was served by a staff, dressed impeccably in black and white uniforms. They whizzed around the table, carefully balancing large silver trays and porcelain china, passing within inches of one another with amazing fluidity. Skillfully removing plates, replacing utensils, filling glasses – all without a spill, a bump, mishap or uttered word. Moving in silence and making no eye contact, the staff moved with such precision that no one at the table seemed to notice them except for me. I was fascinated by their effortless ballet.

Despite the splendor, attending lavish dinners became commonplace when compared to the live entertainment. At the Edgewater Beach Hotel, there were a number of performances by headliner entertainers, including Sarah Vaughn, who routinely played to sold-out audiences in New York, Chicago and Europe. These private shows for the senior executives of Mercury Records were just some of the typical perks of Charles' new position. We had entered into a world that had previously been known to me only through the pages of magazines.

All of these social gatherings would have been simply just fun excursions except for the barrage of questions about my background, education and family pedigree that came at every turn. I felt like I was on a never-ending interview. It was very obvious that Charles and I were being analyzed and evaluated. But we played along with the game, and to this end, we were quickly accepted on some level. Charles also began to ascend up the corporate ladder. With each cocktail party, his responsibilities were expanded along with getting a secretary and an upwardly adjusted expense account. However, the one thing that I disliked about Charles' new position was that he traveled out of town so much. If people would ask me, "Can you remember what you were doing when President Kennedy was shot?" I would respond that I was at home alone with my two-month-old son, Todd, and Charles was in New York on company business.

All in all, Chicago, commonly referred to back then as "Negroes' Paradise" was working out fine for us, in spite of the harsh winters. I never got used to the winters. Oftentimes I would identify with the fabled pioneer women on the prairie who swore every bitter winter that they were moving back East as soon as spring came. But during the winter of 1964, my spirit was upbeat as I was eight months pregnant and was anxiously awaiting the arrival of my second child. Things were going well in my household; the entire pregnancy was progressing smoothly; and I was happy. Just one week before my birthday, I delivered a beautiful baby girl, Cheryle, without any complications.

Back in 1965, it was the policy of Chicago Lying-in Hospital to keep new mothers in the hospital for one week after delivery to insure proper rest. I stayed but I was eager to go home. My mother had come up from Memphis to be with my eighteen-month-old son, Todd, and I wanted to be there with them. Momma remained with me for two wonderful weeks after I returned home. Of course, her culinary skills went to work as she prepared the most delicious meals for us. She spoiled us all. Then, the inevitable happened; my mother returned to Memphis. The time following her departure had its highs and lows. But the worst was a sleeping problem that I developed. Even though having to care for two small children and juggling housework at the same time was a challenge, it was doable. But since Charles travelled a great deal for work and could not help with the nighttime feedings, I was extremely tired. The lack of sleep had taken its toll on me. It was the catalyst for my anxiousness. One of my friends told me that it was probably just part of the "baby blues" that would soon pass and suggested that in the meantime I should take sleeping pills to help me rest. But I did not want to develop the pattern of relying on sleeping pills in order to sleep. Also, I feared that I might sleep so soundly that I would not hear the baby's cry. So, sleeping pills were not an option. Finally, after wrestling with insomnia, I reached my wits end. I did not see how I could bear it any longer. That's when I got up and knelt by the side of my bed and asked God to help me to sleep, vowing that I would serve Him and do whatever He would have me to do. Shortly thereafter, I began to sleep better and had a dream.

In the dream, I was applying for a certain job. Instead of being hired for the job that I applied for, I was given a different position for which I had no qualifications. I was baffled. Why would someone hire me for a position that I obviously was not qualified? Then, I began to rationalize that I would have to buy books and study to prepare myself for this new job. It was at that moment in the dream that the person who had hired me, approached and said to me, "Young lady, we have hired you for this position. We know that you don't know anything about the work, but don't worry. We train our people our way." When I awoke, I knew immediately that God was going to give me a special work and that He was going to give me all that I would require for this work. However, I had no idea what this special work would be.

But my training soon began. Charles had returned from a business trip to Philadelphia and had brought back a Bible for me, which I started to read every morning. Each day, I studied the Bible as if it was a crucial homework assignment and I began to feel a new realm of hope and expectation. My vow to God and that dream had transformed me and brought me back into focus as I asked myself, "What is my purpose in life?" The question had gnawed at my subconsciousness ever since the passing of my father, but my search to discover the answer was fruitless despite great effort – an effort that had stretched over many years leading up to the birth of my daughter, Cheryle. During those years of wandering, I held numerous jobs and took classes at both Northwestern and DePaul Universities, all in an effort to discover my true interest or calling. I even took a stab at writing short stories about my life in Memphis. But despite all of my efforts, nothing soothed my unrest and my sense of being lost, until "the dream." Even though I still did not know what my purpose was, the dream had given me an assurance that I did have a purpose and that the answer to that question and, ultimately, my happiness would only be found with prayer and patience. Knowing this, I took comfort and felt a calmness that had escaped me for years.

Just when I was getting excited about the idea of a special calling that God had for me, Charles had become restless with his work at Mercury Records. His boss had left, and Charles was given his duties. Naturally, Charles, who had grown accustomed to his steady and rapid rise up the business ladder, expected that the increase in his responsibilities would be reflected by a similar increase in salary. But this did not occur, and this caused him great anguish. I knew that he was growing weary and impatient with waiting for Mercury to come around, but I did not know the extent of his frustrations until late one evening when he came home from the office and collapsed into one of the kitchen chairs.

Trying to use my most cheerful voice, I asked, "So, how was your day?"

"Hmmm," he uttered.

"Hmmm...What does that mean?"

He removed his glasses and for several moments, vigorously rubbed his eyes. Finally, after putting his glasses back on, he unconvincingly said, "Nothing."

"Something's wrong? What happened?" I continued.

After a long pause and a deep sigh, he turned and looked at me for the first time and said, "I'm just getting tired of being passed over."

"Charles, give it more time."

"Earnestine, I've given them enough time. Yeah, they want me to do the work, but they don't want to pay me. I'm tired of busting my butt so they can use me and push me around."

I tried to allay his concerns saying, "We'll just pray about it, and I know that the..."

But he interjected before I could finish my statement, "No. I'm thinking about leaving,"

The words hit me like a brick wall; my face flushed with heat. For some reason, I was immediately reminded that I had just received the news of my passing the exam to become a computer programmer for the state of Illinois. I was really looking forward to the challenge, but with this new revelation, I looked up and simply asked, "Leaving?" My mind could not put the pieces together fast enough.

"What would we do then?" I replied with a tremble in my voice.

"I've already started a job search and I think I've got a good bite with a government auditor's job in St. Louis but it's going to require me to do some training there. In the meantime, you can take the children and stay with your family in Memphis until I get everything established."

"Memphis!" I exploded. "Memphis! Not Memphis! You've got to be kidding! Charles, I left Memphis looking for a job. I didn't plan on going back."

He did not respond. My words hung in the air as I stared at him in disbelief. He only looked at me with a stoic gaze. It was something that he had to do, what he thought was best for our family.

Chapter 8

Welcome Back to the Old South

It was the summer of 1965 when we pulled up stakes in Chicago and headed south. The plan was for the children and me to temporarily stay in Memphis while Charles would continue on to St. Louis to set up a permanent residence. My sister, Dorothy Mae, had left Chicago the previous year and moved to California, and now I was leaving, too. Part of me was happy to be abandoning the harsh Chicago winters; I was also looking forward to living around my family again. But I was also feeling a great deal of trepidation about moving back to the South, even for a short while. The country was in the midst of the Civil Rights Movement, and now we were moving into the middle of it. Change was taking place, but I wondered how much change had come to Memphis. In Chicago, our skin color did not hinder us; in fact, we had prospered as tokens of diversity, but in Memphis, I knew that our race would be like a millstone around our necks. Nevertheless, I kept telling myself that my time in Memphis would be short. But the unexpected happened. The job that Charles was seeking in St. Louis fell through, and my initial worries related to the move were becoming a reality. No longer were we just visiting, we were here to stay, and I knew that our daily lives would now be shaped by the hardships of being black in the old South.

My greatest concern was Charles. While he was not naive about the existence of racial prejudice, his untarnished attitudes toward race relations had developed within a vacuum that was not tethered to Jim Crow. That characteristic made him both unique as a black man in America and vulnerable to the emotional shock of the old South. Even though I had exposed him to glimpses of segregation during a brief visit to Memphis before we were married, that exposure was only a taste of the real world. Life was about to get rough, and I was worried about how Charles was going to cope with a culture that was established and maintained on the principles of treating blacks as second-class citizens. Repeatedly, I warned Charles that in the South, life on all levels, was more difficult for blacks and that the color of his skin and not education or talent would be the main determinant in his access to opportunity; in essence, I tried to mentally prepare him and myself for the worst.

Unfortunately, my initial fears were soon realized.

Shortly, after arriving in Memphis, Charles and I faced the first storm of our five-year marriage as we tackled the problem of employment. We had been told that the hiring practices for blacks were slightly better than they had been a decade earlier when I left Memphis. I could not see the difference. Memphis was predominantly a service economy, far from the banking and finance centers of Chicago, and it was apparent that Jim Crow was still very much alive as Charles was turned down by company after company. Charles' resume was packed with impressive references from predominantly white institutions, such as Ohio State, Northwestern, and stock brokerage firms. On paper he looked great, and his resume got him quick notice. But then, there was the interview, and once they saw his black skin and heard his strong northern accent, he was quickly turned away. On one occasion, after applying for an accountant position at DuPont and walking into the office, he was promptly told, "We don't hire coloreds and if we did, we would hire one of our own boys and not some Yankee." His two most obvious traits, skin color and his eloquent voice, which had served him well just months previously, now had become a large billboard announcing his imminent hiring failure.

 Yet, Charles was the type of man who did not openly complain or freely express his innermost feelings. As a result, during those rough times, I often wondered what propelled him through all of the rejections and what had prevented him from simply quitting and running back to Chicago. Of course, there were times when he was frustrated, but with each day he started his search for employment with a renewed energy. Focused and persistent in his pursuit, he never became angry; but the grim reality of our shrinking savings was beginning to take its toll. After fixing up the house that we had rented, we knew that the owner would look for any reason to break our contract so that he could sell the house to someone else for a higher cost. Also, since our furniture was stuck in storage, Charles, Todd and I spent our nights sleeping on pallets on hardwood floors. Fortunately, we had brought Cheryle's baby bed down with us. Our morale was sinking.

Finally, after months of being caught in a cycle of rejections with no end in sight, Charles made a change. He decided to start his own accounting practice where he specifically targeted small businesses and black business owners. Initially, business was extremely slow with little money coming in, but his number of clients grew. Normally in business, an upswing in clients usually translates to increased income. However, most of the people who needed his services were themselves struggling to meet their own payrolls. This meant that sometimes we would have to wait for payment long after services had been rendered and even with payment, sometimes their checks would bounce, creating a greater hardship for us. Times were rough as we precariously measured success on a day-by-day basis.

Seven days a week, he worked feverishly but, strangely enough, he seemed content if not happy. At first, his mood perplexed me. We were in a financial bind, and the long-term profitability of his accounting business was uncertain at best. His clients were not financial gurus or owned large businesses; like us, they were regular people struggling to keep their business afloat and their families surviving. Because of this, it confused me why Charles seemed happy with the current circumstances and was at peace with himself. Then, the answer occurred to me. Charles had found his niche in, of all places, Memphis. Here, his work directly impacted the lives of people around him. They needed him and valued his advice. By helping them with their taxes, financial planning and expanding their business, Charles was doing more than just improving their paychecks; his actions were benefitting their lives. What he did not gain in monetary value, he gained in the personal satisfaction of knowing that he was helping struggling families and communities to survive and even thrive. In Memphis, he finally felt significant, connected to something much larger than what he was doing in Chicago. In essence, Charles had found his purpose in life.

With time, our financial situation did gradually improve. And surprisingly, with all of the racism that Charles had encountered when he first sought employment in Memphis, his first major client as an entrepreneur was a white man. He was the owner of a pallet company who had agreed to have Charles do his books for a modest fee. Although it was not a lot of money, I was grateful for a regular paying client. But after seeing Charles' work, the owner was so impressed that he increased his hours and tripled his original payment. When Charles told me this in his typical casual manner, he did not see the significance of it except that the man was a paying customer, but I saw it as an indicator that race relations were improving or, so I hoped. Personally, things were also improving for my family. Business was going well, and we were blessed with another son, Craig, in the spring of 1967. But just a year later, life would be turned upside down in Memphis and the rest of the nation.

My brother, Jonathan, stopped by my house while I was getting ready to fix chili for dinner. It was April 4, 1968. I vividly remember the date – not because of his visit but because of the horrific event that happened during his visit. It was early evening when my brother sat down at my table. He loved to boast about his cooking and would often tease that his chili was better than mine; so, he took over and made a pot of his "masterpiece." In our usual way, while sitting in the kitchen, we talked, laughed and reminisced about old times; then, the conversation turned serious. The shift in tone was not surprising or unusual. The entire city was on edge as a result of rising tensions from the ensuing sanitation workers' strike, and through the middle of it all, a deeper line had been drawn between black versus white. This type of division was nothing new; it had always existed in Memphis. However, at this particular time, that imaginary line had become a battle line as the white majority dug in with the defiance of the old guard and the black community lashed back with resistance against Jim Crow. What started out as a simple strike was mushrooming into an all-out civil war against years of oppression. Skirmishes had been erupting throughout the city in doses just small enough to release a fraction of the pressure. But the pipeline of hate and oppression that had stretched back to the origins of the city was beyond the critical point and about to explode. Just like the humid haze that hung over the city, fear was everywhere and real. And like everyone else, my brother and I were afraid that something bad was about to happen. It was during that conversation that my brother surprised me with a question.

"Do you believe that when your work on this earth is finished, that God calls you home?"

"Yes," I said emphatically.

Again, he startled me, this time with his response, "Martin Luther King's work is finished."

As a minister I had heard my brother speak prophetically before, still, his comment struck an uncomfortable chord. The word "finished" sounded ominous and had such finality to it that neither of us attempted to elaborate further. From that point, the conversation trailed off as we finished eating. Once completed, he left my house to go home which was just a few streets away, but within minutes he returned and blew his horn. I ran to the door, and he hollered out as he approached me with a look of panic on his face...

"Earnie! They shot Dr. King! Turn on your radio." He knew my television was not working.

I immediately could feel the blood rushing to my face, as I stood paralyzed, unable to move anything except for the thoughts in my head. My brother quickly moved past me toward the radio. Still shocked, I could only comprehend fragments from the radio broadcast, "Shots fired at the Lorraine Motel." I could not believe my ears. What was the world coming to? First, they killed President Kennedy and now this. Later, I found out that the shot was fatal. Dr. Martin Luther King, Jr., was dead, and from that moment, someone or something had unleashed a firestorm into the atmosphere. The previously quiet and lazy afternoon was now being ripped to shreds by the constant squall of police sirens. The civil defense alarm howled as if it were announcing the end of the world.

Sometime during all of this, Jonathan had left, and I sat there in fear, staring at my children and waiting for Charles to come home. I was motionless, knowing that Memphis had become the epicenter of a rage that had reached its boiling point, and my neighborhood was only a few miles from the Lorraine Motel. Finally, Charles walked through the door, and I could tell by the look on his face that he, too, was experiencing the same horror. Looking up into the sky, the familiar black night glowed with a reddish hue – clearly something was on fire. The shrill of alarms continued nonstop, and I shuddered every time I heard gunshots ring out through the night.

Over the next several days and weeks, it was amazing how the entire world outside of the United States reacted to Dr. King's death, but it was terrifying to experience firsthand the rioting and violence that erupted in Memphis. Our neighborhood seemed to turn overnight into a militarized zone. There were troops everywhere, carrying machine guns and roaming the streets in green military jeeps that carefully zigzagged around abandoned torched cars. It was difficult to shop for food; the small "mom-and-pop" stores that once stood on the corner were now boarded up or had been replaced with mounds of rubble and burnt debris. Through the haze of the turmoil, neighbors tried to regain some sense of normality by coming out of their houses to talk and socialize. However, the conversations were usually centered on rumors as to who killed Dr. King and talk of sightings of people being picked up and dragged away by soldiers. No one was relaxed, and everyone constantly looked over his or her shoulders. Before long, it was usually the civil defense alarm, announcing the beginning of curfew that broke up the chatter and forced people to run inside their homes. Gone were the people talking casually in the yards; no longer could you see children playing. The only thing left was desolation and an eerie silence. This was how each day ended with people hidden behind the security of locked doors and suspiciously peering out their windows. It was all unnatural. Only the sound of the television, which we had repaired, helped to provide a little comfort, but the images of devastation on the evening news were so strikingly similar to the images right outside our windows that it only reminded us more of our stark reality.

 Even though I, along with the rest of the world, was shocked at the assassination of Dr. King, I was not entirely surprised. With the rising hostility and the vile rhetoric toward Dr. King, I felt that it was just a matter of time before they got him. While he was revered by the world, as evident by his Nobel Peace Prize, the intense hatred directed toward him was incredible; yet, somehow, I had expected it to occur in some "backwards hick town" in the Deep South. Instead, standing in the kitchen and listening to the news blasting from the television, I had to not only deal with the grief and sorrow of the tragedy, but also with the shame that it had occurred in Memphis, my hometown.

Lost in my thoughts, I was drawn back to my surroundings when Charles walked into the kitchen, carrying Craig who was only a year old at the time. Sitting down at the table, he was joined by Todd and Cheryle as he began to bounce Craig on his knee. He loved playing with the children.

"I talked to Mr. Tooley today," he said in a very nonchalant manner.

Mr. Tooley was the owner of the home we were renting. He had decided that he wanted to sell it and was pushing us on making a decision on whether we wanted to buy it. But he wanted to sell the place at an unreasonably high price. All of this did not seem to bother Charles. He never really liked the house and had only considered it as a temporary dwelling. As a result, he had been looking for something else and had found a really nice, new complex, the Belz Apartments, but there was one problem. Blacks were not allowed to live there. However, a class action lawsuit had been filed against the property to mandate equal housing, and since Charles was familiar with the case, he knew that it was just a matter of time before the lawsuit would be settled. So, along with others, we put our names on a waiting list. But the dilemma with Mr. Tooley had suddenly become a more urgent issue, and once again our immediate future had been thrown into an uncertain transition.

"So, how'd it go with Mr. Tooley?" I asked.

"He wanted to know if we had made up our mind yet. So, I told him that we weren't interested and that we would be moving."

"When do we have to move?" I asked.

"At the end of the month," he casually replied while rising from the table.

"The end of the month! That's in two weeks!"

"I know, but don't worry. I've already got this place where we can stay until the court order passes." He then walked out of the kitchen, carrying the baby.

My mind began to immediately whirl with a laundry list of questions. How would I pack on such short notice? What needed to be done first? How would I get the children ready? Then, all of a sudden, my planning slammed into a wall as the most important question finally hit me.

"Where are we moving?" I yelled out to Charles in the next room.

"One of my clients owns a motel downtown."

Thinking to myself – downtown? I couldn't think of any motels downtown where blacks were allowed to stay except for one. "What's the name of this motel?" I cautiously asked.

"He's giving us a great deal."

With a firmer tone, again I asked, "What's the name of the motel?"

"We can stay there until we move into the new apartment"

"What's the name of this motel?" I waited a moment; then I heard him mumble something. "What did you say?'

"The Lorraine Motel."

My mind went completely blank as I dropped a glass bowl on the floor. Only the sound of the shattered glass brought me back to my senses. I immediately ran into the living room, hoping that what I had heard was a mistake, but the look on his face did not hint at anything else.

"The Lorraine Motel! You've got to be kidding...right?"

"Look, Earnestine..."

"We can't stay at the Lorraine! They just killed Dr. King

there!"

He fell silent for a moment and then said, "We don't have a choice. Besides, we're only going to be there for a short while."

"But, Charles, it's the Lorraine Motel."

"I know," as he dropped his head.

Just a few weeks later, I found myself staring out the window of a first-floor room at a large sign that read, "Lorraine Motel." Rarely did I open the curtains fully due to the fear of "something happening." However, that did not stop me from peering out the window day after day and watching a constant flow of visitors who wanted to see the place where Dr. King was shot. Yet, on this particular day, a much larger, somber mass of people had been steadily growing – slowly engulfing the tiny motel in a thick blanket of remorse.

Grabbing his briefcase, Charles was heading out to work but stopped to look out the window at the sea of people. For several moments we both stood there, staring in silence until I said, "There must be thousands of people out there."

"Yeah, I read in the paper that the Southern Christian Leadership Conference had already scheduled to hold their annual conference in Memphis before Dr. King was shot. But now, since his assassination, they decided to hold a special rally here today in his memory," Charles said.

"It's been three months since his murder, and the people are still coming," I remarked. "Each day, from dawn to dusk, they walk up those steps to the balcony to see the place where he was shot. It's interesting that most of them are white people who are courageous enough to press through the ghetto to come and show respect for a man that they never met."

Slowly, Charles responded, "Yeah, I know."

Chapter 9

A Gift from God

By November of 1968, life had calmed down in Memphis. No longer were there sirens, riots, or patrolling National Guardsmen. We moved out of the motel and left behind us, the daily vigils at the Lorraine; our lives had transitioned to a more tranquil residential life. Thanks to the passage of the court order, we were able to move out of the motel and into the Belz Apartments. But it was not long before we outgrew the confines of the apartment, when in the summer of 1969, I had my fourth child, a girl we named Michelle. Fortunately for us, the wave of integration had not stopped with the apartment complex but was spreading into neighborhood housing developments. After a short search and without conflict or court orders, Charles and I purchased our first home in a predominantly white middle class neighborhood. We were among the first black families to integrate the area.

It was a fairly new development, named Cherokee Heights, complete with manicured lawns and thematic names, such as Robin Hood Avenue and Sherwood School. Previously, the neighborhood had been a golf course with gentle sloping hills. The one thing that I relished most about our new home was the large backyard; finally, my children could romp and play outside – a perk that reminded me of my childhood. No longer did I have to drive them to a park to play. It all felt relatively safe and surprisingly, I did not think too much about the potential of racial strife. Our neighbors were civil, and some were very friendly; but soon after our arrival, "for sale" signs simultaneously started popping up all over the place. Before long, white flight took hold and black families began moving into the neighborhood. The once all-white neighborhood quickly became predominantly black. However, our white neighbors, the Spillmans, who lived next door to us, remained, electing not to move. We shared as neighbors; they gave us vegetables from their garden, and I gave them peaches from our tree. Finally, after a number of years, the Spillmans, at the age of retirement, sold their house and moved away. But before leaving Mr. Spillman gave Gaius, our youngest son who was born after moving into our new home, a parting gift of replicas of great ships from his private collection. It was a gift of love that transcended the ugliness of racism.

Even with all of the racial drama playing out in the background, we were definitely living the American dream: a beautiful family, a beautiful home and a beautiful neighborhood. Everyone was healthy, and our finances were stable, and after years of dealing with the uncertainty of moving from place to place, life was seemingly idyllic. But something was missing. Though I could not encapsulate in words the exact nature of this indescribable void, I could feel the emptiness, and I knew the reason for it. There was one key element that was missing – what was my life's calling? It was the one thing that had eluded me my entire life.

When I was near death as a baby, it was first foretold by my aunt to my mother that God had a special work for me, but thirty-three years later, I still did not know what this special work was. Adding to this ambiguity were two startling dreams that only increased my confusion. In the first dream I found a coin dated 1545; in the second one, I saw myself painting three beautiful portraits of Christ, each was a distinctively different style of art. I did not understand either dream. My discovering an obviously valuable coin drew a complete blank in my mind as far as what it meant, and the dream of my painting beautiful portraits of Christ was farfetched, considering that my propensity for drawing or painting was about as far from reality as one could get. Furthermore, as I repeatedly pondered over their meanings, I was reminded of the recurring dream of my playing the piano. I was completely lost. None of this made any sense, but the dreams had to be important. Somehow, there was something deep inside, beckoning that these dreams were related to my purpose. Yet, an explanation for any of it escaped my comprehension and was beyond logical reasoning. I was in my thirties, a housewife with children, which in my mind, meant that my path was set. Accepting this reality did not dismay me; it was a fact of life that I embraced without reservation, but those dreams clearly represented a radical shift away from my ordinary existence. I just could not fathom how they could have any bearing on my life. But, something was about to happen which was going to force me into a new direction and remove the obscurity of my purpose. With the change in the seasons, a pivotal oddity would occur that would provide both the answer to my prayers and the meanings of my dreams in the most peculiar and astounding manner – an event that would forever change my life.

It was the spring of 1972. The rains had fallen, and the flowers were gradually pushing themselves up. The children played in the yard, and the birds chirped. Each day I did the usual cooking and cleaning, and on the weekends, I shopped for groceries, did the laundry and sometimes visited nursing homes to read to the visually impaired. My daily life, while pleasant, was ordinary. But this was spring and like the season, I was propelled by the inevitable cycle of change. This meant several things, but one in particular was a ritual, which started when I was a child – spring-cleaning. Not your regular cleaning but an overhaul that involved everyone and lasted for days. Everything was polished, shampooed, moved around or painted. While dramatic, the physical changes in the house were largely cosmetic, but the real change was about to happen within me.

That spring, my sister-in-law, Flora, came to me one Sunday after church and asked me to assist her in putting together an Easter program. Flora was the wife of the pastor of the church, who was my brother, Jonathan, and with so many other duties to perform, she actually laid this project in my lap. Over the next several days, I poured over children's books that I had recently purchased from a door-to-door salesman, and I visited stores looking for material for the Easter program. Unable to find what I had envisioned, I decided to write my own material directly from the Holy Scripture.

The days quickly stretched into weeks as I found myself caught up in a whirlwind of writing. I had not written so much since my early years of my marriage, but despite the lapse, the writing came naturally. It felt comfortable. However, there was one thing missing from the program – music. I desired to have thematic and complementary songs, following each scriptural reading, narrative and skit. This seemed like an almost impossible task since I was not musically inclined and was unable to get assistance from the church music director. While the creative energy flowed from me during the narrative writing, the music aspect brought me to a screeching halt. After some time, the reality of this impasse finally forced me to settle on the idea of having the children sing traditional hymns. When I had finished putting together the program, I was pleased with the project. But then, something extraordinary happened.

As I stood in the bedroom of my home, I began to prepare for the first rehearsal, starting with the scriptural reading, St. John 3:16. I opened my mouth, intending to read the scripture, but instead I was singing the scripture. It was not of my own volition. When it ended, I stood there, speechless. I could feel another presence in the room; something supernatural had happened. I felt both fear and delight. Awestruck, I walked over and sat on the bed. My mind was blank, as I tried to figure out what had happened or why it had happened. Finally, I stood up and returned to my program. As I attempted to read the next scripture, St. John 3:17, the same thing happened, I sang the scripture. Now, this was too much. I closed the Bible, folded my papers, gathered my children and headed to church. Driving to church, I was rapturous. The beautiful melodies that had flowed out of me with such calmness and peacefulness resounded in my soul.

Once at church, I spoke with a musician who was visiting from St. Louis and sang to him what I had heard.

"Oh, what a beautiful melody. You should finish the song," he remarked.

I quickly replied, "You don't understand. I don't write music. In fact, I don't even play a musical instrument."

"Huh?" he said.

The musician looked puzzled. So, I explained to him the phenomenon that had occurred prior to the rehearsal. At that point, he confidently responded, "If God has given you two verses, surely He can give you a whole song." Of course, I couldn't disagree with that.

Returning home, I was fully charged and challenged to write my first song. Yet, there was some trepidation about my ability to write music. What would be the next verse? How would the rest of the melody flow? When I first sat down at my desk, the blank sheet of paper looked intimidating; then, I remembered to simply continue on the path that I had started, compiling my story from John 3:16-17. After I had written down the lyrics, I began to sing the melody that I heard as a soprano solo part, with the chorus answering or singing as in agreement with the soloist. It was as though there was a force deep down inside of me guiding and directing me as I composed. I sang the words and arranged the song, as I was inspired; the lyrics were indistinguishable from the melody. My voice became both instrument and sheet music where I mentally transcribed and performed the notes. It was the story within the song that dictated the mood, the tempo and even the melody. Everything was coming together, including my scholastic background. I found myself using mathematical symbols to convey on paper what I was feeling musically. Of course, it wasn't very long before I realized, first hand, how music was so mathematical.

All of my life I had wondered what God's purpose was for me. I had searched relentlessly to know my calling, and now, the floodgates had opened up, and my soul was gushing a never-ending geyser of music. My spirit had come alive with music and I heard it everywhere – while driving, shopping, cleaning the house and even during sleep. Yet, the place where I enjoyed composing the most was the back patio of my house. An extended lawn chair sheltered from the sun by the shade of the house had become my personal studio, largely because I loved the outdoors and because it was a quiet refuge from my children who favored the air conditioning over the heat outside. During the summer, the temperatures would often hover in the upper 90s, but there I was, armed with a pitcher of ice water and pad and pencil, caught up in the ecstasy of a creative explosion; I would spend countless hours singing and directing an imaginary choir, totally oblivious to the sweltering heat.

Sometimes a melody would come to me in a quiet corner of my mind, and at other times, it was like a rapturous chorus of angels performing from a corner in my bedroom. Day and night, I could barely contain my excitement as song after song unexpectedly came to me. After I had completed my first song, "For God So Loved The World," I composed my second song, "O' Lamb of God" followed by "The Crucifixion" and "The Prologue to the Crucifixion."

Although my musical journey had started in the most astounding manner, writing "The Crucifixion" occurred in the most dramatic fashion. It was an overcast, cloudy day, and I was pacing in my bedroom, holding a page full of lyrics and scriptures about the Passion of our Lord. The more I paced, the more the words swirled in my head, heightening my senses and pushing my subconscious beyond myself. Then, something inexplicable happened that I was not initially aware of. My conscious being seemed to transcend and cross a chasm into another reality. I was being pulled to a location almost two thousand years into the past. No longer was I surrounded by the furniture in my bedroom, instead I was caught up, witnessing the trial and crucifixion of Christ – the mockery, the scorn, the final hours of his suffering. I saw the women weeping at the foot of the cross, "weeping and moaning, weeping and moaning." I sang what I saw. It was simply that, as I saw it, I sang it. And as quickly as my journey began, it ended with my standing again in my bedroom, singing "The Crucifixion." With that song, I didn't just compose it, but I told the story of what I saw in my spirit. Once, when "The Crucifixion" was performed, a woman came to me at the end of the concert and asked, "How in the world did you write that song?" I said, "I didn't. I was just an instrument. Absolutely, it was divinely inspired."

Through all of this, Charles would often sit by and watch with amazement. With his background in classical music, he understood all too well the complex structure of this genre of music; as a result, he marveled at my sudden ability to compose classical pieces with ease. With each song that I created and sang to him, he could only shake his head in disbelief. One by one, the songs came to me. I could feel them. Soon, it was Christmas, and my heart was filled with the spirit of the season. As a result, I automatically switched to writing Christmas songs. It was all so simple and easy as if I were a vessel being filled up with music.

During the span of the next three years, everything was happening so quickly. It was so overwhelming that I did not stop to consider the next step. Of course, there was my church, but the idea of pursuing music as a career or avocation was always for the other person and certainly not for me. I had always thought that others were more adept for music than me like my best friend, Mattie Pearl, who had studied music; or my roommate in college who had majored in music; and my husband who was a classically trained pianist. As for me, I had always believed that I possessed no musical talent. As a result, growing up, music was never an option; I was a mathematician. But here I was with a fountain of songs pouring out of me. Then, there was another dilemma of who was going to sing them. All of my songs were Easter or Christmas classical pieces. The question plagued me because I had never heard my church choir sing this style of music. After much deliberation, I made a shortsighted decision to switch to writing contemporary gospel songs. Even with this change, there was still no overall direction or purpose to my writing – at least, from what I could tell at that time.

However, that all changed with one song. After some years of not writing classical music, I was captivated by a beautiful melody. It was clearly classical. I remembered the exact moment because the song was such a radical departure from my current frame of mind. While walking out of the house to shop for groceries, an incredible voice encompassed me like a wave. It was a tenor singing, "I shall be betrayed by someone near." It was so startling that I asked Charles to go to the grocery store without me. I went back inside the house and immediately developed that melody into a song, entitled, "The Betrayal." My mind and hands moved feverishly as if not to lose that moment. As I worked on that song, it finally became clear to me that what seemed like random songs that I had written over the years were anything but random. They were not just a string of songs. Embedded within those years was a well-orchestrated course, and with a sudden awareness, I realized that they all pointed to events leading up to and including the Passion of Christ. I thought that if I composed a few more songs, I would have told the entire story of the Passion of Christ. Over a span of thirteen years from the first to the last song, I completed my first oratorio, "The Crucifixion," depicting the death and resurrection of Christ. What I thought was a path of coincidental events was actually the hand of God guiding me during my periods of befuddlement. Grasping this realization, I elevated my expectations with an eye keenly fixed on Him; and with this gift from God firmly in my hand, I turned toward the future.

Chapter 10

Uphill Journey

After an explosion of composing new songs, I was left staring at a stack of my work on the table and pondering what to do next. The perplexing challenge of how I would expose and promote my music seemed insurmountable because I didn't know where to start. Even though I knew that God had chosen me for this work, the ambiguity of what I was doing and the uncertainty of what to do next was always a constant presence. Yet, there was one thought that plagued me the most, "Why did God choose me?" I showed no talent for music growing up; I was not born into a family with a musical legacy; and I did not have the money, resources or connections for a career in entertainment. I was one of the least qualified. Furthermore, I did not know how anyone, especially me, a housewife, would promote classical music in Memphis, a city known for Elvis and blues. The more I thought about it, the more dejected I became. This was going to be an uphill journey. However, I knew one thing, if I were to succeed, it would only happen if I put my trust in God; and each day I prayed and asked God for direction.

Resolution did not come soon or easy. In fact, it seemed that my mind was being plagued by the very opposite. One day, I had a dream that I was walking down a street. In the dream, there was a strong headwind so intense that I struggled to place one foot in front of the other. But the strange thing about the dream was the fact that all of the people surrounding me were walking normally without any difficulty. The wind was only affecting me. Even though I did not fully understand the meaning of the dream at the time, it was not long before I realized that the wind of opposition was blowing strongly against me in my efforts in getting my music heard. Yet, despite the ominous nature of the dream, something inside me was pushing me, and I earnestly believed that God would not have given me a gift to simply have it tucked in a folder or stashed in a drawer. As a result, I decided to pitch my music to an established record label.

Just a few miles from my home was Stax Records, a recording studio that was known primarily for its rhythm and blues, and artists such as Otis Redding and Isaac Hayes. However, they did have a gospel division, and knowing this,

I put together a demo tape of some of my contemporary gospel songs and made an appointment. It turned out that the person who interviewed me was Mary Peake, the vice-president of the gospel division. She was a very pleasant black woman who patiently and very intently listened to all of my recordings; at times, she nodded her head with the music and gave an occasional slight smile. Surely, this was a good sign. Afterwards, in a cordial manner, she asked many questions about my background, was gracious in complimenting me on my music, and told me that they would be contacting me and then said goodbye. Everything seemed to go well, and since she seemed so sincere in her comments, I anxiously waited for a call of good news from the studio. But after some time had passed, nothing happened. There was no "yea" or "nay," just nothing, and with the passage of time, I realized that signing with Stax was not going to happen. It was my first muted rejection; so, I moved on. Months later, I found out that Stax Records was closing.

Undaunted in my pursuit to have my music heard, I was excited the following year when I was presented again with the wonderful opportunity of putting together the children's Easter program at church. The event was especially heartwarming for me; after all, it was during preparation of a previous Easter program that the revelation of my first song came to me. However, unlike the previous program, I was not nervous about finding music. I chose some of my Easter compositions and modified them for the children and the youth choirs. Their natural energy and receptiveness were mesmerizing, and I was surprised by how easily they learned the material. The enthusiasm of the children rehearsing for the program was infectious, and word of mouth of the upcoming concert began to spread beyond the neighborhood borders of the church. As a result, with each rehearsal the number of participating children grew, and I had to expand the scope of the program by adding more scriptures and rewriting the narration to match the age of each child. The program was well received by the congregation, and it was the first public performance of my music.

Even though several church members commented on how they enjoyed the music, I was still concerned on how the adult choir would accept my music. They were adept at gospel and traditional hymns, but my music was predominantly classical. And there were other concerns. I was not naive about the egos within the human aspect of the church. Even though my brother was the pastor of the church, I knew that the power brokers that governed the choir were very traditional and narrowly focused. Because of this and the politics within the church, the music department and pulpit were at times delicate minefields where careful navigation was an arduous task. Despite the intricate manner of this environment and my propensity to avoid conflict, I could not ignore the desire within me to hear my classical works performed.

While I contemplated this matter, a fellow church member told me that she was going to be performing my music for another church. Her name was Betty Ann Owens, and she had a beautiful soprano voice. I had been quietly teaching her the dramatic classical song, "The Crucifixion." Therefore, it was a pleasant surprise when she told me that she had been asked to sing my song at the Easter service of Bishop G.E. Patterson, who later became the presiding bishop of the Church of God in Christ. The event was a sunrise Easter service before a large concert hall audience of 3,000. Of course, I was thrilled that my music was being performed, but I was also a little nervous. I wondered how the audience would react to the a cappella performance of this classical work.

On the morning of the service, my oldest son, Todd, accompanied me while Charles stayed at home with the rest of the children. Getting five children ready for the regular 11:00 a.m. Easter service was a tough enough job, but trying to attempt a similar feat before daybreak would have been next to impossible. The sunrise program started at 6:00 am. Ellis Auditorium was packed, but despite the crowd, we managed to get center seats in the upper tiers. As I sat there, my heart was pounding with anticipation. I could feel the nervous energy building inside of me as the program moved along. The scriptural reading, the prayer, and certainly the music, all contained a familiar, comforting rhythm. This was a traditional, Pentecostal black church, and the entire service had a certain harmonic flow to it. You could sense it, feel it – the way everyone swayed and moved to its energy. I knew it all too well. After all, my father and grandfather had been Pentecostal preachers. But the thousands gathered in that hall were about to hear something different. My lyrics would be familiar to the crowd, as they were taken straight from the Holy Scripture, but the classical melody would be foreign to many. Quietly, I said to myself, "How will they receive my music?" As I pondered this, I continued to pray. Finally, as Betty Ann appeared on stage, the piano and organ came to a halt and an unusual silence rendered in its place.

Leaning forward in my seat, I watched as she took in a deep breath. The first series of perfectly pitched notes leaped out of her mouth, ripping through the air and tearing the veil of tradition. I could see that the audience around me was captivated. As she performed the song, I became fixated on the music, mentally accompanying the soloist through every note, lyric and gesture until her bow. There was a pause, a brief moment followed by thunderous applause and standing ovation. My heart leapt in my chest; the applause was my confirmation. From that moment, a fire had been lit inside me, and the drive to push my musical gift was burning bright. I vowed to let nothing stop me from pursuing my purpose with passion.

Over the next several weeks, Charles, who shared my enthusiasm, was united with me in my quest. Although we were bursting with grand ideas, we needed to complete the foundation. As a result, we hired Marcel Holman, a graduate student in composition at the local university, to notate my music. Our latest challenge was to have him score, "The Grace of God," a composition that I had just completed. I really liked this song and was eager to get it in sheet music format. Marcel and I worked on it for days to make it happen. As I sang the voice part, he played the melody on the piano and jotted down notes on sheet music paper.

When the score was completed, Marcel came over to deliver my music or, so I thought, but he surprised me when he pulled out his flute and began to play, "The Grace of God." As his fingers danced across the flute, it was an amazing experience to see the notes come alive, leaping off the page into a whirlwind of sound. I could hardly contain my joy. It was beautiful. Then, Charles took the sheet music, sat at the piano, and began to play, "The Grace of God." It was amazing to hear my husband playing my music. It seemed that the very room was rejoicing and about to burst at the seams. We were all lifted to a realm of blissful joy that day.

With each song, I found myself feeling a growing sense of accomplishment as we slowly laid my musical foundation. After a song was completed, Charles would fill out registration forms and mail the sheet music to the copyright office. This type of working relationship where

Charles would handle the business end and I would steer the creative part was a natural fit, borne out of necessity and merged by compatible talents. It was a team approach that would last our entire lives together.

As the weeks turned into months, our ideas gradually morphed into a large planned project. We interviewed, scouted and courted singers along with musicians and locations for a concert. We decided to put together a performance using a nearby college choir. The renowned opera star, Marguerite Piazza, who sang with the Metropolitan Opera in New York, agreed to perform the title song, "The Crucifixion." I was elated and highly honored that a person of Ms. Piazza's standing would agree to sing my music. She never inquired what her fee would be. The only question that she asked, amusingly, as I gave her a score of the music was, "Where are my money notes?" We both chuckled. I was impressed not only with her voice but also with her sincerity and humility. Unfortunately, the choir that we selected could not perform the music despite the music director assuring me that there would be no problem with the new work. Of course, this was disastrous as we struggled to find a replacement, but we were unable to recover. It was our first concert and our first cancellation.

Despite the failure, our resolve was still strong, but the light of our desire did flicker as we tried to understand where we had made our mistake. After much deliberation, Charles reminded me that these types of things were to be expected in the entertainment field and that we probably had not vetted the choir well enough. I agreed, and with very little hesitation, we started again the process of trying to get the music performed. This time we were meticulous in our efforts; we researched choirs at churches, schools and civic groups within our reach. Unfortunately, there was always some degree of disappointment with the outcome. Large experienced groups came with lofty price tags or looked at us with disdain, small choirs with little experience and musical acumen could not handle the music, and others simply made promises only to break them later. Sometimes the disappointment occurred early in the planning phase, and at other times it came later; but failure was the usual outcome. Of all of the various obstacles, money was always our constant threat; it was the enemy lurking behind the corner of every idea and decision. We struggled to support a growing family while simultaneously bank rolling a concert project that seemed to be more of a delusion with each cancellation than a dream come true.

As the months rolled into years, each failed concert attempt took its financial and psychological toll on us; only the children were unfazed by the events. Our savings were gone, and we were back in financial debt. Adding to our plight was the recession that was raging in the 1970s. Inflation had driven the price up on everything from milk to clothing to gasoline, which pushed our strained budget to the edge every week. This forced Charles to work longer hours. He was scouring for clients in an economy that was grinding down and evaporating minority small businesses. To make matters worse, one of his more successful clients was a person for whom I had no respect. Even though Charles had successfully bid and won several construction contracts for him, this client always seemed to find a convenient loophole or misrepresentation to shorten his wages. I often asked Charles why he allowed this. He never gave me a clear-cut answer, but the look on his face showed me that he shared a similar disdain for this client. Deep down I knew that his tolerance for this client's behavior was his way of survival, and, as a result, I felt guilty of the extra burden that the music had placed on him. Yet, it was always Charles who was the driving force that pushed me, relentlessly, in my musical career.

Somewhere during the midst of this, I developed intermittent bouts of stomach aches. At first, the attacks were infrequent and amounted to nothing more than mild annoyance. However, as time progressed, and the doldrums of our situation deepened, the painful episodes increased in frequency and severity. Rarely did a meal pass that I did not experience pain and cramping, but these episodes also occurred with any situation of increased anxiety. Sometimes I could relax and soothe it, but there were other times that the pain would not abate until it crescendoed into a bout of vomiting. Everywhere I went, I carried a handful of Alka-Seltzer tablets or a box of baking soda in my purse. It was so bad that Charles repeatedly begged to take me to a hospital, but I refused. My avoidance to seek medical attention was probably motivated by subconscious reasons, stemming from a past experience when I had similar symptoms. At that time, the doctors were unable to make a diagnosis based upon my symptoms but decided to do exploratory surgery. Despite finding nothing wrong, they removed my appendix. This time I decided to cope with my pain by taking anti-acids, avoiding certain foods and skipping meals when the pain was severe. Even though I learned to manage my symptoms, the condition took its toll on me as I began losing weight due to finicky eating.

With all of my troubles, the joy of that day when I composed my first song felt like a distant memory; my spirit had become bruised from a stampede of disappointment. I was praying for God to heal me from my stomach ailment and for a breakthrough with my music. Even though I never stopped believing God's promise to me and my special purpose, I was perplexed and searched for answers as to why the concerts were not working. I prayed, asking the Lord, "What happened? I know You gave me this music." As unbelievable as it may sound, God answered me in a still, quiet voice saying, "Your vision is too small." I didn't know where I should go from there but apparently, I needed to dream bigger.

Chapter 11

Sounds of a Miracle

By 1978, my family had grown to a size of seven. My five children, who had been born in stair-step fashion, were moving through their usual milestones of childhood, puberty, and adolescence. With each birthday, they grew an inch taller and an inch closer to independence. Witnessing the signs of their predictable growth also had the added effect of reminding me of my own progression. While I was pleased and grateful for the success of my family, the hopes for my music had not followed the same steady, positive trajectory. I was constantly writing, but despite my efforts I was still waiting for something to happen with it. Even though this lack of development was disappointing, I was content with the other aspects of my life. The immediate world around me was in harmony. The children were doing well, and Charles, who had found a balance between managing his clients' financial affairs and spending time with family, had found his stride.

But, for me, the story was a bit different. My daily life was a never-ending decathlon of projects, assignments and deadlines. In the morning, at the crack of dawn everything started with an abrupt jolt as my entire family stumbled out of bed into an obstacle course of rotating turns in the two bathrooms, flying through the kitchen for a quick breakfast and packed lunches, and finally piling into the family car. Once we backed out of the driveway, the station wagon transformed into a taxi as it raced around town through traffic, dropping off passengers at different schools before the dreaded tardy bell. My destination was usually the last stop as Charles dropped me off at the University of Memphis where I was taking classes. Even though the university was only located a few minutes from my home, our "taxi route" made the trip closer to an hour. Later that evening, the entire process ran in reverse but with added events of grocery shopping, homework, school projects and a final destination of everyone sitting around the dinner table.

Dinner was more than just an activity. If there ever was a single moment in time and space where the personality, tempo, and mood of my family was on full display, dinner was that moment. From the time when the food was blessed, the entire family would erupt into a simultaneous chorus of conversation. Everyone seemingly talked at the same time. To an outsider, this spectacle could easily be misconstrued as chaos, but to everyone around the table, it was comfortable and completely natural as we moved in and out of one another's conversations. Talking, laughing, and utensils clanking – it was a symphony of noise that we performed every night.

However, in a household of five kids with varied expectations and schedules, conflicts arose on a regular basis. This was due in a small part to physical limitations. There was only one television set, one radio, one car and one telephone line – no multiple cell phones like we have now. As a result, we had to share everything and do everything together: church, meals, entertainment, traveling or just simply sitting around in the family den. The combination of our sharing, the close proximity, and our differences would invariably lead to problems. However, as quickly as the disagreements and arguments erupted, they were always resolved. Sometimes, this resolution happened with talking and crying, and sometimes it occurred with yelling. But in the end, the peace would always be restored. Our individual differences were clearly evident, but with the passage of time, it was those same differences combined with our shared experiences that somehow produced something far greater – a close family that cheered, rallied and fought for one another despite the odds.

Although I was grateful for the comfort of the unity, it was not complete; there was something else that was missing. Through the din of my busy life, a quiet voice deep within me tugged at my subconscious, reminding me of my music. Sometimes it was an event that reminded me of my purpose, or a musical note playing in my head, or simply a whisper telling me, "You must do what God has ordained you to do." No matter the circumstances, the effect was the same – pulling my focus back to my music – my purpose.

One such reminder walked in with Charles one evening. His days were unusually long and exhaustive because he was splitting his time between his accounting practice and a new project where he offered his accounting services to a local funeral director who was running for U.S. Congress at the time. On most days, he would return home with just enough energy to collapse into his chair in front of the television or at the dinner table. However, on this particular day, his level of fatigue had been replaced with a perky gait and slight smile. Moments after stepping into the house, he made a bold announcement, "We're going to do an album." Then, he turned and disappeared down the hallway.

I was so startled by his statement that his words seemed jumbled and incomprehensible. Even though I continued to move perfunctorily around the children who were helping to prepare the table for dinner, my confusion hung in the air, waiting for his return to the kitchen.

"What did you say?" I asked.

"I decided that we're going to do an album," he repeated as he sat down.

"What are you talking about?" I asked, still confused.

"An album of your music. The idea came to me after I met this guy, named Earl, a few weeks ago down at the campaign headquarters." Readjusting his chair, he continued in a casual manner while trying to suppress his excitement with a little smirk on his face, "Turns out, Earl used to work for Stax Records. So, I gave him one of your demo tapes."

Puzzled and still trying to catch up on the details of the conversation, I asked, "You gave him one of my tapes?"

"Yeah."

"Okay...so which song did he hear?"

"The Lord is Near," then Charles began to chuckle to himself. "In fact, he told me, Man, why you out here hustlin' when you got a million dollars sitting at home?"

"You said that he worked at Stax?"

"Yeah, a songwriter. Anyway, when he started to go on and on about how much he loved your music, I thought to myself that maybe I should start a publishing company."

"A publishing company?"

"You know, the music industry is like any other business. It's a business."

"But, Charles..."

"Don't worry. All you need to do is just focus on the creative work, and I'll take care of the business. Remember I use to work for Mercury Records."

By this time, the children had ceased their conversations and had tuned entirely into ours. I could tell by the look on Charles' face that he had more to tell, but I was still trying to process the earlier news.

"But there's one condition. I will only do this if you sing three of the songs on the album," he said while staring into my face.

This last bit of news hit me like a wall. While the magnitude of starting a publishing company conjured up many logistical questions, it was the last revelation of my singing that startled me the most. That single thought rang out so loudly in my mind that I could barely think of much else. Singing as I usually did during my composing was one thing, but singing as a recording artist was entirely something else. His request touched on two sensitive areas, which I had long perceived as my weaknesses. I was never comfortable with myself as a singer, and I had always attempted to shy away from anything that made me the main focus of attention. After hearing Charles' stipulation, I had a flashback of my excruciatingly awkward performance in high school. After being elected the student body vice-president, I was asked to give an impromptu acceptance speech. Caught totally off guard, standing on a large empty stage, and facing an auditorium filled with students, I was overwhelmed and dwarfed by a monsoon of emotions that paralyzed me. Finally, after a seemingly eternity of standing there in motionless fright, I somehow managed to muster a few words of thanks and immediately turned and ran off the stage. Equally as painful was the day that I graduated from high school. I walked down the aisle alone in an auditorium filled with people, who watched quietly, as I moved along, placing one foot before the other until I reached the stage and took my seat. I am sure that my solo procession as valedictorian was meant to be an honor, but it was a painful experience. I wanted them to simply announce that I was valedictorian, nothing more. Although years of experience had taught me how to mask the shyness, those high school incidents became my recurring, inaudible alarm that cried out whenever I was unexpectedly placed under the spotlight. Now, as I stared back across the kitchen table at Charles, I reflected on the notion of singing on the album and those familiar anxious feelings began to bubble beneath the surface.

"Charles..." I slowly began to say.

Charles immediately interrupted, "No, Earnestine. I mean it. That's the only way that I'll do this. You have to sing three songs."

From his expression, his decision was steadfast and not negotiable. There was no hesitation, no doubt. In fact, he had already started the project.

Over the next several months, the days and nights morphed into a seamless string of events. With the advent of the project, our previously busy schedules cranked up several notches as our daily lives became a whirlwind of activity that was divided into two categories. During the weekdays, the usual chores of school, work, and other personal obligations were shuffled, compressed and somehow made to fit into the traditional 9 to 5 timeframe. During the nights and weekends, it was everything else related to the album – auditions, contracts, planning and rehearsals. Unwittingly, the project had placed us aboard a roller coaster where it seemed difficult to catch our breath or glimpse at any of the blurred images whizzing by.

Of course, all of this took money and that was the difficult part as we financed the entire project with our personal funds. That meant stripping our household budget to the very basics and making sacrifices. However, it was Charles' tenacity and acuity that really pushed the project forward. Once again, he plunged head first with an incredible determination to ensure the success of the project. Doubling his efforts to pick up extra clients and accounting jobs, he quickly raised money, but his experience with Mercury Records was the biggest payoff. With ease, he created the company from the ground up: drawing up contracts, negotiating studio fees, and even creating all of the copyright documentation of my music – a feat that he accomplished by scoring the lead sheets of my contemporary gospel music while I sat beside him, singing the songs. With his resourcefulness and business acumen, he was relentless in saving money. In essence, he became a one-man music production company with me providing the creative focus; and somewhere, in the middle of the commotion, he decided to name the album, "Sounds of a Miracle."

Although Charles was very efficient and frugal throughout the project, studio time is expensive. He managed to obtain most of the funding by taking on extra work, but to underwrite all of the costs, we had to make deeper lifestyle changes. Some of those changes required us to sacrifice items that we had previously considered as essentials; owning a car was one such item. Having no car and living in a large city like Chicago or New York is easier with an extensive mass transit system, but in Memphis where public transportation is spotty, not having a car meant spending hours each day standing at bus stops, waiting on connections, and walking long stretches to your destination. Unfortunately, during the album project, our car ended up in the shop, and the decision came down to either pay for the repairs or continue with the album. We put the car repairs on hold and moved ahead with the album.

With the name in place and all of the preparations completed, we arrived at the music recording studio one spring evening. It was located in the heart of Memphis on an ordinary corner. The facade of the studio was unassuming in its appearance, as the weathered sign, which read "American Sound Studio," seemed so unpretentious in its existence that it barely distinguished itself from its surroundings. But stepping inside, there was a transformation into a different place in time where the building's objects hinted at the glory of its faded past. The main interior opened up into a large room that contained a collection of mikes and musical instruments and its walls were covered with soundproofing foam, creating a vacuum of sound. There was another room, smaller in size which was barely noticeable and simply labeled "souvenirs," that served as half gift shop – half shrine, displaying gold records and memorabilia of the studio's past performers and giving notice of its most famous alumnus, Elvis Presley.

As intriguing as the studio was, there was no time to reflect on its history. Studio time was very expensive, and Charles ran a very tight schedule. He did not tolerate anyone who was tardy or unprepared, including us. Since we did not have a car, we did not want to run the risk of being late for recording sessions due to tardy bus schedules. As a result, we took a cab to the studio, but afterwards, to save on costs, we would catch a bus, which dropped us off near our home, and we walked the rest of the way. Normally, I would have enjoyed the walk as a relaxed opportunity to talk business with Charles, but because of my anemia at the time, I dreaded it. My condition was such that each block seemed to stretch out like miles. After walking only a few blocks, I would invariably be forced to stop and sit down on the curb to catch my breath. Sitting there, trying to slow the pounding of my heart, I would look down the street, mentally measuring the remaining distance home and dreading getting up. The only thing that provided comfort was the fact that it was dark so that none of my neighbors could see me like that. It was often at times like this when I thought of my brothers and sisters and how they used to tease me about how fragile I was, calling me a "cream puff."

Sitting on that curb, I would occasionally look up at Charles who patiently stood beside me. By his silence, I could tell that he felt sorry for me and was grieved by his inability to make the situation any better. Despite my state, I felt no self-pity; after all, sacrifices had to be made, and this one was mine. So, I never complained. Charles had made sacrifices in embracing my dream. He had poured everything that he had into it and believed in me when others laughed me to scorn. So, I just smiled with assurance, stood up and pushed myself onward. Those trips from the studio did not become any easier, but with each struggle to make it home, I embraced something far greater than the discomfort. This was my chance for people to hear my music, and with each step, I was closer to achieving my dream.

With a disciplined approach, Charles coordinated an ensemble of musicians, soloists and choir members and squeezed their performances into precise time slots, allowing us to record the entire album within a few days. On the last day, it was my turn to record. The first song I chose to sing was my favorite, "The Grace of God." I was isolated in a separate recording booth with nothing more than a mike, a barstool and a set of headphones on my ears. As the music was piped into my ears, I closed my eyes and felt my music flow in me. Everything around me disappeared; only music remained. My previous anxiety and reluctance were quickly replaced with melody and tempo as the music pulled me in and encompassed me. Then, with an internal cue, I began singing; the lyrics flowed out of me with ease, and fortunately for me, only a few retakes were required. After the first song, I quickly started and finished the other two songs, "A Time and a Season" and "Born Again," which were both contemporary selections that I felt the most comfortable performing. While standing in front of the mike, my grasp on time escaped me, and before long, it was over. The recording session transpired with ease that was surprising to me since I had dreaded that moment from the time Charles first requested that I sing on the album. It was only the second time in my life that I had ever publicly performed a song. The first time occurred when I was around ten years old and that was a duet with my cousin, Malvolia, on Easter morning. Just as it was when I was a child, the hardest part was the time leading up to the performance and all of the nervousness associated with it. But after finishing my recording, I smiled; I was glad that Charles had forced me out of my comfort zone.

Chapter 12

Vanishing Hope

Once we completed recording, the plan was to sell the album via regional television ads until we could either sell it to a larger record company or attract the interest of a distributor. That exact plan did not materialize, but something else quite remarkable did happen. Surprisingly, we received local and national acclaim. When Nancy Hart, a reporter for the local NBC affiliate heard about my story, she came to my home and did an interview of me, which aired on the evening news. That interview led to a bigger expose of me on "The Minority Report," a popular public affairs program, also an NBC affiliate. Along with my interview, the "Memphis Community Singers" choir was invited to sing songs from my album, "Sounds of a Miracle." Charles also flew in accomplished soloist, Ernestine Dilliard of Oklahoma to sing "The Crucifixion" on the show; her dynamic performance was outstanding. After this presentation, I was told that the TV station was flooded with calls from people asking them to air that episode again.

We gained national exposure when writer, Rose Clayton, penned a glowing review of our album in "Billboard" magazine. She called my contemporary songs, "easy-listening gospel." Finally, my music was getting out. I was overjoyed as people came up to me even when I was running errands to say that they had seen my inspirational story on TV and enjoyed my music.

Of course, I took this increased awareness to mean that our success was guaranteed, but ironically, we became a victim of our own success. As the commercials ran, the orders feverishly poured in, and the stack of records in our garage began to shrink in size. With the money generated from the record sales, we were able to pay off the debts from the album. It was wonderful that we were succeeding, but something else was happening. What most companies dream of – demand being greater than supply – had become our curse. Although we no longer had debt, we also had no cash reserve and were unable to get a loan. As a result, we were unable to manufacture more albums. Where there was once a stack of albums had now been replaced with a stack of unfilled orders. Success was not just within reach; it was in the palm of our hands, but we could not hold onto it. Experiencing the combination of success and failure was like feeling joy and sadness at the same time. It was a perplexing emotion that left me feeling numb, a feeling that lingered long after the last television commercial went off the air. The enormity of it all choked my spirit and withered my hope. Promise had been taken from us.

Months later, I stood in my living room, looking out the window and continued to reminisce about the promise of the album. I was trying to swallow the disappointment of its unfilled potential. Some mornings, I just simply stared out the window at the spot where the UPS truck used to park, a spot where filled orders took flight from our home, heralding our imminent success. Now, I just stared at an empty spot filled with nothing. Reflecting on the cancelled concerts, the failed album and our current financial downturn, I came to a single, succinct conclusion. That was it. I was done with the music, and with one defining act, everything related to the album, every printed letterhead and every piece of sheet music was packed in boxes and shoved into the garage. I was moving on with my life.

Four years had passed from that moment. Time and my life had drifted by without incident; it was the summer of 1983, an extremely hot, sweltering summer. The pain from the album failure had long faded into the background as the daily routines of family life, and the pursuit of studying philosophy at the university consumed me. The classes captured my interest and seemed to push time forward, and before I knew it, I had completed my bachelor's degree in philosophy. There was no great fanfare associated with it. It was simply a matter of crossing it off of my "to do" list. I was ready to move onto the next item…which did not include music.

Although from time to time, thoughts of my music would occur anecdotally, but I was always quick to push it away from my daily existence. I made it my objective to constantly preoccupy my mind with whatever task that was at hand, and during that summer, I was focused on my oldest daughter, Cheryle. She was preparing for her freshman year at Northwestern University. When Todd, my oldest son, started college a couple of years earlier, getting him ready was a simple matter of filling up a footlocker with all of the basics; but with Cheryle, it was a different situation. Finding clothing and dormitory items that were functional was not enough; everything had to be fashionable with a unique flair that expressed her presumed style. So, there I was, roaming down aisles of a store and probing through racks of clothing with Cheryle and Michelle who were flanking my every turn when I heard someone frantically calling my name.

"Earnie! Earnie!"

Looking up, it was my sister, Doris Jean, walking hurriedly with her child clutching on her hip.

"Girl, you won't believe what has happened," she said while out of breath. "I just came from your house," pausing for a moment before continuing, "Your house caught on fire," she said in a seemingly nonchalant manner.

Reaching for her baby, I casually responded, "Uh, huh."

"Did you hear what I just said?"

"Oh, yeah," I replied while playing with her baby. "I've had so many grease fires in that kitchen."

"No, you don't understand," interrupting me and grabbing my shoulder. She repeated herself but this time with a more forcible delivery, "Your house caught on fire!"

Now, I became frozen as I stared blankly into Doris Jean's face. I could hardly believe what she was telling me.

"Earnie, there are strangers, firemen walking in and out of your house. They were sweeping water out the front door." Still not sensing the expected shock in my reaction, Doris delivered the final blow. "You can stand in your den and look straight up into the sky."

Finally, with that last statement, my legs buckled as I slid down to the floor. My mind had simultaneously exploded with a flood of thoughts and vacuum of nothing; the next thing that I remembered was my daughters trying to raise me from my sitting position on the floor. Doris Jean finally satisfied with my response, began to fill in the details.

"Nobody got hurt, but all I know is, Craig was at the house by himself when the fire started." Doris began to chuckle. "When I drove up, the fire was already out, and Charles was shaking Craig down for information. The boy looked scared and kept mumbling something about cooking a bologna sandwich," at which point Doris burst out into laughter.

"Oh, no!" I exclaimed, "The boy has burned our house down."

"Yeah, that's what Charles thought until the fire chief came up to him and told him that the fire had started up in the attic with some kind of electrical problem."

"Really?"

"Uh, hum, you know it's been so hot. Probably had something to do with the air conditioner. Anyway, when are you going to go by your house?"

"Girl, I can't go there now," I replied.

"What?" Doris said, surprised by my response.

"Let Charles deal with it. I can't handle it right now."

Doris started laughing again. "Girl, you're crazy."

"I need time to prepare myself to face this. Maybe in a couple of hours, I'll go. But right now, I am going to finish shopping."

When it got dark enough, I showed up at the house, and it was just as my sister had said. The greatest fire damage to the house was in the den. The room, which had once been the focal point of our home, was now a colossal mess. Water covered the floor. There was a large hole in the ceiling. The sofa, with its pillows missing, was pushed against a wall while another wall had been cut through with an axe. Chairs were overturned, the television lay face down, and books were strewn all over the room. Plaster and soot saturated everything. The constant dripping of water could be heard as pieces of plaster continued to fall. The aquarium, which had once housed beautiful tropical fish was now broken, and pieces of glass and dead fish were all over the floor. Curtains had been pulled from the windows, which were now opaque from the black smoke that was caked on them. The clock on the wall had stopped at 1:17 PM. But I was amazed when I looked and saw on another wall the beautiful picture of boats docked in a harbor with vibrant colors of the sunset, remained intact, unmarred by the destruction around it. It was the only reminder of the beauty and charm that once graced this room. The memory of that day is forever etched in my mind. It happened to have been one of the hottest days of that summer; also, it just happened to be my sister Doris' birthday, July 29th.

The rest of the house sustained only smoke damage, but roofing and electrical repairs had to be made. Of course, Charles had already contacted insurance agents and contractors. In fact, to my surprise he seemed a bit excited like it was some kind of great project. But I was not surprised at my youngest son, Gaius, who was leading a group of his friends into our home while making the announcement, "Okay, I'm going to show you how the fire burned down our house."

For the next several months, we lived in a hotel while our home was being repaired. This extended transition of living in hotel rooms with five children would probably have been viewed by most as a time of predictable confusion and frustration, but as the months flew by, the whole ordeal seemed like an extended vacation. But just like the end of any vacation, it was good when we returned home. Sometime after moving back, it dawned on me that I had not taken any antacid for my stomach problem. For years I had prayed that God would fix the problem. And now, after years of suffering, He had answered my prayers – my stomach ailment was gone. I do not know exactly when it happened, but sometime during that summer, it left and never returned.

Gradually, everything returned to normal. I made the usual carpooling stops of picking up and dropping off at school, cheerleading and basketball practices – all courtesy of our three children who were still at home. However, with my two oldest away at school, college expenses became an added responsibility. I wanted to help out. Even though Charles had never complained about tackling the financial hardships of the family by himself, I knew that it was a strain on him. He never opposed my working before I started having children, but now whenever I mentioned getting a job, he would simply tell me that one person out there punching a clock was enough and that I should continue with my music. It had always perplexed me how he continued to push and encourage me to write, even with all the disappointments. However, this was no longer an issue as I had shrugged off my music. As a result, I started accepting offers to substitute teach in the Memphis public school system.

Even though I felt a sense of abandonment with regard to my music, I rationalized that we needed the money and that I needed to pitch in. We were never able to break even with the music; in fact, I reminded myself that all of our previous music endeavors had repeatedly driven us into the hole. This kind of thought process always seemed to provide me with some temporary comfort and justified my pushing the idea of music to the back of my mind.

Right now, the task at hand was getting extra income, and substitute teaching was a good and honorable option.

After all, I was good in math. Taking math classes from four different universities over the span of twenty years gave me considerable experience, and the logic of numbers and equations was as comfortable to me as a second language to a linguist. Standing in front of a classroom of children with the challenge of maintaining order as well as their attention was a daunting task, but the mechanics of it came fairly natural to me. Undoubtedly, this undiscovered talent was most likely due to my unsung resume of years of orchestrating children's church programs and teaching Sunday School; not to mention raising five children; overseeing an endless pilgrimage of children through my home; and helping them with their math homework that included everything from multiplication tables to algebra and trigonometry.

Surprisingly, the hardest part about my new job was getting there. For some reason, there was always something that blocked me, either scheduling conflicts, transportation woes or something. This time it was our car...again. Just when I had signed up to teach, Charles and the children were involved in a car accident. The car was totaled. Although no one was seriously injured, the children came home very much shaken with glass in their hair and clothing. Days later, I was called to teach. Charles got one of his clients who owned a limousine company to drive us to school. For two days we were dropped off and picked up in style. By the third day, we were unable to get limousine service, but I was determined that I was going to work. Nothing was going to stop me, and since I was scheduled to teach at the same school that my children were attending, I decided that a cab would take us all.

I remembered that morning well. In Memphis, humidity is as common as the sky is blue, and there's plenty of it. That particular day was no different from any other; it was so humid that the streets were covered with a thin veil of moisture. At a quick glance, anyone would have assumed that it had rained. But there was not a single raindrop – no fog, just a calm Southern morning filled with a thick haze of moisture. It was a usual humid day.

    The children and I piled into the cab for what should have been an uneventful trip to the school, but no sooner had we pulled out of the driveway, I noticed a peculiar odor. Not wanting to believe what my nose and brain were telling me, I distinctly smelled alcohol. Sitting in the backseat, I attempted to position myself to see the cabdriver's eyes. As I tried to avoid thinking the "unthinkable" of riding in the cab with a driver being under the influence, I hoped to trace the smell to the seats or floor. Maybe, it was coming from a spilled beer can. Maybe it was something else causing the odor. Hopefully, just maybe, there was another reason for this alcohol smell. But as I leaned toward the driver, my fears were confirmed, and then, that's when it happened.

    From the corner of my eye, I saw the moist, slick street and the approaching curve, a treacherous section of Prescott Avenue well known to anyone who lived in our neighborhood. My eyes quickly darted back to the speedometer. As I trained my sight on the gauge and its red needle, everything immediately blurred. All at once, I heard gasps filling the mouths of my children as the car started to lose control. Within a flash of several moments, our bodies bounced inside the cab as the car spun and spun. Images beyond the cab became a dizzy spin of colors and blurred flashes of light. Finally, after what seemed an eternity, we came to a jarring halt as we slammed into the side of the street, hitting the curb and causing our heads to bang against the taxi's interior roof. Then, for an endless second, time became frozen and our perceptions numb. Everyone momentarily had swallowed their shrieks and paused with abated breath; the only remaining noise was the exploding sound of the tires being blown. Paper, books and pencils were strewn all over us like debris as we sat there in stunned silence. Slowly, time and our senses returned to normal along with our panting breaths. Needless to say, none of us went to school that day.

We all suffered injuries; thankfully most of them were minor. The children recuperated quickly, but my injuries, on the other hand, were more severe. It seemed that my back had taken the brunt of the trauma. As I went through the ordeal of medical visits and physical therapy, I didn't think too much of it initially. Of course, it was understandable that I was going to experience pain; I was in an accident, and with time the pain would gradually fade away, or so I thought. But as time went on, the pain did not improve; in fact, it lingered then it grew. What started in my back seemed to slowly involve other parts of my body. For some reason, my stomach felt like it was going to drop out of me. The chronic pain and mounting symptoms left me with the inability to work and unable to do simple things. Household chores, such as standing to cook, or vacuuming turned into monumental tasks. Despite therapy, pain treatments and even sleeping with plywood between my mattresses, the pain persisted. But that was not the worst of it. In the process, something far more sinister began to develop. In the most insidious manner, the pain had, without my awareness, leapt from its physical realm and began to affect my mood.

When and how it had started, I wasn't sure, but lying on my back, the first thing to surface in my mind was thoughts of my music. I mentally recounted all of the past years, the highs and the lows. Despite my successes, seeds of doubt that were borne out of years of deferred dreams began to sprout. With each passing day and week of agony, my misery watered those seedlings until they towered in my mind, casting long shadows on my entire existence. The past ideas and failed opportunities that I once envisioned as great successful experiences, were now being reexamined. With my current state of mind, I saw them as nothing more than a waste of time. It did not help matters that prior to my accident, rumors of my music being stolen began to circulate. From time to time, people would call to tell me that they had heard one of my songs on the radio. This should have been a good sign that my music was getting airtime except for one key problem. They were not my original songs from the album; they were copies that had been stolen and altered. Those who knew my music recognized the changes when they heard it on the radio. One day while I was teaching the song, "The Lord Is Near," to a young lady who was interested in singing it, she stopped me and said, "Oh, I see you have rearranged this song." I promptly replied, "What you are hearing from me is the original. What you heard on the radio is a rearrangement of 'my' song." Finally, one day, my sister called me.

"Earnie, when you are going to do something about them stealing your music?"

The question pierced me because it reminded me of the circumstances related to the theft. I actually knew the woman who stole my music. She visited me in my home. This realization was especially disheartening and added to my woes. However, I decided not to file a lawsuit, but I was prepared to fight if her producers tried to argue that I had taken the music from her as opposed to the reverse. Regardless, I felt humiliated. Someone had stolen and recorded my music and what was I was doing – nothing but struggling to walk from room to room. Obviously, something was wrong. Almost every venture using my music had ended in disappointment, financial ruin or both.

I thought my efforts were about as significant as my dipping a teaspoon of water out of the Mississippi River; and on top of everything else, I was now faced with the fact that someone else had taken my song and made a hit out of it. It was a hard slap to the face. While I wholeheartedly believed that God could do anything, I could not answer why I had not advanced with this work. I thought that there had to be something wrong with me, something lacking in my character or my faith. With the rising self-doubt, I was unable to formulate any answers or resolutions.

As this wave of self-realization poured over me, it rapidly amassed into a tsunami. What had started as a journey of reminiscing, ended with my recounting all of my shattered dreams and the reality that I never had a desire to go into music. In fact, I never wanted any of this. I asked myself what purpose did it all serve? Was this all wrong? I thought my life should have been different. It seemed as if I had gotten off track in life and chosen the wrong path. But where was the split – the point in time when things went wrong? The only place that I could trace it back to was – my father's death. Why had God allowed him to die so young? I didn't know, but I did know that the trajectory of my life was impacted by it. It was no surprise that this was my first and only answer and that I was so quick to draw the conclusion; it had always been a constant thought in my mind since that day in 1957. Decades later, I was still trying to make sense of it. Now, frozen in my present state and perturbed with a twisted reality of hopelessness, I continued to trace my life backwards. I searched for some significance, some purpose, some truth; it seemed I had found nothing until I thought about my sickness as a toddler when I almost died. Then, the realization hit me with a chilling and almost shocking calmness... "maybe it would have been better if I had died as a baby."

Chapter 13

Rebirth of Purpose

Several months had passed since the taxi cab accident. Although my back pain had improved, I still experienced discomfort. It was a lingering reminder that refused to go away. There was also the other problem that remained; and despite my being acutely aware of my state, I did not speak of it out loud, but it had a name. It was called depression. Lack of interest, hopelessness and sleep disturbance were some of the symptoms that greeted me in the morning and escorted me to bed at night. They were a constant beacon of my misery. Each day I prayed for some kind of flash or twinkle of new life. Every night I lay awake for hours, tossing and turning, and praying that something would happen that would lift me from this dismal state. Then, one night during one of my brief lapses into sleep, I heard this soft, still voice.

"Chantez."

A single word in a voice that was still, yet forceful. After waking up, the word, "chantez" kept echoing in my mind. Although my study of French was not extensive, I knew enough to know that chantez meant, "sing." Translation of the word was the easy part, but I could not lift my spirit to sing. My burden was too heavy. The thick clouds of my depression prevented me from exploring anything that might expose any ray of light on my gloomy existence.

The significance of my hearing "chantez" would not reveal itself until weeks later when I came across a box stuffed with papers. For years, it had been collecting dust in a dark corner of my garage, but with the fire, it had been dislodged from its forgotten place and moved to my bedroom. I had passed this box many times, walking to my bed, but for some mysterious reason it sat there quietly untouched. Clearly, its close, intimate location in my bedroom meant some kind of importance when I placed it there, but that significance had tarnished with the passage of time. Now, I stared at it and noted its disheveled appearance. The box had become camouflaged and overlooked, disappearing into the background that existed just a few feet from my bed. Through the lens of my despair its contents might as well have been pushed into a crevice of some remote cave on a different planet. However, sitting on the edge of my bed on this particular day and staring into the corner, the image and purpose of that box started to come into focus. Buried within me, I knew what it was, but the importance of its contents had faded until something inside me, at that moment, forced me to pick it up. It was my music.

Leafing through the first sheets of music, my mind began to point back to a different time where another version of myself existed. Slowly, the music began to creep back into my soul, and the most unusual thing happened. Without notice, I started to hum. The musical notes that were stretched across the page began to dance inside me. The energy from this musical turbulence began to slowly sweep away the dust and cobwebs from my heart that used to house my music. The stagnant air of despair started to lift, being displaced by the breeze of song. My eyes captured the lyrics; and, finally, my mouth and heart opened up and I began singing. All at once, the previously whispered word, "chantez" had become a reality as I began to sing, and in the process, I was renewed.

Now, I spent my days raptured in my music. Each day was a new day of discovery, a rebirth of my purpose. No longer were there feelings of hopelessness. No longer did I walk in discomfort; the pain had miraculously dissipated along with my grim outlook. It was all replaced with a spring in my step that raced to keep pace with the tempo of my singing and the bounce of my spirit. Once again, I felt alive, and it was wonderful.

Digging through the box, I eagerly searched the forgotten past and found pages and pages of my music. Everything felt comforting until I came across something odd. While thumbing through my music, I found something peculiar. Normally, humming the songs was as familiar to me as knowing my name. The melody flowed from my soul like living water. There was nothing unusual about this. Composers know their music just as babies know the sound of their mother's voice. It was my music, written by me from my soul. But there was something else that had been added that quickly became odious to me. The introduction and finale sections of my oratorio were not mine. Something foreign and unwanted had been inserted into my oratorio, and its jagged edge stabbed at me. It was clearly not my style of music. I immediately said to myself, "Oh no, I'm not going to allow this."

Stunned that I had allowed this invasion in the first place, I quickly began to search the past recesses of my mind, trying to figure out how this intrusion had occurred. Then, I remembered. One of the people, who we had hired, took the liberty of adding an orchestral introduction and finale to the oratorio. Those foreign sections were his creation and not mine, and with that revelation, I immediately discarded his musical renditions and began to write my own intro and finale. Within the span of that one single event, I immediately returned to my abandoned path. I was back to composing.

Later that evening, Charles walked into the bedroom, smiling, "It's good to see you singing and writing again."

"I know. It feels good. Do you remember that recurring dream that I told you about, where I would see myself playing the piano?"

"Yeah."

"You know, I haven't had that dream since I started composing music. Anyway, I was thinking that maybe I should take some music theory classes"

"I wouldn't do that," he quickly responded.

"Well, the chairman of the music department at the university suggested that I should take composition..."

Charles interrupted me, "If you do that, then your music will sound just like theirs. Right now, you only write what you feel. That's what makes your music different." And with that last statement, he turned and walked out of the room.

His words resonated with me long after he left. He was never one for lengthy discussions, and he always had a blunt approach whenever he shared his thoughts, but he was a deep thinker. Plus, he had a unique perspective. While he had studied classical piano for years, he was one of only a few individuals who actually saw me writing my songs. Therefore, he knew, more than anyone else, my unusual manner of creating music and how it differed from the norm of traditionally trained classical composers. The more I thought about it, the more I thought that maybe he had a valid point. Maybe I would corrupt my style with structured theory. As a result, that was the last time that I considered formal musical training. God had given me this talent and placed me on this unique path, a path that had already been chartered. It was finally clear to me that I should never deviate from its course.

Fully engaged in my writing, I completed the introduction and finale sections of my oratorio that consisted of three parts. I named it, "The Crucifixion," and although I was pleased with the songs, I felt like something was missing. That's when I decided to add short segments of narration, dispersed throughout the oratorio to help guide and illustrate the story. With my oratorio completely reworked with the added narration, I spent the next several months editing it.

There was something powerful inside me that was propelling me at that time to an unforeseen goal. No longer was I was pursuing a career in teaching. I worked day and night, rewriting my narration and researching design layouts. I wanted my oratorio to look as professional as the works of the classical music masters. My renewed enthusiasm felt good and I took delight in the level of my research. To know that I was completing a task gave me a sense of accomplishment, but there was more to this. Ironically, I did not know what it was until one day when I had a realization. I do not recall exactly when it hit me, but it was as though someone had gradually pulled back the curtain, revealing the prize. After countless visits to the library during my research, the hidden secret was suddenly crystal clear.

"I don't believe it...I've written a book," I murmured in disbelief.

All that time, it was right in front of me. While praying for God to show me what to do next, he was guiding and directing me in my next project. My intent was to complete my oratorio, but I was totally unaware that by doing so, I had written a book. It took days for it to sink in. A book. It seemed so logical, and it was right in front of me.

With the awareness of this new idea bubbling inside me and propelling me, the family typewriter became my new companion. Every day I made my way to the laundry room and hoisted the heavy IBM electric typewriter from its perch on top of the dryer. I paid little attention to its weight as I carefully lowered it onto my workstation, which was usually the floor of the den. Surrounded by an array of books, the sprawling mound of paper served as a visual testimony of my enthusiasm and its very presence seemed to give me confidence with each stroke of the typewriter. Although I typed away with a tenacious determination, I was not naive about the enormity of my new task. An idea and a typed page were a long way from the professional typesetting and printing of the books that encircled me. From my former creative endeavors, I was very aware of the costs associated with my new project; previously, Charles and I had been given an estimate of several thousand dollars by a printer just to typeset and print some of my sheet music. In those days, choices of printing services were limited, and self-service printing venues were all but nonexistent. As a result, I could not even imagine how I would cover the cost of producing an entire book; it was a problem that seemingly had no solution. Yet, none of this seemed to matter as I moved that typewriter every day back and forth between the laundry room and the den. I knew that God was telling me to do this because I could feel the joy in my heart whenever I thought about it. Therefore, I did not focus on the problem, only that God would provide the solution.

It was the fall of 1985, and Todd had graduated from Colby College in Maine and was attending medical school at the University of Tennessee in Memphis or as he called it, "UT," an acronym that was common to anyone familiar with the university. I was glad that he was back home but a bit surprised at his decision to attend school in Memphis. He had seemed most excited when he was accepted to the medical school at Brown University, but despite this, he decided to return to Memphis and was quite content living at home. It was getting late one evening when he walked through the front door, carrying a large stack of books and hunched over with a large backpack.

"Wow, you look serious," he said as he collapsed on the sofa.

"Uh, huh," I said glancing at him. "Have you eaten?"

"Yeah, I grabbed something at school." He paused for a moment, observing me as I resumed typing, "You know, you can do that on a computer."

"The typewriter is working just fine," I said without looking up.

"But the computer would be better," pausing to see if I would respond but I continued typing. "I usually work in the computer lab at night. You should come down to UT and work on your stuff while I'm doing…"

"Why?" interrupting him and looking up from the typewriter. "I can do the same thing right here."

"Yeah, but they've got computers."

"Look, Todd, I do know a little something about computers. I studied computer programming."

With a bit of exasperation, he responded, "But Mom, this is different. I've been playing with this new type of computer called Macintosh Plus. It's really cool. You can write papers on it, draw pictures, graphs, all kinds of stuff."

"Well, that sounds fine," as I resumed typing, "but unless there is some way I can put the words of Jesus in red, I'll just stick with my typewriter."

He became quiet for several moments before speaking, "I don't know about putting His words in red, but on the computer, you can highlight them."

Now, I stopped typing and looked at him, "Highlight?"

"The lettering. You can make it bolder...darker, so it stands out from the rest of the text, and it looks really good."

"Really?" I said.

"Uh, huh," nodding his head. "You can also make the words stand out by italicizing them."

"All this on a computer?" I responded.

"Yup. And get this. They even have these printers, so you can print it out. It looks really professional. In fact, I've been thinking about buying a computer and a printer. UT has this special deal, so students can purchase them..."

With that last statement, the volume of his voice trailed off. I was stunned. Once again, a solution had been provided and was awaiting me even before the problem was fully aware to me. The barrier of printing costs had been completely erased in one brief conversation with Todd, who had just happened to get a job working in a computer lab. Yet, a part of me was having difficulty fully embracing what Todd was discussing. I was no stranger to computers nor was I intimidated by new technology, but my mind had a hard time conceptualizing this new idea of a personal computer. When I trained as a computer programmer, computers were large, intimidating machines that were housed in enormous air-conditioned rooms. Then, there were the stacks of data punched cards and long scrolls of computer paper containing seemingly cryptic lines of data. This was my mental image of computers. That is why a few days later, I was speechless when Todd and I sat in front of a Macintosh computer. It was an unassuming small box with a screen, keyboard and a device called a mouse. I was even more apprehensive when Todd turned it on, and a little smiley face appeared. However, after typing for an hour and a click of a button, a printer spat out a sheet filled with a beautiful landscape of text with razor sharp letters. It was amazing how easy it was, and within weeks, we had completed typing the narration. But that was only half of the story; we had yet to deal with the music.

In those early days of personal computing, desktop publishing was a new field, and although there was plenty of software for creating text documents, the availability of inexpensive programs for developing and publishing sheet music was entirely a different matter. As a result, the section of my book, which dealt with sheet music, had to be put together without the use of a computer in such a tedious manner that it could have been easily described as "manufactured and assembled."

The original score had been completed in stages by two different individuals; as a result, some of the original sheet music varied in size while others had slightly faded print. Therefore, the first step was copying the music one page at a time, checking for contrast and either enlarging or reducing the print until uniformity was achieved. Each line of music on every page had to be a certain length. It was a process that was often trial and error and required Todd and I to spend long hours at Kinko's, a popular self-service print shop located near the university. After photocopying and obtaining the correct size, each line of the score was cut into strips, placed on a page, and arranged so that either three or four lines of music appeared evenly spaced apart on each page. Once we agreed on the proper layout, each individual strip was carefully lifted and glued back into place. We used a special adhesive paste, which allowed the pieces to be lifted and repositioned with relative ease. Unfortunately, the readjusting was a process that sometimes recurred so frequently that the glue would lose its adhesive properties. Furthermore, there was another unforeseen drawback of this pasting-readjusting approach; the paste seemed to be an incessant magnet for dirt. Any trace of dirt or lint along with the slightest smudge on the glass plate of the copier would invariably end up on the photocopy. We tried everything to minimize this aggravation, but despite all of our meticulous efforts, it was a problem that we could never fully prevent. That's when we developed our last line of defense – liquid paper. A small bottle of white substance, liquid paper could be applied to any smudge using the attached brush, and like magic, when the liquid dried, the spot was gone. The whole ordeal from beginning to end was a painfully slow process, but when everything was finished, the reward was a sheet of music that had a quality appearance, a feat that required hours of standing with stooped necks and strained eyes.

Once we completed the music section, we combined it with the narration and headed to a local bookbinder. Because of our modest budget, we had a total of only five hardback books created. Despite the small number, my overwhelming sense of accomplishment was not diminished. When I first opened the box containing our finished product, before I even saw the book, I breathed in deeply the crisp scent of the fresh print. Slowly reaching in, I grasped the book on top, tracing my fingers along the spine. Seeing the lettering of the title, "The Crucifixion" and my last name, Rodgers-Robinson took my breath away. I could not speak. I had labored for thirteen years to get to this moment. I was overcome with joy. I kept thinking in awe, "I had written my first book."

Charles submitted the copyright forms to the Library of Congress, making it official. But I did not want to waste too much time basking in the glow of this accomplishment. The hard truth was that though the book was put together well and tastefully, it was basic in design, and I was not satisfied until my book looked like the ones on library shelves. As a result, Todd and I immediately started on the second edition.

This time, my daughter and second oldest child, Cheryle, joined our efforts. She had graduated from Northwestern University with a degree in painting and drawing and had continued her studies at the Art Institute of Chicago. But she decided to transfer to the University of Memphis graduate school to pursue a degree in graphic design. Like Todd, I was surprised to see her back in Memphis, but here she was, sitting in a medical research lab with Todd and me, legs crossed, and flipping through the pages of a fashion magazine.

"What are you doing to those poor mice?" she said with a look of disdain as she watched Todd carrying a cage of laboratory mice.

"I'm not doing anything to them. I'm just moving them. That's someone else's project. I work with adrenal cells," he responded.

"Adrenal what?" she exclaimed.

"Adrenal cells. They're from a gland next to your

kidneys," Todd replied, very matter of fact. "On Tuesdays, Mom and Dad sometimes go with me to this cattle slaughter house in Mississippi where I get them."

"That's disgusting," Cheryle said.

"No, it isn't. It's part of my research project. We're studying hypertension."

"It's still disgusting."

"I don't know why you're tripping. You've probably eaten hamburger meat from this place. They say some of the local restaurants buy their beef from the same slaughter house."

"I think, I'm going to be a vegetarian," she said as she returned to reading her magazine.

Todd moved around the lab swiftly, setting things up before we started with our work. This was our usual practice. He was enrolled in a combined degree program where he was earning his MD and PhD at the same time. He had already completed his first two years in medical school and was now spending his days and nights doing research in physiology. Whenever he ran a late-night experiment, we would often work on the book in the lab.

Settling into a chair next to me and glancing at Cheryle, he said, "I thought you were working on designing the book cover."

"I am," she said nonchalantly, without looking up from her magazine.

"Shouldn't you have some paper, pencil or something?"

"Look. Don't worry about it. I'm working on it."

Todd looked at me and shook his head. But over the next several months Cheryle took a strong interest in the project. Not only did she design the cover, but she also redesigned the entire book. In fact, on some occasions, Cheryle and I would barricade ourselves in an art studio or computer lab at the University of Memphis for an all-night session where she would work tirelessly, splitting time between her own graphic project and my book. For safety reasons, we would lock ourselves in and not leave the room until daybreak. When I was not working with Cheryle, I was spending time working with Todd down at the lab. The three of us worked feverishly.

Even though my expectations for the second edition were elevated, I felt that they were not unrealistic. I knew that with Cheryle's background in graphic design, the cover and layout of the book would surpass the first edition. In fact, where Todd and I had previously relied on manually cutting and pasting sections and photocopying the pages, Cheryle was arranging everything on a layout grid that was specially lit underneath and then taking pictures of the finished individual pages. But there was the other issue to deal with – the music section. Our earlier crude methods of duplicating the music for the first book would not yield the desired professional quality that I expected this time. However, something crucial had occurred since our first attempt. The technology in computer music publishing had improved, giving us options that were now within our financial reach. We were now able to purchase music composition software that was considered "cutting edge" at the time. However, the software was the 1.0 version, which meant glitches and bugs that would randomly result in notes shifting or entire tracts of previously, entered music disappearing. It was frustrating, but it was a small price to pay, considering that the program produced beautiful, publish-quality sheet music. As we learned the software, we realized that the most reliable method that resulted in the fewest headaches was entering the music one note at a time. It was a slow, mammoth task that took eight months of my working with Todd to make sure that each note, time signature and slur which he entered was what I intended it to be.

At the same time, while I was finishing up with the second edition of my book, I realized that I had not received any information about my copyright submission from the first edition. It had been months without any reply. So, I called the Library of Congress to find out why. The person on the phone was very pleasant and apologetic but repeatedly placed me on hold for long stretches of time. Finally, she told me, and I distinctly remember her words, "If it is any consolation to you, your book has been requested by the Library of Congress for its Special Collections." I was very relieved that everything was in order and elated that I had been selected. I knew that this was an honor, but it would be years later, before I would fully understand and appreciate the significance of my book being selected for the Special Collections. Upon finishing the second edition, I also forwarded it to the Library of Congress.

While visiting Washington D.C. several years later, Charles and I along with Todd went to the Library of Congress just for the experience of actually taking a glimpse of my book. Instead of the beautifully bounded second edition, I found a generic hardbound book of the score that I had previously forwarded for copyright purposes. When I first saw it, I was shocked at its rudimentary appearance. It obviously had been put together by the Library of Congress. Immediately, Todd and I went upstairs to the administrative offices to determine the procedures in replacing the book. The first office we entered had a counter with several desks behind it. At one of the desks, a man sat with his back to us.

After standing at the counter for a moment without being acknowledged, I spoke up, "Excuse me."

"Yes," he responded but barely looking up.

"I have a question. Who do I talk to regarding my book? It was selected for your Special Collections?" I asked.

"What is your question?" he responded in a slightly annoyed tone.

"I was just downstairs, and I saw my book. I wanted to know where are the hardback books that I sent in for the Special Collections."

"You mean to tell me that your book is housed in our library," he said.

"Yes, but it was just the edition that I sent in for copyrighting purposes."

Now standing, the clerk had an astonished look on his face as he said, "You actually saw your book?"

"Yes, they allowed us to see it, but we weren't permitted to take it out of the room," I said in a nonchalant manner."

Still appearing to be shocked, he interrupted me and started to walk toward us, "Your book is actually downstairs in this library."

"Yes, we just looked at it a few minutes ago," I slowly answered, puzzled by his reaction. "Is there a problem?" I asked.

"Oh, no, quite the contrary," he responded with a more relaxed expression.

"What do you mean?"

Answering me with another question, "Do you think that we keep everyone's book here in this library?"

"Well...yes," I said, realizing that there was more to the question.

"Oh, no!" he responded emphatically. "When we receive a submission and after cataloguing its information into our system, the actual book is transported and stored in a warehouse. There is simply not enough room in this building to house all of the materials we receive. So, the fact that your book is actually on the premises is amazing in itself. But being selected for the Special Collections is an unbelievably rare honor."

With his last statement, I was stunned. As the enormity of my accomplishment finally started to hit me, I said nothing. The Special Collections, as it is formally called, has several divisions and represents a remarkable treasure of items ranging from the unique to the extremely valuable. Its vastness and diversity include everything from one of only three Gutenberg Bibles known in existence; the autographed scores by Beethoven and Gershwin; and the personal library of Thomas Jefferson from 1815. The Special Collections, which also contains such titles as the Benjamin Franklin Collection, the Susan B. Anthony Collection, and Rudyard Kipling Collections, is a testimonial of the incredible stature of the Library of Congress, and there I stood, listening to the librarian's explanation and for the first time understanding what it all meant. I thanked him for his time and left. Stunned with our new revelation, Todd and I caught the elevator down to the ground floor and walked outside. We could barely contain our joy as we shared the news with Charles.

Chapter 14

Battle on Many Fronts

Sitting in a parked car in front of White Station High School, I sat alone with only my thoughts to keep me busy. It was the calm before the storm on a cool December afternoon. The last stretch of quiet time before a frenzied dash to cram as much as possible into the remaining hours of the day. School had been out for almost twenty-five minutes, and while that may only seem like a brief lapse of time, it was more than long enough to normally clear out the grounds of a school. The sound of the final bell at the end of classes was universal in its purpose of starting a massive and quick exodus of students. It was chaotic to watch but a ritual that was just as common in my day. Within minutes after that closing bell, gone were the yellow school buses, the long lines of carpooling vehicles, and the droves of running children. Yet, despite this regular occurrence, I sat there waiting because this age-old tradition did not seem to include my children. For reasons that were rarely related to academics, my children never immediately left the building. They were always, invariably, some of the last ones to show up after school had ended. According to them, their popularity necessitated their delay; club meetings, school projects and other extracurricular activities were some of their reasons, but no matter what the reason was, the waiting was always the same.

During such stretches of solitude, I had learned to take advantage of the still moments with a well-honed practice of reflection. Watching the trees in front of the school, I momentarily caught the wind as it blew the few remaining leaves off the trees, and my mind seemed to drift with the freedom of a single floating leaf. It was relaxing, but fleeting as the leaf hit the ground, ending its journey and switching my mind back into the structured mode of a checklist. Today was my mother's birthday, and I had a long list of unfinished errands for a planned birthday dinner. Sitting there, drifting in my thoughts, I glanced past the dashboard of my car and saw one of my children slowly emerging from out of nowhere at the far end of the school – finally, then one by one the rest came. With everyone in the car, I pulled out of the parking space and started down my long list of errands. Stopping by the grocery store always seemed to be on the list; it was the norm but today there was a special item to pick up – the birthday cake.

My mother was turning 77, and although I always treated birthdays as special, this one was even more endearing. My mother's health was fading, and as I had with my brother, who had recently passed, I was spending a lot of time caring for her. She had severe heart failure, and the condition of her heart was so weak that simple tasks became difficult feats of will and stamina. Not being able to fully do for herself was the thing that troubled her most. She would often tell me how it puzzled her that she never had any chest pain, but it was the shortness of breath that stopped her from doing the things that she liked. Her breathing difficulty was always present; most times it was controlled with her medicines. At other times, her breathing would progress to such a labored status that the only viable option was an emergency room visit. It was during those severe episodes that I would see her sitting up, struggling to use her entire body to breathe. It was hard to see her like that, leaning forward with her head slightly tilted and chest heaving. At times like this, she did not lie down, speak, or stir, just struggled to breathe. Sometimes the symptoms happened gradually, and sometimes their onset was swift. No matter what, her response was always the same as she fought to beat back another trip to the emergency room. Unfortunately, she rarely succeeded in her efforts, and with each episode and ER visit, her overall condition seemed to worsen, thereby, leading to more frequent hospitalizations. She was gradually becoming weaker and requiring more assistance. It was a fact that she was well aware of.

Yet, she was resilient, and there were two things that she fought to maintain: her independence and keeping her apartment. She lived in a building that was associated with the Catholic Diocese and catered to senior citizens. Her apartment was part of a complex that included a library, hair salon, small convenience store, and a park and recreational center. There was a long waiting list to get in, but Charles knew the managers of the building and helped to get Momma accepted. Despite the amenities, I was a little doubtful that she would like to live on the eighth floor, but surprisingly, she liked it. However, she did not like, as she used to say, "just sitting around." As a result, she worked out an arrangement and decided that either one of my two sisters, Doris or Odesser, or I would rotate picking her up several times throughout the week based on the type of activity. Odesser was mainly responsible for driving her to and from church services. Doris was the designated driver for any social events that usually involved relatives; and I picked her up for doctor appointments, shopping, paying bills and any other miscellaneous errands. Sometimes, all three of us would be involved in picking her up and dropping her off during the same day. Her neighbors would often comment on how she had the most visitors of anyone in the building and was always on the go. However, as her medical condition gradually took its toll on her, she began spending more time at my house. Eventually, she ended up living with us, but she never gave up her apartment, and to maintain her last hold on independence, she would, on occasion, have us drop her off her at her place in the morning just for a few hours.

Because of the severity of her symptoms, it was reassuring, having her close by. Besides, everyone enjoyed my mother's company, especially her sharp wit. There was also another reason that I found beneficial from her staying with us. I was becoming concerned about Charles and needed to talk to someone, and that perfect someone was my mother. There was no denying that she had a keen perception of analyzing the unspoken and obscure perplexities of life. With a pause and a squint of her eyes, she could deliver a succinct assessment of most problems in a manner that anyone else would only achieve with a lengthy discussion.

Several times I attempted to discuss my concerns about Charles with her, but each time I simply turned away and buried them within me. There was never anything specific to trigger these feelings, but all at once I would feel the anxiety swelling and pushing against the seams of my heart. I had to tell someone what I was feeling. Yet, I did not know how to broach the subject of something that I was barely convinced of myself. After all, I kept thinking that Charles had not displayed any significant changes – nothing alarming. Most of my concerns were stemming only from a few incidental things like the way he would at times jumble his speech. Charles, who rarely got sick, just shrugged off any change in his health, and whenever I asked if something was bothering him, he simply denied that anything was wrong. In fact, his answer to all of my inquiries was always the same, a quick and decisive "everything is fine," but none of those emphatic denials and casual reassurances could placate my doubts. Something was amiss. It was like catching a whiff of the slightest vapor, having it linger long enough in your nostrils to alert you to the presence of something, but not long enough to pinpoint its source.

All of this had another effect on me. It had alerted me to a dream that I had about Charles some years earlier, and now I was afraid. For a brief moment, I thought that if I ignored the dream, it would go away. Maybe I had the dream because I had become overheated while asleep or maybe it was something that I ate prior to going to bed that had caused the premonition. Yet, despite all of my rationalizations, I could not shake it. Like all of the dreams before that God had shown me, the images and message of this dream were real and not to be ignored. However, I did not want to accept this dream. Even though I was afraid to mention it to anyone, I knew that I had to get it off my chest, if only to simply get past it. Now was the perfect opportunity. My mother and I were alone in the kitchen. She was sitting at the kitchen table and I was standing at the stove, finishing up the meal for her birthday party. So, after months of deliberation, I decided to bring up the subject.... indirectly.

"You know, Charles has been taking these long baths lately. He always liked taking baths, but now, every night he takes these long baths. Kind of strange?"

"Hmm." she murmured and continued to stare at the floor.

I paused a moment to gauge her reaction, but she was stoic. I continued, "I don't know what to make of it. It's odd for Charles."

"Uh, huh," she said.

"I'm probably just making something out of nothing," I added.

"Oh, no. There's something wrong."

In an instant, my heart quickened, and all of my muscles instinctively tightened. For it was more than just her words; it was her tone. I did not want to hear anything else. I was not mentally prepared for this. So, I quickly countered to change the direction of the conversation, "Anyway, you know, Charles can do strange things sometimes."

Hoping that she would agree with my last statement, my body remained tense as I waited for a favorable response. Several moments went by, but she said nothing. Well, at least, she did not say anything negative, but the silence was deafening. Finally, I got up enough nerve to look over at her. She was still looking down at the floor, and I quickly thought to myself that I was making an issue out of it and started to brush off the conversation.

"Momma, do you want me to fix your plate before the rest of the gang gets here?" I asked.

Then, out of the blue, she finally let it all out, "I had a hard time accepting it, too." She paused for a second before drawing in her breath and continuing, "But God showed me your father's death long before it came to pass."

Her words drove straight through my heart, and the pain felt so real that I almost dropped her plate. This was not happening. My mind was racing as I filtered through the conversation, searching for any clues of why she would mention anything about death, especially about being a widow. I drew a blank; there was no way she could have known about my dream. Finally, I turned toward her, and I was sure that she could see the astonishment on my face.

"Yes, God showed me," she said calmly.

Immediately, my dream came back into clear focus. In it, I was standing before a mirror, getting dressed. Wearing all black, I could barely see my eyes staring back at me. A black veil covered my face, burying the lifeless stare beneath it. There were no words or sound – just me standing alone, dressed in black. As my mind returned to the present from the dream, I could feel a chill run through me, and I looked at my mother.

"Well, I also had a dream...about Charles being gone. But that was some time ago."

"Just because it hasn't happened, doesn't mean that it's not going to happen," she promptly replied.

"I don't know. Maybe…"

She interrupted me. She did not mince words to cuddle my emotions, it was too important.

"I was pregnant with you when God showed my mother a dream that I was alone, left with several small children. It was nearly twenty years later that James died. So, don't ignore it; stay prayerful," she said.

She knew and now I knew. As my lips parted, I heard the front door open. It was Charles. His entrance into the kitchen with a smile on his face was so jarring that I struggled to collect myself.

"Euber, look at you," he said in playful manner upon seeing my mother. "Out of the hospital one day and having a party the next."

"Yeah, yeah," she sheepishly replied.

Chatter quickly filled the air as everybody made their way into the kitchen and the adjacent family room. The private moment shared between my mother and me was gone, and the topic that we discussed, ever so briefly, never came up again. There was no need; we both understood.

The next day Cheryle and I went to my brother Jonathan's church where he served as pastor. He had just purchased a commercial printing press that could produce documents in large volumes. My brother allowed us to use the machine in exchange for design work that Cheryle did for the church. This arrangement offered us the opportunity to print my books at a fraction of the cost. It was a perfect solution and an ambitious plan except for one problem – neither Cheryle nor I knew how to run a printer. There were only a couple of people in the congregation who knew how to operate the press and they did not have the time to help us. As a result, we had to teach ourselves.

Looking at the printing press for the first time was a bit intimidating. Cheryle and I just stared at it. It was a large metal labyrinth of levers, knobs and plates. Slowly, we walked around it, circling it in silence in an attempt to determine our best approach. Gradually, the magnitude of our project began to wash over and pass us as we started to put the pieces together. Eventually, we found the instruction manual and turned it on. We smiled as we figured that we had cracked the code to part of our problem

– just follow the directions and we will be on our way.

Days later, we were still trying to conquer the machine. Our efforts had become a never-ending marathon of trial and error. The only thing that we were successful in doing was increasing our frustration and spilling ink on our hands. Just when we were at the point of declaring that something had to be wrong with the press and not us, Cheryle remembered that she had a friend who used to work with a commercial printer and called him. He gladly accepted our call of distress and showed up the following day. Chuckling throughout our explanation of our problem, he was a refreshing breath of air as he joked and teased us about our tall order of learning how to run a professional printer in only a few days. There was nothing wrong with the press; according to him, it just needed to be used by someone who knew what they were doing. We watched as he glided around the machine, confidently pushing buttons, flipping levers and adjusting knobs without the slightest hesitation or contemplation. His maneuvers were as effortless and smooth as a well-rehearsed waltz, and within moments, the printing press roared to life. The noise, although loud and mechanical, had a human quality to it. The machine's rhythm was pulsating like a steady heartbeat, and with each beat we could see paper spitting out the opposite end. We smiled because we knew that we were back on track.

The next day we started the press with a renewed sense of confidence. The tutorial that we received proved to be very valuable in getting us up to speed. In a rare occurrence, Craig, my second son, decided to join us. Initially, I was not sure that his appearance was out of a need to help us or just plain old curiosity. As a child, Craig had a fond fascination of taking things apart to see how they worked. Once he had found out that we were working with a large machine, it was just a matter of time before he showed up.

"You guys haven't started yet?" he asked, with a smirk on his face as he strolled into the room.

"We're about to go through our checklist. Grab that manual," Cheryle said, while pointing to the desk.

"Don't worry about that."

"What?" Cheryle said, slightly annoyed.

"We don't need it."

"Look here boy. We've been struggling to figure this thing out and you're supposed to start with..."

"Why don't you just relax," he interrupted.

It was a universal fact in our household that all of my sons seemed to take great pleasure in teasing their sisters and Craig was no exception. While they traded barbs, I handed Cheryle the manual which included our startup checklist, and, before long, the machine was up and running. Our film was on the drum, and the paper was feeding smoothly through the machine. Everything looked and sounded good. Then, everything went haywire. Instead of finished sheets flowing out the end, paper was flying up in the air from somewhere in the middle of the machine.

"Shut it off! Shut it off! Craig shouted.

Cheryle immediately turned it off and looked at Craig and said, "Well, everything was fine until you showed up."

"I thought you knew what you were doing," he quipped.

"Craig..." Cheryle said in exasperation.

"Wait," I quickly interrupted them. "It seems that the problem is happening somewhere in this area. Let's run the machine slowly and maybe we can see what's going wrong."

After running the printer at a reduced speed for a period of time and all three of us bent over, staring at one particular area from different angles, Craig finally pops up with a declaration.

"I found the problem!"

He then ran out of the room, only to return several minutes later with a wire hanger. While bending an end piece repeatedly back and forth, he finally succeeded in breaking off a small piece.

"What are you doing?" Cheryle asked.

"There's a slot where the paper comes through," he said while reaching into the midst of the press. "It's loose but I think that this could temporarily hold it in place"

"You've got to be kidding!" she snapped back.

"No, I think it might work," he responded.

"Okay, Mr. Fix-it, you turn it on.. but slowly," she said.

Eureka! Within moments, the printer started to run but this time without paper flying into the air. All three of us were ecstatic.

With the problem solved, we returned to our main objective. Our comfort with the press grew which assured us that we would complete our task, but there was always an emergency. In those days, the emergency was usually related to my mother's worsening medical condition. The scenario of relapse and recovery involving her health occurred with such regularity that I had learned to adapt my life around it. Just as quickly as I would stop everything to take care of my mother, I would return to my music once things had settled.

The stopping-and-starting was always difficult, but I did not let anything stop me. Even with the frustrations, my excitement was never diminished. The idea of having a concert of my music was always a persistent, yet elusive dream of mine. As a composer, I had always envisioned that my music would be performed and heard by others, not just a melody heard only in my mind. Yet, the sad reality was that no one had ever heard my oratorio, "The Crucifixion," in its entirety; only a couple of songs from the oratorio had ever been performed. Besides the album, very few, including my mother, had ever heard a choir sing any of my music. But there was always something inside me that pushed me, driving me to get my music performed no matter the odds against it.

Because of this, I was especially enthused when my sister, Doris, introduced me to the director of a popular local gospel group. He had charisma, a devoted choir and was very eager about my project. Immediately, I thought that this was a wonderful opportunity to have "The Crucifixion" performed. However, my excitement was soon blunted when a professor from the music department at the University of Memphis told me that the gospel choir would not be able to handle my music. Surprised by his comment, I felt frustrated, asking myself who then could do my music, and I asked myself why God would give me music that no one could perform. I did not receive an answer and did not know which way to turn. So, I pressed ahead and started planning with the gospel group. The preparations went smoothly; everything was falling into place. The date was set, advertisements and radio announcements were running prominently, and we had decided on the Orpheum Theater for the concert. Located in downtown Memphis, it was a popular venue that had been recently restored to its previous opulence of the 1920s. Everything was ready.

As the publicity for my event grew, the popularity and appearances of the gospel choir seem to grow as well. Then, one night I decided to drop in on the group during one of their rehearsals and experienced a familiar pain. The director, choir and musicians were totally lost with my music. It was a fiasco. Several months of planning and rehearsals, and they had nothing to show for it. At one point during my shock, the manager of the group came up to me and tried to console me with empty reassurances. It was hopeless. There was nothing else to do but to cancel. Once again, I had to accept another failed concert with my music, and despite all of the preparations and hard work, I had nothing to show for my efforts, well almost nothing.

Days later, Charles unfolded the local newspaper and handed it to me. Displayed very prominently across the page was a very large advertisement for a cellular phone company. With my initial glimpse, there was nothing of concern to me. But a second later, I saw it, and my eyes could not believe it. Covering nearly half the page was a photograph of a businessman talking on his cell phone. He was standing in front of the Orpheum Theatre, and behind him on the marquee in large bold letters was, "THE CRUCIFIXION ORATORIO." The irony was unmistakable. The half page ad ran throughout the summer in the newspaper. Though the concert was cancelled, something good had come out of the crushing defeat.

Chapter 15

No Rest for the Weary

My resume of failed concerts was growing, and although I was naturally disappointed by this, my fervor of attempting yet another concert was undaunted. While I had not been as successful as I had wanted, the string of failures had unknowingly succeeded in another arena. My resolve had been strengthened by the years of adversity. With each cancellation, feelings of despair would rise, and then fall; and in its place, the spirit of promise would automatically spring back. Despite all of the negative outcomes, I continued to feel hopeful, but there was something else that was developing.

It was a subtle feeling of apprehension and dread that was not directed toward my music – just a sense that something was wrong. I did not think much of it at the time because I was too busy to think about anything else. But, in retrospect, it was fatigue. I first noticed it after the death of my brother and the years of taking care of him. Unfortunately, time did not allow me the luxury to heal from his passing. Right on the heels of my brother's death, my mother had made a turn for the worse, becoming so fragile and weak that she had become bedridden. The doctors said that there was nothing else that could be done; their recommendation was just to make her as comfortable as possible. Therefore, out of necessity, I converted my sons' room into a makeshift hospital room, complete with a hospital bed. She required total care around the clock. During the day, I prepared her meals, fed and bathed her, and rotated her support pillows in order to avoid bedsores. Todd, who did most of his medical studying at night, took the nightshift, and the rest of the children helped out where needed. We all knew that her time was short. Over the past ten years, I had been involved in every aspect of her medical care from her first symptoms and up to those final moments; yet, despite all of that time of reflection and mental preparation, the ending was still a bitter pill to swallow.

The beginning of the end for my mother started one morning with a more pronounced struggle to breathe, a condition that we were familiar with and knew how to manage to a certain degree. With Todd there and all of my experiences with her, I knew that fluid was building up in her lungs. Instinctively, as a medical student, Todd listened to her chest, monitored her blood pressure, and adjusted her medicines based on a protocol prescribed by her cardiologist. I learned that elevating the head of her bed was a technique that helped her to breathe better. Unfortunately, with all of our maneuvers, we were only able to mildly ease her discomfort but not the inevitable. Then, later that day without any warning, she began sleeping more and even becoming exceptionally drowsy during the times when she was awake. I knew that this was not your normal kind of sleep. Gradually, she fell into a deep slumber, and we could not arouse her. She had slipped into a realm that was far away from ours. It was a sleep that prevented us from administering her oral medicines, and more poignantly, I was no longer able to communicate with her. With that transition, her breathing slowed and became erratic, and although all of this was unsettling, there was a peace. As we watched this unfold, we all knew what was coming, but it was not until several other family members showed up to visit and witnessed the change, that panic settled in and the paramedics were called. There was nothing the doctors could do for her and within a few days, she passed away.

Despite being emotionally fatigued, the task of putting together the funeral program became my duty. Fortunately, I had Cheryle and Todd to assist me with the layout and printing. Both of them also stood in for me when they met with my brothers and sisters at the funeral home to pick out a casket. It was just two days left before the funeral, and I was still running around town taking care of errands. There was one final detail that was important to me – the dress that she would wear. My mother was a very fashionable dresser, and I wanted her funeral attire to be reflective of this. Dress, hair, jewelry – it all had to be perfect for her "homegoing" service.

Within the black church, it is common to label the

funeral service as a "homegoing." When Christians, or as they are commonly referred to in my church, "saints" died, they were going home to heaven. It was inevitable that on such occasions, anyone in attendance would hear during remarks or the eulogy, numerous repeated references or scriptures from the Bible stating that, "beautiful in the eyes of the Lord is the death of His saints" or "to be absent from the body is to be present with the Lord." So, at my church, a "homegoing" is, in effect, a celebration, and I wanted everything to be perfect.

Finally, after gathering all of her clothing, I sent the items to the funeral home and crawled into bed. I was both physically and emotionally exhausted and just needed to rest. My eyes had not yet begun to close when the phone rang. Moments later, Charles came into the bedroom.

"Earnestine, that was the police."

Immediately, my head turned around to see his face. Surely, I did not hear him correctly, but his expression did not mislead me. Before I could ask, he continued, not allowing me time to think.

"Craig has been in an accident. He was hit by a car while crossing the street."

Immediately, fear seemed to choke the escape of air from my body. I kept telling myself, "Exhale. Try to exhale."

"They say he has internal injuries."

Finally, all at once, the air rushed out of me, "Oh, no!" Right away, I got up, and Charles and I headed to the hospital.

We were driving in silence, not knowing what to expect. Todd and Cheryle were meeting us there. By the time that all of us arrived at the hospital, my mind had already assumed the worst. It was only natural to feel this way, considering the timing. I was in the midst of planning my mother's funeral when I got this catastrophic news about my son. Now, standing in the hallway of the trauma unit, I was about to lay my eyes on Craig. Charles continued down the corridor to see him, but I could not face it. I stopped; my legs would not allow another step. Then, I looked up and saw Todd and Cheryle approaching me.

"I can't," I murmured to them. "I can't go in there. Todd, you go first and get a report."

He paused a second, nodded his head, and without a word stepped down the corridor and disappeared from our sight. I thought that Todd could soften the blow. As a medical student, he worked there and knew the medical jargon, but as my son, he knew me. I felt that the news would be better coming from him. For what seemed like a prolonged stretch of time, I leaned against a wall and waited and continued to pray. The place was extremely busy. Hordes of people passed by me, but I did not see their faces. The noise of the frenzied activity was loud, but I heard no words. Finally, through the chaos, I spotted a glimpse of Todd heading toward us. I held my breath as I tried to look past the throngs of people to see his face. I could see a smile on his face, and immediately my heaviness began to lift.

Todd walked up and was eager to tell me the news, "He's stable and alert. A little drowsy from the pain meds but he's awake. They did a CAT scan of everything, and the good news is that there is no brain injury and no internal bleeding. He does have a broken jaw and leg, but it's a miracle when you consider that the car that hit him knocked him twenty feet. But he's doing okay."

Now, I was able to see Craig. Pulling back a dark green curtain that separated him from the rest of the trauma unit, his appearance startled me at first. His familiar thin frame was stretched out and strapped down to a long, rigid board on a stretcher that was crisscrossed with belts, straps and tape. Every inch of his body seemed to be covered by something medical, including his neck, which was wrapped in a brace, and his head was taped to the stretcher. The only exposed part of his face was swollen and bruised. I could feel a knot in my stomach that started to increase in size. I braced myself against Charles, who was standing alongside the bed, and leaned in toward Craig. He was completely motionless.

"Craig?" I asked softly.

I paused and waited. I was not sure of the type of response that I would get from him, but unexpectedly, he raised his hand ever so slightly and gave me a "thumbs up." My heart melted; he was going to be all right.

I was happy with a sense of relief when Craig was discharged home. However, this emotion was also being shared with the sadness of burying my mother. Her passing, unknowingly, reopened the recent wound of my brother's death. I had taken care of both of them to the very end and had buried them both. The sense of loss was inescapable. But there was not much time for reflection on my grief because again I was busy taking care of the sick. I had to convert the bedroom, the previously makeshift hospital room used for my mother, back into a space that would accommodate Craig and make him comfortable with his broken leg. As a result of his fractured jaw, his mouth was wired shut, which meant that all of his food had to be pureed. Craig, who was already thin before the accident, had lost a considerable amount of weight during his hospital stay, making him look frail. Now I was under pressure to boost his nutrition and weight on a diet that had to be both appealing and able to be administered through a straw for the next six weeks. Everyone helped out to keep his spirits up. My youngest son, Gaius, developed a task with Craig, whereby they made a list of all the foods and restaurants where they were going to eat once the wires were removed. The list was ridiculously long.

By now, I had become extremely weary and worn. In fact, one day while waiting at a stoplight, I put my car in park just in case I fell asleep while waiting for the light to change. Fortunately, I stayed awake. But, despite all of the issues surrounding me and my growing exhaustion, I knew that I could not stop with the music. I would not allow anything to derail me from my purpose of getting my music out. As a result, Cheryle and I returned to the printing press and finished the choral books. I was making some progress, but they were only tiny steps toward my goal. After printing the books, we purchased a machine to spirally bind the books, which I began selling to academic institutions and libraries. But with all of my efforts, there was still something missing – a concert. We had tried everything. Even after several months of planning a benefit concert with a regional university, the concert was cancelled. Nothing was working. Then, we thought that maybe we should try our efforts with an established professional organization that was local, and the Memphis Symphony Orchestra immediately came to mind. We did not have the money to hire them, but we thought that maybe we had something else to offer that would be enticing to them. At the time, the symphony did not have a significant presence within the Memphis black community. To counter this, we thought that pitching the idea of a concert, featuring the work of a native black Memphis composer, would be a perfect opportunity for the orchestra and, of course, for us. It was a bold idea, and the more we thought about it, the more we liked it.

It was a beautiful morning when Todd and I pulled into the parking space in front of the administrative office of the Memphis Symphony. Surprisingly, we were able to get an appointment with one of the staff members fairly quickly. I hoped that this was a good sign, signaling that the organization was eager to hear more of our idea, but deep down within me, I felt that this was going to be a hard sell. For some unknown reason, I had never been successful in getting my music heard within the establishment of Memphis, but whatever the reason, it was certainly not for lack of trying. Sitting there in the receptionist area, waiting to be called, I tried to focus only on positive thoughts as I rehearsed through my mind all the points that I wanted to stress and how to counter any possible opposition. My thoughts were finally interrupted by the receptionist, "Mrs. Robinson, you can go in now."

Upon entering the office, we were promptly greeted by a tall, young, conservatively dressed man who stepped from behind a desk with an outstretched hand. His face was stern and rigid; there was not a single strand of hair out of place. There was nothing warm or inviting about this man. He flashed a perfunctory smile, introduced himself and without saying hello, he asked, "How may I help you?"

I immediately started my pitch, "We are planning a concert for the spring of next year of an oratorio that I wrote. And, of course, we would be delighted if the Memphis Symphony would be involved."

"And what music will we be performing?" he asked, cutting me off.

The sly way he emphasized "we" came across as being distinctly condescending, a fact that he did not try to conceal. In fact, his entire behavior was so blatant that it initially almost startled me as I was slow to hand him my score of "The Crucifixion."

"It's an oratorio which I wrote called, "The Crucifixion."

Continuing in his demeaning manner, he quickly started flipping through the pages without any obvious intent of real interest, "So, who wrote it?"

Again, I briefly paused before saying, "I did." My

response was a mixture of irritation and bewilderment. I questioned if he had heard me when I previously mentioned that I had written the music or was he just ignoring me. I was not sure, but nevertheless, sensing his growing disdain for the work, I became more forceful in my pitch. "This particular work has been selected by the Library of Congress."

"Okay. So, why should we perform this music?" he asked but this time with a more arrogant tone.

Not to be fazed by his attitude, I immediately jumped into my sales pitch. "As I said before, 'The Crucifixion' oratorio was recently selected by the Library of Congress for its Special Collections."

"Well, that's nice but…"

And before he could finish his statement, I quickly added, "Also, as you already know, the percentage of the black population in Memphis is roughly half, but the Memphis Symphony has had difficulty in reaching this audience. And since I'm from Memphis, I thought that a concert of my music would be an excellent public relations event targeted towards the local black community, specifically the black churches. It has a huge potential to reach this large untapped market."

No sooner than my last words had escaped out of my mouth, he promptly replied, "Sounds like an interesting idea and I'm sure that your music is very nice. But the symphony is not interested in any new projects at this time. Besides, our calendar is booked."

The delivery of his last statement was so blunt and so cold that the finality of its message left both Todd and I stunned, frozen to our seats. He had already stood, thereby ending the meeting. The next few moments were a blur of handshakes, nods and steps out of the office. It was not until we stood in front of our car that we began to fully realize what had just happened.

"Wow. Can you believe that?" Todd said.

I was still shocked and offered no response.

"That was the worst meeting I've ever had. It would have been better if he had just put a sign on the front door saying don't come in," he continued.

I gave no response; Todd was talking to himself.

"That guy treated us like something on the bottom of his shoe. How long were we in there? Maybe, three, four minutes? He didn't listen to a word you said. I don't think we were there three minutes."

After several moments, I finally made a comment, "Sometimes, I wonder why I continue doing this."

I was becoming tired of the struggle. I worked, I planned, and I failed. There were those who could do the music, but would not for whatever reason; then, there were others who readily agreed to perform my music but were unable to pull it off; and I was stuck in the middle. This recurring scenario was making me weary with my efforts.

When I told Charles about the meeting, he was not surprised or angry; in fact, his reaction could best be described as calm and matter-of-fact. He had already figured out that I would not be well received because my pathway into classical music was so non-traditional with no formal training or degrees in music. Despite his knowing this and even talking about it out loud, he was never the least bit daunted by these "so called" disadvantages. His resolve and his encouraging me to keep pushing for a concert of my own was unwavering. In fact, he immediately came up with the suggestion that we simply hire musicians from the local music union whose membership also included one black violinist who played for the Memphis Symphony.

Our first step was to hire a conductor who would be

responsible for assembling a group of musicians. The person we chose came highly recommended. During the first meeting with him, we explained the nature of our problem – that we were having difficulty in finding quality talent who could perform the music. He asked the usual questions of who the composer was, the type of music and the event, and after receiving our answers, he quickly accepted the job and told us his fee. It was very quick, and in retrospect his quick decision should have been reason for concern. It was not because of his answer, but the way that he answered it. There was no detailed analysis of my music, no in-depth discussion of potential problems; in essence, there seemed to have been very little contemplation. After all, I was presenting to him a completely new and original oratorio. This was the same oratorio that the music department chairman at the university had examined and afterwards told me that my music was a new style of music, a concept that I was slow to fully accept. Furthermore, my experiences had taught me that performing a new work like mine was going to be difficult. Yet, despite all of this and the fact that he would have the sole responsibility for assembling the orchestral group of fellow union members and conducting the rehearsals himself, his response was a quick, "Yeah, I can do it." He seemed confident, but the question on my mind was could this group do it. However, we reminded ourselves that they were paid professionals. Maybe we were being apprehensive due to our past failures. So, we paid him the money.

On the night of the first rehearsal, I was excited, but that excitement would soon leave. It was difficult to express what I felt or heard, but if I had to describe that first rehearsal in a single word, that word would be, disjunctive. Only the string section provided some resemblance of my music, but everyone else, especially the brass section, was playing something that was completely foreign to me. The timing, the melody, everything was off. Nothing seemed to flow with my printed music. Out of shock, I began to think that surely this was not happening again. They were professionals, but when I looked at Charles, with his faintly disguised look of disgust, I knew that he had drawn the same conclusion.

The music was well over their heads, specifically the conductor. It was obvious that he had initially dismissed my music as something that would be simple. After all, they were just songs written by someone with no formal training, no music degrees – how difficult could it be? His words, "Yeah, I can do it" came back to haunt him as he stood there bewildered and confused, struggling to understand the music, coordinate the group and camouflage his ineptness. His previous confidence and underestimation of my music was borne out of arrogance. But, more importantly, his decision to accept our project was formulated out of an assumption of what he thought I was and not based on the content of my music. Now, in a vain attempt to salvage his ego in front of his contemporaries, the man, who we had paid as the conductor, threw his hands up and made an absurd announcement.

"As of right now, we don't have a conductor," he exclaimed.

I couldn't believe what I was hearing. And just like that, our money was spent. It was a huge loss in such a short span of time. Not since the album had Charles put so much money into a single project. At least with the album project, our efforts did result in something that was tangible and successful – although it was fleeting, it was successful all the same. In fact, all of our endeavors even the ones with disappointing outcomes had yielded something of value; the previous failures taught us about the business and strengthened our resolve. But this defeat was different. It left a different kind of scar. We had spent months saving up the money to hire this group; and on the appointed day we showed up, expecting the fruits of our labors. Unfortunately, during that rehearsal, even before the clock could strike the following hour, we learned that we had been led astray and that our hard-earned money, thousands of dollars, had been thrown away within the span of an hour. This failure did not feel like a lesson or an added experience; it felt like we had been taken. Charles and I were stunned beyond words. More than any other time, we felt the crushing defeat, and it was hard to swallow.

It was so bad that I did not know how I would recover from it. My emotions ran the gamut from anger to disappointment to hurt, and when my feelings became exhausted, I felt numbness. How could I continue? That was the question on my mind, but there was no answer. Even Charles, who had been unwavering up to this point, also seemed to give up. After that rehearsal, he told me, "That's the last hurrah." He was finished with the music. It was the first time that he had given up.

It was during dark times like this one when I often questioned what I was doing. I reflected and thought about all that God had shown me – the dreams, the revelations and the quiet words in my sleep. Now, I wondered, was I misunderstanding what He was telling me, and should I continue? Similar questions had plagued me after the previous cancelled event. During that time, I heard the words spoken softly in my sleep, "You must not let anything stop you. FIGHT to overcome every obstacle!" But this time my spirit was fatigued and broken; I was tired of asking questions. I prayed for understanding and to know His will, and God reassured me in the most unexpected way.

The next day, Charles approached me and unexpectedly

said, "We must not stop. We can't quit. We have to continue." I do not know what motivated him. But within a span of one day, he completely reversed his earlier decision to give up. I did not ask him what made him change his mind, but I also knew within my heart that we had to continue.

Chapter 16

Leap of Faith

It's incredible how occurrences that seem insignificant can impact your life. A single event, one moment in time, can happen without any fanfare or notice, and only after looking back under close scrutiny can the wonderment of that moment be truly appreciated. The year was 1956, when I first met Merle Anderson. She was an upperclassman and my dorm counselor when I arrived at Fisk University, and as a freshman, she gave me a request to take some clothes hangers to her boyfriend who was standing only a few feet from her. It was a silly and frivolous tradition whereby upperclassmen, during the first week of school, ordered freshmen to do meaningless tasks. That was one of my enduring memories of first meeting Merle. Now, nearly 37 years later, after not seeing or speaking to one another, our paths once again crossed, and our friendship blossomed when Merle moved back to Memphis. As heartwarming as it was to be reunited with an old college mate, there was much more to the story that was about to unfold.

One day out of the blue, Merle's mother, Beulah Anderson, called me and asked to stop over at my house. It was a bit unusual since it was the first and only time she had ever called with such a request; nevertheless, it was not remarkably odd for people to drop by my house on short notice. My home is located in the heart of the city. The airport was only a seven-minute drive to the south, and 10 minutes away to the north was the University of Memphis. Traveling 15 minutes to the west was downtown Memphis, and the city's major shopping malls were located only a few minutes in the opposite direction. This geographic convenience was quickly realized by anyone who knew where I lived. As a result, it was a very common practice for friends and relatives to often stop over while en route to somewhere else. On this particular day, it was Merle's mother who was stopping by for a visit. She was nearby running errands and asked if she could wait at my house until her granddaughter got out of school. So, several minutes later, she sat in my kitchen, waiting, and watching me prepare her a light snack. The time was well spent as we laughed and made small talk, but then, she made a surprising comment.

"Earnestine, Merle tells me that you've been having some

problems getting your music performed."

"Yes, it's been difficult."

"Well, I'm going to call Carol, my daughter in Oregon, and ask her if she knows anybody who can help you."

As I listened to her, I smiled. It was a nice gesture on her part to show what seemed to be a genuine concern, but I had been down this road many times. Over the past twenty years, I had heard this type of conversation over and over again. The details and the people that were involved changed from case to case, but the scenario was still the same. It always started with someone who knew someone, who, in turn, had some kind of connection. From there, the story usually ended quickly, but on those other rare occasions, that "someone" would lead me down a trail of promises that would meander through a growing list of ideas and contacts, all of which resulted in nothing specific except for a rise and fall of enthusiasm. So, it was with very little excitement that I listened to her talk about her daughter in Oregon who could possibly help me.

"Did you know that Carol plays violin for the Oregon Symphony?"

"No, I didn't."

That last piece of information was unexpected and caught me by surprise. I thought what an odd coincidence, and for a brief moment, my mind toyed with the idea of a symphony playing my music. But the memory of my meeting with the Memphis Symphony quickly sprang to mind, and my hopes immediately dissipated. I was not getting my hopes up – not another disappointment, not this time. That was the one thing that I was determined to avoid; and as a result, I just nodded and smiled, but I did not inquire any further about her daughter. We were just having a pleasant conversation, and I simply told myself not to read anything more into it except that her suggestion was a well-intended and sincere gesture.

A couple of days had passed without incident, and I had largely forgotten the details of my conversation with Mrs. Anderson about her daughter. I ignored the possibility of her idea, not due to some lack of truth on her part, but because it seemed like such a random event. The mother of a friend, whom I had only recently reconnected with after more than 30 years, happens to show up at my house on a whim and somewhere between sandwiches and lemonade, she just happens to connect me with someone else who was affiliated with a major symphony on the other side of the country. It was a wild stretch of the imagination and the odds of something developing out of it seemed extremely remote. Furthermore, I was too scarred from all of my previous disappointments to see any potential of her random visit. However, only four days after her visit, I received a call from her daughter, Carol Neff, in Oregon, I was stunned.

Just like her mother had mentioned, Carol was well connected within the musical spheres of Portland, Oregon. I remember that day so clearly. It was a Sunday morning when she called and told me that she had passed my name and information onto Dr. Jonathan Griffith, who was the choral director of the Oregon Symphony. Slowly, I could feel that something was happening. Then, she gave me his phone number and asked me to call him. By the time she had hung up, excitement was bubbling inside me. This was all brand new to me – a choral director of a major symphony wanting me to call him. I just could not believe it. For years, I had tried everything, only to be ridiculed, taken advantaged of or just plainly ignored. Now, an opportunity without any effort on my part had fallen into my hands. The words, "choral director of the Oregon Symphony" kept rolling through my head. This was too good to be true, and for the next several hours I mulled it over, thinking of the possibilities. The seed of faith planted deep inside of me began to grow.

Later that day, just hours after Carol's call, the phone rang again. I answered.

"Hello, may I speak with Earnestine Robinson?" the caller said.

The voice on the other end was unfamiliar to me; his speech and dialect quickly alerted me that he was not from the South. My mind scrambled as I tried to determine who was calling me as I responded, "This is she."

Then, with a very casual and unassuming tone, he said, "Hi, Earnestine. This is Jonathan Griffith. I was about to go out of town, but I wanted to call you before I left. Is this a good time to talk?"

Again, I was absolutely stunned. Usually, as the composer, I was the one who took the initiative in starting a new project, but by his calling me first on such short notice, it was very obvious that he was interested. He did not have to talk about his excitement or feign enthusiasm about the project, his actions showed it. This was a nice change from what I was accustomed to. After the usual introductions, Jonathan began by quickly presenting his credentials, and while his musical background was impressive, it was his demeanor that grabbed my attention. He was very professional, and throughout the entire conversation he exhibited a comfort and ease with himself that was matched only by the energy in his voice as he talked about music. His career was definitely his passion, something that was also reflected by his list of conducting experiences, including performances at Carnegie Hall. Yet, despite the disparity of our successes, we talked as equals, and of course, he had many questions about me, my music and the journey that had led me to the phone call with him. At one point during the conversation, when I expressed my hesitations and concerns about how I had been burned so often, he was quick to identify with my plight. But if there was one thing that he said during that lengthy talk – one thing that stood out from the rest – it occurred when he told me, "I'm not afraid to do a new work." With that single statement, I was hooked. Even though Oregon was so far away, I knew that I had to explore this opportunity. I still needed a little more reassurance, some type of confirmation that I was not chasing another dead end. For that confirmation, I knew that I had to go to Portland to meet Jonathan face to face, and although I was guarded in my expectations, the conversation with him left me feeling optimistic. It looked like things were finally starting to turn around for my music.

My spirit was elevated with the thought of this new opportunity, and I was in an especially good mood because Michelle, who was taking a vacation from her job in Peoria, Illinois, was in town. We headed to the local PBS station and picked up Cheryle from work. The three of us chatted nonstop as we drove back home to get Charles; we were all going to dinner. However, we were surprised when we got home and found Charles sitting in a chair in the dining room. This was unusual because he always sat in his recliner in the den to relax and watch television. But there he sat, with his body twisted to the side. I knew that something was wrong.

"Charles, what happened?" I asked

He was slow to respond, "I had just finished taking my bath and came to the front door to turn on the porch light for you. I dropped my towel, and when I tried to pick it up, I slipped and fell."

He was not moaning in pain, but his movements did suggest that he was in discomfort. Instinctively, I looked at the spot where he had fallen. The flooring of the hallway was made of a gray and white mosaic marble, which was beautiful when polished, but unforgiving when falling on it. I cringed at the thought of him landing on it. Over the years, when my children were small, I had often worried about the health hazards of the marble and brick flooring in the house. However, no one had endured any serious injuries from it…until now. I stared back at Charles, trying to put together the pieces of the story.

"Where are you hurting?" I asked.

"My hip." And before I could ask another question, he continued, "I'll be alright."

But that did not ease my concerns. He was not making any eye contact; I knew he was in pain. I could picture in my mind what had happened during the fall, but the real question was how serious it was. Somehow, Charles managed to make it back to our bedroom, not allowing anyone to help him. He then decided to take a bath in hopes of easing the pain, but it did the opposite. By the time he made it to bed, he was exhausted and in more discomfort. It was a rough night, and by daybreak, the pain had increased and was so unbearable that he readily agreed to go to the emergency room. Under normal circumstances, Charles did not like going to doctors, much less hospitals; so, I knew that something was seriously wrong.

Standing next to his stretcher in the emergency room, I was swallowed up by all of the activity around me. Cheryle and Michelle, who were with me, were also mesmerized by the beeping machines, loud voices, and scurrying medical personnel. It was the same hospital where I stood next to Craig after his accident. It was still the same – chaotic. Patients in wheelchairs and on stretchers whirled around us with doctors and nurses barking out orders in their unified mission. It was a marvel to watch, but a very stressful environment, one that I could not imagine working in. Yet, despite all the excitement and the noble quest of the staff in attending to the sick, emergency rooms are cold and uninviting places. But this time was different. When the doctor pulled back the curtain surrounding our stretcher and touched Charles, I smiled. It was Todd. Wearing scrubs and a traditional white lab coat, he was on duty and working in the ER. This was my first-time seeing Todd working in his official duty as a physician in a hospital. It felt a little odd but comforting to see his face among a sea of unknown doctors, and I am certain it was strange for him that his father had now become his patient. Of course, he had excused himself from being directly involved with the case. Charles was also glad to see Todd. He had already been treated by another physician with intravenous morphine and was starting to feel more comfortable. Returning to his usual self, he was asking Todd a barrage of questions of who his doctor was, what was going on and what was taking so long.

From the very beginning, everyone that attended Charles all suspected the same thing, a fractured hip, which was later confirmed by a series of x-rays. Although I was not completely surprised by the diagnosis, I was shocked that he had walked with a broken hip. The orthopedic surgeon, who seemed impressed with Charles' resilience, explained how the clean break on the day before was probably perfectly aligned at first, but after the bath, the surrounding muscles relaxed, causing the bone to shift and resulting in the increased pain. In the emergency room, the main concern was obviously admitting him to the hospital and the treatment of the fracture, but it did not take long before the doctors started to ask questions and investigate the other problem, the one thing that Charles had tried to minimize over the years – his balance problem. After days of testing and an exhaustive parade of doctors, a meeting with the neurologist was scheduled to discuss the final outcome. Prior to this meeting, Todd, who was careful not to alarm Charles, had already prepared us about all of the concerns, but this was the official version.

"Mr. Robinson, how did you sleep last night?" the neurologist blurted out cordially, but in a perfunctory manner as he entered the room. His voice was so loud that it quickly filled our room and probably the adjacent hallway.

"Fine," Charles responded, lying calmly in the bed with his hands folded over his stomach.

"Well, we have finally determined what's causing your equilibrium problem. All of our testing point to a disorder that's called oligocerebellopontine degeneration. Basically, symptoms of this disease occur when healthy brain tissue that is responsible for your balance and movement is replaced with scar tissue."

"So, what does this mean?" Charles asked without hesitation.

"Well, unfortunately, we don't have any treatment for it, and the symptoms that you're having now are going to get worse. In fact, even your physical therapy is going to be very difficult and prolonged because of it.

"How long?" Charles asked.

"Beg your pardon?" the doctor said, looking puzzled.

"How long is the therapy going to be? I plan on being in Oregon for a concert in the fall. Can the therapy be finished by then?"

"It's not that simple," the doctor responded. His words were initially slow to come out, but he quickly regained his composure and reasserted himself. "Mr. Robinson, you've got to remember. You just had major hip surgery. It's going to take time to heal, and then, with your neurological problem, learning how to stand is going to be difficult, let alone retraining yourself to walk if it even happens at all."

His statement stunned my heart, not so much as his words but his tone. It was not what I was expecting to hear. I was not in denial about the seriousness of Charles' diagnosis or his prognosis. Todd had already explained the results to us, being very truthful, yet, with hope. But the neurologist's delivery was filled with such gloom that I was momentarily speechless. With his cold, factual approach, he had unknowingly stripped any shred of hope from the situation, leaving only emptiness and despair. For several moments, there was a stillness in the room as we all sat in silence, a silence that was only broken by the sound of the doctor's beeper.

"I'm sorry, but I have to get this," he said as he turned and left.

When I looked over at Charles, he had already looked away from the doctor and was staring past the television set, which was bolted to the wall in front of him. I thought that maybe he would be disappointed, but when I looked in his face, he seemed unfazed by the news.

"Charles, did you hear what the doctor said?"

"Yeah, I heard him," he said without any expression and continued without pausing. "I'm going to Portland."

I knew that expression. He had made his decision; he knew what he was going to do, and the prognosis given by the doctor was not going to stop him. From that point forward, he never talked about what the doctor said or discussed at length anything about his neurological problem. He became more determined as he pushed through his therapy. As a result, his rehab went very well, better than anyone expected in a short three months, and despite the rigors of therapy, he eagerly pushed me to go to Oregon to have my initial meeting with Jonathan Griffith.

A couple of months after my first conversation with Jonathan, Cheryle and I boarded a plane for Portland.

Throughout the lengthy plane trip, thoughts of apprehension repeatedly rolled over in my mind, and I mentally rehearsed all the points that I needed to cover. If there were any problems, I was determined to expose them immediately and avoid prolonging the agony. My mind kept reverting to all of my phone conversations with Jonathan in an attempt to pick apart what was said, but the same, basic conclusion always presented itself: he was definitely qualified and seemed so nice. There was one particular conversation that I recalled when he laid the phone receiver near the piano and played through some of my songs, pausing several times to ask questions. Of course, I was glad to be discussing my music, and it was reassuring to hear him play my songs. But it was the way he asked for my input that I found interesting. This type of interaction from someone who was so accomplished felt strange at first. Throughout those sessions, he would often comment on the complexities of my music, acknowledge my talent, and genuinely inquire about the motivations behind my music. He would ask me technical questions such as key and tempo changes without any reference to his doctorate or my lack of formal training. He was neither arrogant about his extensive musical experiences nor did he slight my humble beginnings. Never did he gloss over my music with an air of superiority; instead, he spent time, methodically examining and discussing every detail which I imagined was scribbled as notes in the margins of the sheet music, propped up in front of him at the piano.

It took us almost half the day to reach our destination, and with our arrival into Portland, my feelings of anxiety grew. It was a mixture of excitement and apprehension, feelings that had been bottled up by years of hope and disappointment. After arriving at the hotel and settling into our room, we went immediately down to the hotel lobby to meet with Jonathan; I tried to imagine what was about to take place. I knew what he would look like from his resume photos, and I could hear his voice in my head, but I was eager to see him in person. Would this be the break that I had longed for or would our long trip out west simply be a waste of time? The answer and the moment were at hand as Cheryle and I entered the lobby and began scanning the area.

Suddenly, Cheryle nudged me and said, "Dr. Griffith?"

"Cheryle! Earnestine!"

Cheryle and I extended our hand for a formal greeting.

"Oh, no. Give me a hug," as he opened his arms. "Welcome to Portland. I have spoken with you so much over the phone, I feel like we are old friends," he said while giving us both hugs.

Although his exuberant approach definitely caught me by surprise, his friendly embrace did succeed in breaking the ice and melting some of my apprehensions. All of my previous experiences had taught me to be cautious and somewhat guarded when embarking on new projects. Over the years I had learned to always be mentally prepared for the usual sternness of such new encounters. But this was nothing like that. His unorthodox approach and introduction were completely void of emotional detachment. Subsequently, our meeting did not feel like the beginning of an awkward interview of a new conductor; it felt more like a pleasant invitation.

"I hope you are hungry. I know this wonderful restaurant where we can grab a bite to eat and talk business."

"Oh, yes that sounds good," I politely responded, but I was still trying to process it all.

Jonathan had this abundant energy. His words seemed to bounce as he talked, but, once again, what struck me the most was that it was refreshing to interact with someone so humble. During our trip to the restaurant, the three of us laughed and passed the time with small talk that was surprisingly easy, considering the brief time that we had known each other. Once we had finished ordering, the conversation shifted to business as Jonathan pulled out a copy of my oratorio. He immediately started flipping through its pages, pausing at moments to study and hum certain sections. The pages of my oratorio were dotted with barely legible notes in the margins, as I had previously imagined. I glanced at Cheryle to gauge her response; she also seemed captivated by our host's enthusiasm. Returning my gaze to Jonathan, my eyes noticed his right hand, which was moving in rhythm as if he were conducting my music. Finally, after several moments of reading and humming, Jonathan abruptly stopped, nodded his head and looked up from the sheet music.

"Earnestine, I absolutely love your music."

"Well...thank you."

"I love your melodies," he continued without interruption. "You know, what's so amazing about your music? It's a different style of music. It doesn't fit any single genre."

"What do you mean?" I asked.

"Your use of repetitions gives it a gospel feel. Of course, that's understandable. Your music is going to be influenced by your background. But your harmonies and rhythms are more like jazz. And somehow, you bring it all together under a classical format."

"Hmm, that's interesting."

No sooner than the words had left my mouth, Jonathan was back to scanning the sheet music and humming to himself.

"Earnestine, I would love to do your music," he said abruptly, as if making an announcement.

"Well, we've been looking for someone to perform it. But, in the past..."

"I know. People have really taken advantage of you. And I'm sure that some of them probably looked at your musical background and automatically assumed that your music was not anything significant."

"That has been a problem," I responded.

"Then, you're a black woman in a male dominant field. Off hand, I don't know of any African-American female composers who are writing major works. And you're in Memphis. Now, I haven't been to Memphis, but I do know that it's mainly known for Elvis Presley and blues, not classical."

"This is true."

"But your music – you write from the heart. You write what you feel. That's what makes your music so different."

"Yes, I've been told that before."

Throughout the conversation, we volleyed comments back and forth with ease. He seemed to anticipate my concerns and understand my struggles without my having to articulate them. But I still had a concern that I wanted him to address.

"Jonathan, the biggest problem that I have had is that this is a new work."

"You're right. Taking on a brand new work is difficult. As a result, most people are afraid to perform a premiere work, but not me. I love the challenge."

At that very instant, Cheryle and I looked at each other and smiled. We both knew that that was the one statement that we needed to hear.

"Jonathan, you don't know how long I have searched for someone who felt that way."

Throughout our time in Portland, everything that I saw and heard reassured me that this was the right path. It was comforting. With all of the years that I spent toiling in Memphis and doing everything in my strength to have a concert, anguish and disappointment were the usual feelings, but this time I felt a peace. I remembered before the trip I prayed and asked God to show me why I was having so many failed concerts. The unexpected answer, which I had heard in my sleep, was simply, "Your vision is too small." Reflecting on that simple message, I thought of the enormity of this new project, and I was no longer reluctant in stepping outside of my comfort zone. Flying back to Memphis, it was clear that the trip was a success.

    Back home, I had a captive audience. Everyone was eager to hear what had happened: the conversation with Jonathan, his enthusiasm, and how he drove us around Portland to point out possible locations for the concert. As I poured through my narrative about the trip, Charles flashed a half smile, which he repetitively and unsuccessfully tried to suppress. Oddly enough, I knew that this was a good sign. This was his usual reaction whenever he was trying to contain his excitement; as a result, I knew within minutes into the conversation that I had the "green light." He was not the least bit hesitant about taking on such a huge venture; in fact, I think the vastness and complexity of the project is what really excited him the most.

    After agreeing on the amount to pay Jonathan for the use of his choir and signing the contract, we were set. However, securing and paying for a choir was not our only concern. The logistics of producing a concert had its own set of inherent problems and headaches. Obtaining permission and recording rights, discussing ticket sales and disbursement percentages, and the cost of advertising were just a few of the usual roadblocks that had to be navigated, and their terms negotiated. The distance further complicated all of these issues. As a result, right from the start, these and other problems started to grow in significance. The hurdles were rapidly becoming more pronounced, and although we were far from failure, the whole process was starting to deteriorate until we made a radical change. A decision had to be made or the decision would have been made for us; so, we decided against having a concert. No concert – it was difficult to formulate the idea at first. For years, we had been chasing this elusive goal and once again, our limitations were halting our efforts. But this time we adapted to our hardships, made a paradigm shift and abandoned the concept of a traditional concert. In its place, we opted for a performance of my music in a church without an audience. Even though it was a decision made out of necessity, that single move eliminated the majority of our problems and steered us back from the brink of disappointment. Instead of a live audience, we decided on recording the music and filming the performance for a television audience. In retrospect, it is interesting how we averted the looming misery of another failure by not thinking small or conceding to defeat but stepping out on faith and going bigger. Although we had not secured any television contracts, we figured that we would edit the video into a documentary format and shop the final product at a later date.

By this time, my household had shifted into full-blown project mode, and just like all the times before, all unnecessary spending came to a halt; all available money was redirected toward the project and sacrifices were made. Each day was filled with impromptu brainstorming, a frenzied pace and excitement. It was all familiar. I had been down this path many times, but this time was different. Before, it was Charles and I who alone faced the challenges, but this time we had help.

Years ago, I had a dream where I saw a cluster of small

houses that, individually, were not striking in any obvious manner, just ordinary houses, but collectively, they seemed to be linked to one another and represented something far greater. I understood that the houses were representative of my family, Charles and the children, but I did not fully grasp the implications of the dream until now. As we pushed through the Portland project, the meaning of the dream became clearer to me. Everyone in their own way was contributing, and the amazing part of it was that I did not plan this. It all seemed to be occurring automatically. Yet, there was something else that was more striking, something that was unforeseen until that moment. Over the years, everyone in my family had pursued and cultivated their own interests, but in the time leading up to the Portland event, those developed interests and talents seemed to converge in a way that was amazing.

    Although Charles was recuperating from hip surgery, I continued to rely on his business advice. That was usual; he had been encouraging me and supporting my music from day one. But now, Todd, who was finishing up his medical training, was adding money to the project. He was moonlighting, picking up extra hours in emergency rooms and taking extra overnight hospital call. Although he helped previously with the book, his new financial involvement was a big boost. Cheryle, who did graduate studies at the Art Institute of Chicago, had recently landed a job as art director at the local PBS station. In this position, she developed a working relationship with another staffer who expressed interest in helping us to package our final product for broadcasting. Then, there was my younger daughter, Michelle. Upon finishing her master's degree in journalism at Northwestern, she took up a news reporting job in Peoria, Illinois. However, after realizing that she needed a break and help in planning her wedding, she made plans to move back to Memphis. With her background in broadcast journalism, it was only natural for her to join the project as the narrator for the oratorio and to assist with the filming part of the project. The meaning of those small houses from the dream was now more evident than ever, especially when I thought of the words that God spoke to me, "I'm going to converge gifts, talents and abilities for My work." It was all coming together.

As the months flew by and the days pulled closer to our planned concert recording, the cost of the project had grown. Fees for the choir, recording engineer, film crew and, not to mention, travel expenses and accommodations for the family were mounting. Time was running out and our money was running short. Despite all of our planning and efforts, we had a dilemma that was facing us as we sat in the kitchen, just one day before we were scheduled to leave for Portland. In the weeks leading up to that moment, we had refused to entertain any possibility of defeat, not this time. This time was going to be different. I had been praying that God would make a way, but the clock had run out on us, leaving us with one ugly fact of reality. We were out of money. We had paid everyone their sums in full, airline and train tickets had been purchased and hotel rooms booked. There was only one last detail – the last installment for the choir. We had scrapped every possible source of funds to make timely payments for the choir, but the last payment was due upon arrival in Portland. We did not have it. It is the worst feeling to see, hear, and even touch victory, but only to have it fall inches away. In that kitchen, the three of us, Charles, Todd and I sat in despair. No one was willing to be the first to say it out loud until I spoke.

"We don't have the money." I said, betraying the silence. No one said anything. The seconds passed like hours.

"Well..." I responded to my own words.

Again, nothing.

"Do we need to cancel?" My heart ached just to say the words, and it felt like someone had let all the air out of the room as the words hung in space for what seemed like an eternity until Todd broke the silence.

"No." he said only one word, paused and then two more, "We can't."

"We don't have the money, Todd. There is nothing else for us to do," I responded.

"How much do we need?" he asked.

Finally, Charles who had been sitting quietly and thinking, spoke up, "We're about $2,500 short."

Again, we all went silent. Everybody withdrew into their own private deep space of thought. Twenty-five hundred dollars was so close but seemed out of reach. No one responded, not only out of disappointment and despair but also out of exhaustion. Our struggle to raise the money had drained us of every resource, every sacrifice and every idea. There was simply nothing left.

Then, right to the very edge of quitting, Todd spoke up again.

"I'll get it." His words were concise, direct and confident. There was no hint of wavering, no hesitation. He spoke as if he already had it.

Stunned by his response, I quickly asked, "Where are you going to get it?"

"I don't know…maybe, I'll borrow it or something."

"Todd, I don't know. I just feel so badly. Everybody has put so much into it. I can't ask you to do that."

"No, I want to." Then, with a defiant stance, he turned toward me and said, "Tomorrow, you and Dad will leave, and I'll meet you later in Portland with the money."

"Yeah, we need to go through with this," Charles added with a calm resolve.

Then, with a leap of faith, I stood, feeling a peace come over me as the very atmosphere of the room seemed to lighten, and gave the concluding statement, "We're going."

Chapter 17

The First Victory

It was early morning, a little after 6:00 when Charles and I walked onto the platform of the Amtrak station to board the train. The train whistle had yet to blow; so, we had plenty of time to find our passenger car that we would be riding in during the first leg of our journey westward. Joining us was Michelle, Craig and a friend, Brenda Miller, who had assisted me with the children's Easter program so many years ago and who now wanted to share this moment. This day was a long time coming. For years, those who were close to me, had witnessed me either singing, composing or planning concerts, but also during those years they had witnessed no performance of my oratorio in its entirety. Now, after years of anticipation and hope, we were making a pilgrimage to Portland, Oregon, to see the fulfillment of my dream, the first complete performance of "The Crucifixion."

Of all the people who were planning to attend, we were the first ones to depart for Oregon. Ironically, the first part of our itinerary headed in the opposite direction away from our ultimate destination. We had to travel south to New Orleans to change trains before heading westward. Typically, this would not have been the most direct or optimal route if traveling by car, but on the train the extra day of travel seemed to add to its overall ambiance, making it feel more like a leisure indulgence instead of prolonged time. From start to finish, the entire trip was scheduled to take four days, plenty of time to unwind before the concert, and over the course of the following days and nights, we immersed ourselves in the scenery outside our window and the conversations of the people inside the train. As we made our way past southwestern deserts, we talked and laughed; through the Californian mountain pass, we dined; and along the stretches of the Pacific Ocean shoreline, we looked in awe.

Although our journey was convoluted, the planning of it was a relatively simple process. However, for other members of the family, making reservations was much more complicated because of conflicts with college class schedules and work obligations. Fortunately, dealing with those type of frustrations was Charles' forte; for some reason, any trip planning that was wrought with complexities, obstacles or a tight budget was a welcomed challenge for him. Assembling difficult travel arrangements was as rewarding as completing a massive jigsaw puzzle where all the pieces appeared to be similar. His planning task was all the more challenging because during those times prior to the internet, there were limited options; the newspaper was the only real resource for locating the best fares. Beyond that, you either contacted a travel agent or called the train or airline directly. Of course, Charles chose the indirect approach of searching on his own.

Travel by train was less expensive and a great choice for anyone who had the extra time. But for three of my children, it was not an option. My youngest son, Gaius was a freshman at Tennessee State University in Nashville at the time, and we did not want him to miss too many days from classes. As a result, Charles decided to fly him out on Friday and return him to school on Sunday since our event was on a Saturday. Work restrictions also required Cheryle and Todd to fly, but they had to leave at different times. Cheryle used the days while we were on the train to fly to Portland early in order to tie up loose ends. Her friend, Charles, who lived in Berkeley, California joined her to help and to be a part of the experience. Todd was the last to leave Memphis because he was on call at the hospital. Then, there were friends of Todd, one of whom who lived in Texas and who Charles also assisted with making travel plans. After weeks of marathon phone sessions and stacks of newspapers, his labor resulted in the coordinated exodus with a common destination of Portland. By that Friday, the day before the big event, after I had mentally rehearsed many times the details of my debut event, we rolled past the lush forests of the pacific northwest and into Portland. Almost everyone had made it to Oregon and assembled at the church for the dress rehearsal.

I could hardly wait to hear the choir at this final

rehearsal. Sitting there and focused on the singers in front of me, I was caught up with the thrill that my dream was actually taking shape. Lost in the excitement of the moment, my skin tingled with glee that it was going to happen. From the first few lines of the music, I knew that this was different from any of my other attempts. For the first time, I finally heard a conductor and choir actually delivering on the promise that they could perform my music, and just like that, gone was the pain from years of cancelled concerts and disappointments. The music swirled in my head and filled my heart with joy. There were no thoughts or threats of cancellation. In fact, the previous conversation with Charles and Todd that tethered on the brink of making another cancellation had faded into the background, completely camouflaged by the energy of the moment. I had forgotten all of it until Todd walked through the side door of the church, and all of a sudden, everything came flooding back. By some automatic reflex, my thoughts quickened. In an instant the sounds and images surrounding me went blank as I searched Todd's face for some clue. With his appearance, the harshness of reality came rushing back – we did not have the required last payment. We had left Memphis, traveled for days and sat in on rehearsals, all without knowing if we had the remaining money. Not only did we not have the money when I left Memphis, we also did not have any idea of how to get the remaining funds. It was a mystery that I had comfortably pushed to the back of mind; it was a leap of faith. But Todd's appearance had redirected my thoughts, causing the dilemma to resurface. Now, the only thing that I could think of was, did we get the money? The rehearsal was drawing to its end, and payment would soon be expected. Promises and apologies would not be enough. There would be no time to regroup. It was now or never. I leaned forward in a subconscious effort to draw myself closer to the answer. Finally, our eyes met, and from Todd's sparkle and nod, I knew; no words were needed. The jubilation was loud and clear. We had succeeded. The last hurdle had been crossed and the race was won. With that realization, my spirit relaxed, bringing the angelic sounds of the choir once again back into my ears. The rehearsal ended on a joyous note; everything was in place and everyone smiled.

Later, back at the hotel, Todd revealed the incredible details of how our problem was solved.

"You won't believe how we got the money," he started his story.

"What happened?" I eagerly asked.

"It was unbelievable. You'll never guess it in a million years"

"Todd Vincent, will you just tell us what happened?" Charles interrupted with a smirk on his face.

"Okay, on the day you guys left, I immediately started to ask everybody that I knew who could loan me some money. That didn't go far. Only one person said yes, and it wasn't very much. But I was pleasantly surprised. Anyway, by the second day, I had run out of people to ask and to make matters worse, I got a call from the Bursar's office. They only call you when something's wrong. So, I didn't call them back. I was on call that night, and I didn't feel like hearing any bad news. Anyway, by the third day, I was panicking, I had only one more day left before I had to catch my flight, and I was way short on the funds. I didn't know what to do. And in the middle of me freaking out, I get another call from the Bursar's office. I'm thinking, 'just great.' Well, this time I went over there, and you won't believe what happened."

"What?" I asked.

"When I got there, the receptionist, who's looking all serious, tells me that they've been looking for me. Then, she tells me to have a seat and goes back to typing."

"What did she want?" I asked.

"I had no idea. I must've sat there for 15 or 20 minutes, thinking what could be taking so long. The whole office only has three people in it."

"Todd," I interrupted, growing anxious by the moment.

"Okay. Finally, this woman comes out of the back, hands me an envelope and tells me that she thought I may have wanted this," with this last statement, he paused.

"And?"

"I opened it up, and it was a check for...$2,500!"

"What!! That's the exact amount that we needed to pay off Jonathan." I exclaimed.

"Exactly! I couldn't believe it. So, I'm just standing there in shock, looking at this loan check."

"You didn't know about it before?" I asked.

"Nope."

"Maybe you applied for a loan and forgot about it," I said.

"Mom, I would not forget anything like that. In fact, I know that I wasn't eligible for a loan, and I've never even heard of this bank. Anyway, I'm just standing there, staring at the check when the clerk asks me if it was the correct amount."

"Well, what did you do?" Charles finally jumped in and asked.

"I signed for it and walked out the door," Todd replied.

For the next several moments, we all sat in silence and marveled at the chain of events. My head was filling up with so many questions that I did not know which one to ask first, but Todd was not finished with his story.

"You know what's really weird? As the day went by, I started feeling badly, like I had taken something that didn't belong to me. It was really starting to eat me up because I didn't want to get into any type of trouble; so, I went back to the Bursar's office and told them that I didn't apply for a loan."

"And what did they say?" I asked, moving to the edge of my chair.

"She told me to hold on and went to check the paperwork, and when she came back, she told me that everything was in order. So, I said okay, paused for a moment and walked out. Then, I went immediately to the bank and deposited it, just in case, they changed their mind."

With that last statement, we all laughed. Of course, weeks later, the Bursar's office discovered that Todd had, indeed, never applied for a loan and demanded repayment; by that time, we were able to pay back the money. However, to this day, no one has been able to explain how the "mistake" happened in the first place. In any manner, it was simply miraculous how we got our last payment for the performance.

The next morning, the light of dawn had started to crack past the curtains of the hotel room; it was my usual time of reflection and meditation. My mind scanned through the past several years that I had spent either planning or wondering what to do with my music. But on this October morning in 1993, as I lay in bed, thousands of miles from my hometown where I thought my music would have taken flight, I watched the sunrise embrace me in a new light. There was a new excitement that caused my heart to flutter with joy. The anticipation of this long-awaited day was finally here.

It was not long before everyone else started to stir. Everybody was moving quickly through the preliminaries of getting dressed and having breakfast with the unified focus of getting to the main event. We loaded into the rental van and started our drive to St. Anthony's Church in Tigard,

Oregon. Leaving downtown, we eventually found ourselves driving through suburban streets that flowed with autumn colors. The church was beautifully nestled within the surrounding neighborhood. Once inside the church, there was a stillness that filled the air of the sanctuary. It was the last moment of expectation; I thought to myself that this was really happening. I was on the cusp of hearing a choir perform my oratorio, "The Crucifixion." The reality of the moment was almost beyond my imagination and my heart danced with excitement. I kept reminding myself that it was truly happening, but it was almost unbelievable. The choir members had started to file into the church, but the film crew and audio engineer were already there and fully engaged in their set up. Watching the crews move through their hurried pace, my gleeful anticipation turned serious as I focused back on the objective. There was work to be done.

I was especially interested in seeing the film crew. My curiosity stemmed from the fact that I had never met them. When we first came up with the idea of filming the performance, I did not fully realize that finding a video company was going to be such a daunting task. This arena was outside of Jonathan's expertise, and we had no other contacts in the region that could give us any advice about available videographers. In fact, the only resource that was readily available to me was the phone book. Browsing the internet was not an option since it did not exist at that time. As a result, I spent countless hours at the main Memphis public library, searching the yellow pages of the Portland, Oregon phone book. Flipping through the pages, I looked at businesses until one caught my eye. Their listing made the standard claim of great service and reasonable rates, which was the usual description of every other company, but this one particular business mentioned their experience with filming projects involving Billy Graham events. It was that one single detail that put them head and shoulders above the rest. I figured if they had such experience with large events, then, filming my small event would be a breeze, and with their history of doing religious programs, I thought that they might be more sympathetic to my cause. Although I had much experience in making "cold calls" and conducting business with various vendors, I was never totally comfortable with it. Outwardly, I was relaxed, confident when engaged in the business task at hand, but inwardly, I often wished for someone else to do this. But this had to be done. Therefore, with dread and boldness, I dialed the number listed in the yellow page advertisement. The person on the other end of the line was informative and pleasant which was reassuring. That first phone conversation went so well that it led to a second one, and after sensing a comfort and satisfaction with their answers, I hired them without viewing their work or laying eyes on them. Therefore, on the day of the performance, it was of particular interest that I carefully noticed one of their cameramen as he approached me.

"Mrs. Robinson, it is so nice to finally meet you," he said while reaching out to shake my hand. He continued, "Well, your big day is finally here."

"Yes, it is. I just hope that everything works out."

"Oh, you'll do fine," he said with a reassuring tone. "Excuse me for a second, but I need to place this mike beside you."

He moved and talked at the same time. His maneuvers were quick and decisive and seemed to flow effortlessly without hesitation or much conversation, traits that were shared by the rest of his crew. Watching them work feverishly through their set up, it was clear that they were proficient at their craft.

"Did you get a chance to meet with my daughter,

Cheryle?" I asked him.

"Yes, she has already given us copies of the layout of your program. And all typed up," he said while pausing to smile and search for something." He continued, "Man, you guys are really organized which is good because it makes our job easier. Okay, we need to do some sound checks," he said while adjusting the mike.

As the film and audio crews completed their setup, the choir, which had fully assembled, was running through their warm up paces with Jonathan. It was not long before everything was in full swing. Cameras were posted in the balcony and near the choir, and another one was designated to roam around and zoom in for close ups. Initially, I was a little self-conscious whenever the camera moved in close to me, but I soon forgot about it as I became totally immersed into the sound of the choir. It was truly amazing. Some of the songs like, "Thy Will Be Done" and "The Betrayal," I had never heard sung before except in my own voice. After years of only singing them to myself, it felt different hearing a professional choir sing my music back to me. It was a new and truly wonderful experience.

Another first was watching Michelle. Standing at the podium, which was stationed just above and to the left of the choir, she waited for her cue from Jonathan, and at the appropriate time, she became the only sound in the church. In the traditional structure of an oratorio, she narrated the story of the Passion of Christ. With each gesture and breath, she took, I sat there waiting for each word. For years, I had spent writing and editing those words, sometimes staring at them until they blurred into the page itself; for years, I had read them out loud over and over again to myself until they spoke to me in my sleep; but now, I sat in awe. For the first time I was hearing the words spoken to me. Michelle was only three years old when I first started to write the oratorio, and twenty-one years later she was the first person to narrate my words to me.

It would have been easy to lose track of time if it were not for the necessary interruptions. Either the sound engineer, who had worked at NPR and came highly recommended by Jonathan, would yell out "action" or "cut," or when the choir made a little mistake. Then, there was Jonathan himself. He always seemed to know exactly how to capture the attention of the cameraman. While singing, "Hallelujah, Christ Arose," he abruptly stopped the choir because he was not satisfied with their intensity. Turning and pointing to my friend, Brenda, who was sitting in the very back of the church, he exclaimed, "You see that lady in the back? Sing to her." On the very next take, they got it right. At other times, he would request an impromptu consultation with me whenever he encountered a problem or needed to counsel a soloist. The singers were superb and more than adequately prepared as they moved from song to song with ease. Soprano soloist, Leslie Williams, sang the title song, "The Crucifixion." Her passionate and dramatic performance was outstanding. When she finished singing, there was a loud burst of clapping as we all stood to applaud her extraordinary performance. The hours seemed like minutes until Cheryle approached with a statement that immediately prompted a little of apprehension in me.

"Okay, Mom, you need to get ready. After the break, we're going to start doing interviews of you and the singers," she said.

Slightly startled by her announcement, I responded, "I thought you were going to start with the singers first."

"We are but I wanted you to start getting ready."

Michelle joined the conversation. "Yeah, we need to work on your makeup."

"Well, that's fine; and, maybe, since we have time,

Michelle, we can go over your questions."

Cheryle quickly interjected, "No, Mom. We already agreed to this. We don't want any practiced, canned answers."

"That's right. I want your natural response," Michelle added.

"But, if I knew the questions ahead of time, I could give you better answers," I countered.

Michelle piped in, trying to be reassuring, "Mom, it has to feel natural. And we all know that you don't like doing this. But don't worry. That's why I'm interviewing you; so just think of it as a conversation between the two of us."

Although I had done radio and TV interviews before, I was a bit nervous, but it was not long before I forgot about the camera and relaxed. Michelle's chatting and her interviewing me was a nice and comforting touch. I had watched her reporting news stories but during all of those times I was simply a spectator; now I was not only watching her in person, but I was also the story. Our interview seemed to end as quickly as it started, and that's when I realized the passage of time. The rays of the setting sun, shining through the stained-glass windows of the church, were more muted. Without a watch or looking at a clock, I had lost track of time. Several hours had seemingly evaporated with barely a blink of the eye, and there was still one last song left, "Go Tell The World."

As the choir members, dressed in concert attire and Jonathan in tuxedo tails returned to their places, my heart was completely filled with joy at the sight of it all. Positioning myself in the second pew in front of the choir, I sat poised to capture every remaining moment. Before making the first note, there was a hushed pause; then, with a raise of Jonathan's arms and his baton, the chorus started to sing, and the last leg of my long journey began. The sound of their voices started softly before taking flight in a rapturous chorus. Rushing past my ears, my spirit caught the music on its ascent and floated up with the a cappella melody to the vaulted ceiling. For ninety-seconds, the entire length of the song, my jubilation whirled and hung in the air with the angelic sounds until the final note of "amen." Higher than their voices and through the walls of the building, my emotions soared past the concluding hum, beyond the reach of the music, and transcended the physical bounds of that church. Twenty-one years from my first written song of the oratorio, I had waited for this moment; now I had finally completed the task of having my oratorio performed.

Long after the performance, when everything had been packed up and even after checking out of the hotel and boarding the train, I was still in a state of euphoria. On our return trip to Memphis, the memory of the concert was on the forefront of my mind as we made our way through the Northern Rockies and into the Prairie states. With all of the wide-open spaces, the empty scenery provided the perfect tranquil backdrop for my thoughts. There were no distractions to compete with the sounds and images of my mind. I replayed the music in my head while Charles, who was sitting beside me, listened to the music at various times on a portable tape player. The audio engineer had given us a preliminary cassette tape of the performance, and Charles had spent his time with headphones to his ears, immersed in his own private concert. As the click-clack sounds of the train raced beneath our feet, he seemed content in his own private world, offering very little in the way of conversation until he abruptly pulled off his headphones, looked at me and made a single statement, "You can forget trying to explain to people how you wrote these songs. I saw you write them, and I still can't understand it." I found out that his remark was prompted while listening to a certain section of "Hallelujah, Christ Arose." He had listened as I made changes in the later part of this song. I wanted this section to be more challenging and to crescendo into a dramatic finale. Now, as he listened to the finished product, he was simply amazed.

The remaining trip passed by quickly despite an eight-hour layover in Chicago. That gave us the opportunity to relive the experience as we shared it over lunch with Michelle's fiancé, John, who lived in Chicago. When the train finally rolled into Memphis, I had returned to the familiar. But it's interesting how an event can change one's perspective. After Portland, the familiar now felt different. My outlook was different. No longer would I spend my days trying to encourage myself past the bitter taste of recurring failures; the Oregon event changed all of that. I was standing in new territory. My family and I had for the first time successfully completed a large-scale project. More importantly, it was a project that we had steered past the struggles, around the repeated threats of cancellation, and into the realm of victory. My decades-long dream had finally become a reality. Just as rewarding was the tangible proof of the recording that I could show for the accomplishment; every time I played the tape and heard the choir singing my music, there was an overwhelming feeling of victory, and it felt good. With this success, my expectations had grown beyond the basic desire of hearing my music; the question now was, what to do next?

We had a box of videotapes, containing eight hours of footage from the performance and an audiotape of my music. Our previous idea of putting together a documentary was just that – an idea. The journey from an idea to finished product was an entirely different matter. I knew that it was going to be involved, but before I could struggle with the difficulties of completing my newest project, there was the more immediate problem – where to start. I, nor anyone else within my circle, had ever done a documentary. I simply did not know where to start. At first, the box of tapes sat inside my house. There was no urgent need to start; my thoughts were still celebrating the Portland concert. However, it was not long before my mindset shifted. The growing reality that I needed to move to the next step started to gnaw at me.

My first in-depth conversation regarding the documentary involved Cheryle and Michelle. The three of us sat inside our home office, which was actually our garage that Charles converted years ago during the album project. It was a large space that was connected to our home on one end by a door that lead to the laundry room, and on the opposite side it was enclosed by an overhead garage door that had been sealed shut. Over the previous 25 years, the garage had been used as everything from storage to playroom to office – everything, that is, except for a car garage. Despite its multiple uses, we had never taken the time to outfit the converted room with central air or heating. As a result, the three of us sat there in front of the TV during the winter season, discussing the documentary while wrapped in sweaters. Michelle started things rolling by inserting a tape, labeled "Portland footage," into a video tape player. The involvement of my two daughters in this new project was a logical choice. Both had connections with the television industry. Cheryle was the art director for the local PBS television station, and Michelle's degree and experience were in broadcast journalism. However, this also led to some interesting and occasional diverging point of views.

"What are you doing?" Cheryle asked, watching Michelle hit play on the video tape player.

Michelle then grabbed a pen and a writing tablet, "We need to log all of the videos."

"I thought that we should first discuss the artistic direction that we want to take with the project," Cheryle responded.

"Artistic direction? It's a documentary, okay. That's your artistic direction. Besides, we first need to know what's on the tapes," Michelle countered.

"Look, Michelle! I don't want our documentary being presented like the 5 o'clock news."

"I know what I'm doing. In fact, I believe that I'm the only one here who is a trained professional," Michelle quickly responded.

Cheryle breaks out into laughter, "Trained professional!"

"Cheryle, you don't know the first thing..."

"Wait," I interjected. Although I thought their exchange was humorous, I quickly interrupted before things got heated, "Why don't we do both? Michelle, you can focus on the logging while Cheryle and I work on an outline for the project." There was a long pause, as they both seemed to contemplate each other's position.

Finally, I added, "That way, we can make more efficient use of our time."

"Well, that could work," Cheryle slowly responded.

"Fine," Michelle consented.

Michelle's logging of every scene and every word was a huge help in organizing our thoughts, but I was still feeling lost. The actual process of constructing a documentary was overwhelming. We had all the pieces, but I was not sure how to put them together until we received some valuable advice from Norm Reynolds, a friend of Cheryle. He was a very pleasant gentleman with an easy-going demeanor and more importantly, he had a great deal of experience in producing various local television broadcasts. When I first met him, I listened intently as he talked about the "ins and outs" of the editing process, and from his words, there was no doubt that he was experienced and had enthusiasm about our project. He seemed like a natural fit to produce our documentary, but my expectations of an easy solution were quickly dashed when he said, "You all are going to have to put it together."

My mind was back at square one as to what to do. But then, it occurred to me to simply start at the beginning. In fact, this approach was so easy that it was startling that I had not thought of it sooner. Before that moment, I had always viewed the box of videotapes with apprehension, focusing my attention primarily on the enormity of the problem and the complexity of tackling something that was outside my normal sphere. But the recent revelation had changed that; now, emboldened with a renewed spirit, Cheryle and I started our newest quest of assembling a musical documentary.

Thanks to Michelle's exacting details of writing down every word said and logging the moment they were uttered and which camera recorded them, adding the interview clips was made easy. The difficult task was the creative aspect of streamlining a massive collage of images and sound into an hour-long film that conveyed our story in a seamless manner. With the first song of the oratorio, "For God So Loved The World," we started to formulate a storyline, inserting segments of interviews whenever the song was mentioned and adding video of pictures from the Bible that enhanced the music and provided variety to the timeline. Then, we moved to the next song and restarted the process. Sometimes, after putting together a section, we would smile with a sense of accomplishment, but after further review and noticing something disruptive in the background of the video, our joy would be short-lived as we erased our efforts and started all over again from scratch. It was a tedious task that made our eyes fatigued and our minds anxious as we constantly struggled to decide which clips to add, clips that were often only seconds in length. From seconds into minutes, minutes into hours and hours into days and months, we were learning and editing at the same time. It was painfully slow. However, our toil began to take form and grow as we marched through the oratorio song by song. In the end, Cheryle named our finished documentary, "A Woman and Her Music."

Completion always has a satisfying effect, but in this case, our job was only halfway done. We needed to get our documentary on television. Getting any type of film project on network TV is a formidable process with the usual vast number of film projects never seeing the light of day. As a result, our task was not going to be easy, but with the assistance of another colleague of Cheryle's at the television station, we were able to navigate our documentary through the standard PBS protocols in order to have our project submitted to the regional headquarters in South Carolina. Once our documentary was officially included in their database, it was readily available to any acquisition producer throughout the country, who was looking for content, to obtain and broadcast at their individual PBS stations.

Two years after I had first watched the choir in Portland perform my oratorio, the television in the family den was set to the local PBS station in Memphis as I waited to see the choir perform again – this time on television. The public service announcement ended, and the television screen came to life with, "A Woman and Her Music." Sitting there with my family and watching my oratorio being televised on Easter Sunday in 1995, my heart was full of joy. Though I spoke no words, thoughts raced through my head of all the failed concerts and all of the sacrifices that had been made that seemed, at times, to be in vain. For years, I aspired to have a concert with an audience of maybe a few hundred. And now, by the grace of God, the oratorio was being viewed by hundreds of thousands in home audiences across the nation on PBS stations. I thought of the old adage, "You can't beat God giving." He had given us much more than we ever dreamed. I was grateful and overcome with joy.

The Portland concert and the PBS documentary – two victories in a row, it was a reality that I could hardly believe. There was no disappointment, no defeat, only the warm glow of success. From day to day, I found myself just smiling. I was simply relishing in the triumphs of my recent victories. I knew that I would continue to put on concerts, but I had no concrete plans or a well-formed idea of my next move. As I had done before, I was trusting God for directions.

From when I first met Jonathan in 1993 to when the documentary aired in 1995, my life outside of my music was also quite full. After the Portland performance and during the editing of the documentary, I had two weddings to help plan. Michelle was the first of my children to make the trip down the aisle. Seven months later, Gaius, my youngest child, got married to his college sweetheart, Maria. Although I was well accustomed to juggling several things at once, all of this was challenging. So, once my film had aired, it felt wonderful just to mentally relax, think about my recent successes, and not have to weigh the consequences of an impending deadline. But the hiatus was short-lived; my next adventure was about to start.

I received a call from Jonathan Griffith. He had shown my documentary to certain individuals at Mid-America Productions in New York. He went further to explain to me that the production company had decided to present a Dr.

Martin Luther King, Jr., Commemorative Concert at Carnegie Hall, but here was the shock. They wanted to use my oratorio, "The Crucifixion." The news was electrifying. I know that Jonathan said more, but frankly, I do not remember anything else. When I got off the phone, I rushed to tell my husband and everyone else the astounding news. There was an explosion of joy. Even so, it was hard for me to embrace the fact that my music was going to be performed at Carnegie Hall. Several months earlier, when I sent a copy of the documentary to Jonathan so that he could see the finished product, I had no idea that anything would come out of it – and now, a world premiere of my oratorio at Carnegie Hall. It was an unimaginable feat. The first thing that I did was hiring Francisco Nunez in New York to orchestrate my oratorio. Once again, all hands were on deck as we prepared for our next project.

But life always has its unexpected twists and turns, ones that you can never plan for in advance. One day, Michelle joined Charles and me for a late lunch after she got off from work. She was working as a morning reporter and news anchor at a local TV station in Memphis. It was a very hot summer day, one of the hottest of the year. As the three of us sat in the restaurant, Michelle and I chatted away while Charles listened, but then something happened. It was subtle, but I noticed that it was definitely unusual. Charles had only eaten half of his meal; also, he was more quiet than normal, and he was sweating. But this was not your normal perspiration due to the heat; the sweat came on suddenly and was profusely pouring off of his face. Something was wrong.

"Charles, are you okay?" I asked.

He nodded yes but said nothing.

"Are you in pain?" I asked more firmly.

He calmly and faintly said, "No."

I was not reassured. With his elbows on the table, he was now holding his head in his hands. I knew that something was, indeed, wrong. There was something deep inside me that made me think of a heart attack, but I was not sure. Not believing his calm denial, I asked Michelle to go and call Todd. At that time of the day, it was a long shot that we would easily reach him. He was living in Bethesda, Maryland, and his days were split between seeing patients and doing research at the National Institutes of Health. Remarkably, we got him immediately on the phone. My fears were confirmed when he told Michelle that Charles was most likely having a heart attack. Minutes later, an ambulance arrived, and soon we were in the emergency room. Even the admitting doctor was surprised with the short time frame from the onset of the first symptoms to Charles being in the ER, and he credited our speed with saving Charles from having severe damage to his heart. Unfortunately, Charles did require heart bypass surgery. Of course, during that time, I did reflect on my conversation with my mother and the dream of being a widow. But Charles did so well, and since he successfully made it through without complications, I quickly pushed any ominous thoughts out of mind. Eventually he was discharged home to continue his cardiac rehab.

Within a few months, by the spring of 1996, he was back to his usual self, and our household was back to its normal hectic pace. Cheryle was getting married, and Michelle and I decided to throw her bridal shower on the back lawn. I had always liked our big backyard for the children to play in as they were growing up, and now the spaciousness was paying off for a different reason. We rented a large white tent, outfitting it with tables draped in billowing white linens, which were enhanced by the natural beauty of the surrounding trees and honeysuckle bushes. It was a beautiful spring afternoon. All of the guests had arrived, and the bridal shower was in full swing. My attention was fully engaged in making sure everything was being done. In the middle of this, I heard the phone ringing in the kitchen but chose to ignore it. I knew that Charles would get it. There were two things that he loved to do – one was getting the mail out of the mailbox and the other was answering the telephone. It seemed to give him great pleasure in knowing all of the comings and goings of everyone in the house. Moments later, Charles came to the patio door and yelled out, "Earnestine, telephone!"

"Charles, you see that I'm busy. Take a message."

Without hesitation, he said, "It's Jonathan from New York."

Since it was not a common event to receive a call from Jonathan, I immediately dropped everything to answer, and I was glad that I did. His voice always had a musical lift to it, but he seemed even more excited than usual. He had good news, and it seemed like he could hardly wait to tell me, and my ears could not wait to hear it.

"It's official!" he exclaimed.

He told me that the date for the world premiere of "The Crucifixion" at Carnegie Hall has been set for January 20, 1997. For the rest of the evening, I floated on cloud nine.

Chapter 18

Center Stage

Carnegie Hall, world premiere, my music, collectively, were words that I never dreamed would be used in relationship to me. But the extraordinary was happening. For the first time, my oratorio would be performed in front of a live audience – a real concert at the famed Carnegie Hall, of all places. After the failed concerts, the prospect of this seemed unimaginable. Even as the pilot of our plane made the announcement of our final approach into New York and despite my staring out the window at the massive expanse of buildings, I still found it hard to believe that the moment had arrived. A Carnegie Hall premiere of my music felt like a dream. But both the destination and my dream were real. It was as real as the throngs of people that pressed against me as I made my way through LaGuardia Airport or hearing the many varied languages of the people talking around me. I was definitely in New York.

The blaring of overhead announcements, flashing signs and scores of information monitors acted as our guide through the maze of ordered confusion at the airport. Charles and I navigated our way through the chaotic flow of people down walkways, escalators, through baggage claim and finally found our awaiting car service. Our vehicle was soon swallowed up in a sea of cars, a massive congestion of traffic where the predominant objects were darting yellow cabs as we entered Manhattan. Of course, the hustle and bustle were nothing like Memphis, which was not surprising, but I was a bit surprised by the temperature. Although it was January, which meant the expected winter climate, it was unusually cold. The forecast for that weekend had been predicted to be one of the coldest on record. It had been years since I experienced such coldness; it reminded me of Chicago. As we entered through the main doors of the New York Hilton, ice had formed on the inside of the hotel windows. It was really cold, a fact that was also confirmed by the clerk at the front desk. But we weren't bothered by it, as it seemed to add to the uniqueness of the experience. It was not long before friends and relatives, who were beaming with excitement, started to check-in and gather in the main lobby. We were in New York, and we were going to hear my music performed at Carnegie Hall.

Moving past all of the final rehearsals, the day had finally arrived, January 20, 1997; it was the day of my music's debut on one of the world's most renowned stages. Although I was living the moment, I was struggling with believing that this was really happening. Several years ago, as I prepared to go to Portland, Oregon, to record my oratorio, I heard in my sleep the words, "after this, center stage." I remember it so vividly. The words were so clear, so distinct and focused, but I wondered how "center stage" pertained to me. When I first heard those words, I asked Michelle for her thoughts. We both concluded that it referenced something of prominence but how it related to my music was still a mystery. However, it was now 1997; I was in New York, and the mystery had been solved. It was the day of the world premiere of "The Crucifixion." My music had reached "center stage" at Carnegie Hall.

That evening, just hours before the concert, a reception was being thrown for the Carleton College choir, which was one of the choirs performing my music that night. A wealthy alumnus and patron of the college hosted the event, and I had been invited as an honored guest. It was a special honor that I had only learned of the day before, but there was an added bonus – CNN would be there. In addition to interviewing me and covering the concert at Carnegie Hall, the producer wanted to capture some footage of my family and me at dinner. As a result, my invitation to the reception was the perfect video opportunity.

How CNN came to cover my Carnegie Hall premiere in the first place is a unique story. The circumstances leading to their arrival at that reception started more than three years earlier in a chain of unpredictable events that were far more convoluted and remarkable than anyone could imagine. When we were planning the Portland performance, we desired to have some type of media coverage of it. One of the news stations that I watched often was CNN; so, one day, I sat down and began making calls to the CNN studio in Atlanta. Since I did not know who to speak to, I started with their main operator and asked for information, which lead me on a trek through different departments. Each person that I talked to transferred me to a different extension. This went on for a countless number of times, but I had three things working for me: patience, time to make the calls and the determination to get a name of the appropriate contact person. Finally, my efforts paid off as one pleasant lady informed me that she was the person that I needed to speak with and after a brief description of my project, she requested that I send her additional information. It all seemed too easy. Later, I received confirmation that CNN decided to cover my Portland event. It was a stunning victory, but on the day of the performance, no one from CNN ever showed up. With the excitement of the choir and everything else happening on that day, I did not think too much about their absence. My euphoria at that time had pushed their no-show from my immediate awareness, but after returning to Memphis from Oregon, I called my contact at CNN to follow up. From the first time that I spoke with her, she had always given me the impression that she was a sincere person; therefore, my calling her was not out of disgust but simply to inform her of the outcome. Once on the phone, she quickly told me that there had been a mix up and that the crew went to a wrong location. Apologizing for the mishap, she made a gracious statement, "when you put it up again, just let me know." I did not forget her words.

Fast forward, three years later, thumbing through my address book, I pulled up her name and made the call to CNN. Even with the years, she remembered the details of our previous conversation, and after I told her about my upcoming Carnegie Hall premiere, she was thrilled and immediately requested more information. Soon thereafter, a friend of Cheryle's, who worked as a producer at CNN in New York--called her and said, "Guess whose music is sitting on my desk?" After that call, all the pieces fell into place; CNN would be at my premiere to do a story about my concert and me.

    By the time the camera crew made their way to the banquet room, the reception was in full swing. My family and I were surrounded by a crowd of people who were affiliated with Carleton College. There was clearly an air of excitement in the room. Members of the Carleton choir dressed in formal attire, bounced around the room with a giddiness and anticipation of the upcoming event. The fellowship was wonderful as different individuals approached me, introducing themselves and offering congratulations. There was a collective pulse in the room that seemed to rise by the moment as everyone talked of the imminent concert. Adding to the palpable energy of the reception was the CNN camera, which moved around the room, encircling the tables where my family and I sat, and capturing the growing excitement. As the time rapidly inched closer to the event, everyone in the room was aware of it. Commemorating the event, the president of Carleton College gave remarks that were brief but inundated with jubilation. I was a bit surprised when after introducing me, he asked me to stand, causing the entire room to rise to their feet and erupt in applause. It was my first bow of the evening, but it was not going to be my last.

    A short time later I found myself standing in front of Carnegie Hall. The temperature outside was well below freezing, but it did not seem to matter as the glow of the occasion warmed my heart. The corridor leading to our private booth was lined with photos of musical greats, a veritable roster of Carnegie Hall alum. The surrounding images swirled and danced in my head with each step as my exhilaration swelled. After finding my way to my box seat that sat just opposite the famed stage, I was immediately captivated by the grandeur of the concert hall. After a year of anticipation, my music was finally being performed at Carnegie Hall. I sat with my family and friends, eagerly awaiting to hear the 300-voice choir with orchestra perform my oratorio, "The Crucifixion." But, shortly after taking my seat, and moments before the concert, I started coughing incessantly, eventually having to go out into the hallway. I wondered if the coughing was brought on by my high level of excitement or was it a simple cold showing up at the wrong time. In any case, after drinking water and taking several deep breaths, the coughing subsided, and I returned to my seat. My sister, Doris, suggested that I put on my coat and I did not cough again for the remainder of the evening.

With my coughing bout behind me, again, I returned my attention to the stage where the singers had assembled. I marveled at the large choir, and of course, the orchestra was an added delight. Finally, an incredible, magical sound rang out like nothing I had imagined. This was the first time that I heard my music performed with an orchestra and I was ecstatic, oblivious to everything and everyone around me, with my eyes fixated on the stage, totally absorbed in the music. There were times when I held my breath as I flowed with the music. It was more beautiful than I ever dreamed it would be. And then came the finale and as the audience applauded, the conductor, standing center stage, pointed to me in the balcony. I stood, bowed and mouthed "thank you." It is a moment in time that I shall never forget. It was incredible! Surely, I was lifted to the portals of heaven.

In the hours after the concert, I continued to float on air, reliving all of it. Never in my wildest imagination did I ever dream of such an event happening to me. It was so far away from my beginning. For anyone looking at the start of my life, it would have appeared illogical, if not impossible to extrapolate the points leading to this moment. There was nothing in my past, nothing in Memphis and certainly nothing given at birth that would hint at my ultimate destination. Yet, here I was, and no explanation of chance could be given to shed light on how a person like me, with no formal musical training, could leapfrog from searching for my purpose as a homemaker to my bowing as a composer at Carnegie Hall. Again, I could barely believe it, but it was not over yet. Just as remarkable as the performance was, another event was waiting for me at home.

Back in Memphis, the overwhelming jubilation lingered with me. The concert was two days behind me. Everything felt wonderful, and this particular morning was especially poignant. I could barely contain my excitement; it was the day when my story was to air on CNN, and my television was already turned to the station from the night before in anticipation. The camera, the questions during the interview, and my responses that occurred prior to the concert were all a haze, blurred by the excitement of the premiere. Therefore, it was with great expectation and a bit of nervousness that I waited to see the story. I knew the approximate time that it was scheduled to air, but waiting for the surprise had my entire family and me energized with anticipation. Only minutes left to go, and Charles was still in the back bedroom. Then, a teaser appeared announcing the upcoming special segment, "All About Women." The clip mentioned me, a composer having my debut at Carnegie Hall and a video snippet of the family at the pre-concert reception. Among the faces prominently displayed was Charles.

I yelled out with excitement, "Charles, you better come in here. They've got a shot of you on TV!"

As Charles and I sat in awe watching the story twice that morning on CNN, again, it was surreal. But reality hit when friends from different parts of the country started calling and saying that they had seen and enjoyed my story on CNN and Headline News.

I could have easily spent weeks watching a videotape of the CNN story, basking in the glow of that experience, but I had a more immediate task before me. Carleton College, whose choir had participated in performing "The Crucifixion" at Carnegie Hall, had now decided to present my work as part of their Master Works Concert Series at the college campus in Minnesota. They invited me to come and serve as convocation speaker for the event. Only Charles and Cheryle could join me. First there was the Carnegie Hall premiere; now I was having another new experience, giving a talk at a prominent college. Taking the podium and standing alone, I was initially a bit nervous as my voice barely registered past the mike. But an official quickly came to my aid, thinking that there was a technical error and adjusted my mike. I knew what the problem actually was and projected my voice. Several minutes later as I finished my speech, there was a thunderous applause. I was both surprised and pleased that it was well received.

From all of the banquets and receptions before the concert to a grand reception after the concert at the campus home of the president, everyone's warm hospitality exceedingly compensated for the frigid temperatures outside. Being from the South, I thought that the event would be poorly attended because of the extreme cold, but the concert was packed. I found out later that some individuals had traveled great distances to be there. My heart overflowed with joy as one person after the other came to tell me that they had enjoyed my music. One man approached me and asked if I had seen the article about me in the newspaper. When I said no, he reached inside his pocket and pulled out the article that he had clipped from the newspaper. I was touched. It was moving to see the phenomenal outpouring of support, not only from the people at Carleton College but also from the surrounding area who came to the concert.

Chapter 19

A Time of Crises

It was a beautiful September morning. The sunlight seemed exceptionally bright that day, intensely blinding. I commented to myself, "There are going to be a lot of car accidents today." It was a thought that I would soon regret. I was driving west with the sun at my back, en route to meet my sisters. They had invited me to join them for a special sale at a home store. For me, it was just an outing to fellowship with my sisters; in fact, I was not even interested in buying anything. However, driving to meet them, it was hard not to enjoy everything that was around me. The air, flowing through the sunroof of my car, seemed especially crisp and invigorating that morning, and the warmth of the vibrant sun against my skin was soothing. The hue of the autumn sky was a deep blue; there was not a cloud in it. Nature was on full display and I relished its beauty. But even with the postcard perfect weather, it was just another day. There were no planned events or special engagements to attend. Nothing was scheduled that morning to explain my uplifted spirit; yet, I felt particularly euphoric. The elevation of my mood stemmed not from what was happening that day but from the promise of what was on my horizon.

Four years ago, at my Carnegie Hall premiere, an event, which proved to be very successful, the conductor, Jonathan Griffith, informed me only hours after that concert, "I heard that you are working on another oratorio. When you are finished with it, we would like to perform it." My heart immediately leapt with joy. Another Carnegie Hall concert, it was amazing, and although I had only recently started my newest oratorio, I accepted the invitation without hesitation. The fact that it took me thirteen years to write my first oratorio did not enter my head. Having an offer placed in my lap was all the incentive I needed to push myself to finish my second one. Besides, this time was different. I knew where I was headed; I knew I was writing an oratorio, and I was both focused and energized by my recent string of successes. Furthermore, an unexpected perk would also aid my latest quest. Todd, who had recently started flight surgery training with the U.S. Navy in Pensacola, Florida, was renting a beach condominium. Initially, it seemed odd that he, being single, would decide to move into a three-story residence, but after the concert when he invited Charles and I to visit with him, it was the perfect retreat. Away from the cold of winter and the routines of Memphis with all of the usual distractions, being in Florida was refreshing. Walking on the beach during the day and listening to the surf at night was the perfect getaway and muse for my writing.

Within the span of six months, I had nearly finished my newest oratorio, which I called, "The Nativity." It was not long after that when the date of my latest oratorio was tentatively scheduled for the winter of 2000 at Carnegie Hall. Of course, I was excited, but I was especially delighted when I realized that the performance would happen during the 2000th anniversary of the birth of Christ. Unfortunately, due to logistical conflicts the concert date was eventually changed and set for the Thanksgiving weekend of 2001.

Now, as I drove to the shopping center to meet my sisters, I was beaming with joy. It was the 11th of September, only a couple of months before my second Carnegie Hall premiere. Along with the surrounding sunlight filling my car, I was aglow with the thought of the approaching concert. As a result, I was feeling especially gleeful as I neared my shopping destination.

The shopping center was at an intersection that had an unusual layout. Several streets converged at one point, and adding to the traffic woes, especially on this morning was the sunlight, which would be shining directly into the eyes of the driver going east. I was very familiar with this intersection and its potential treacherousness from years of driving through it. As I approached the entrance of the parking lot, I carefully looked down the street, noting that there was no oncoming traffic and the nearby traffic signal was red. As I made my left turn, the left side of my face caught the brunt of the intense sunlight while my right view was clear from any threat. My front wheels rolled safely onto the driveway; then, there was a sudden and deafening crashing noise, followed by a puff of smoke and a flash of swirling images before coming to a halt. I thought, "Oh, no, I've been hit." My mind immediately raced to the possibility of an explosion. Quickly, I unlocked my seatbelt, opened the door and got out. Despite my automatic reflex to move myself away from the danger, I was still a bit dazed, but slowly, the fragmented pieces of thoughts began to unscramble and reshape back into a coherent meaning. My face felt strange and its discomfort was becoming more apparent. Glancing back at my car, its rear end was mangled. It was unbelievable that all of this seemed to occur within a split second.

After I had fully collected my thoughts, I started making calls. I first reached Charles and informed him that I had been in a car accident, but I was fine. Shortly thereafter, Todd, who had gotten the news from Charles, called me and said that he was on his way over to check me out. Michelle, who was getting ready to go to work at the news station, headed over to the site of the accident after speaking with me.

The deflated airbag had done its job in preventing me from hitting my head on the steering wheel, but its deployment had caused something else. I could not see the damage to my face since there was no mirror around, but touching the area around my left eye caused an immediate burning sensation. My vision was fine, but each time I changed the direction of my gaze there was increased soreness of my left eye. Looking at my car, I was still in disbelief and amazed at the damage. Mentally, I kept replaying the timeline of the accident in my head until I finally got Cheryle on the phone. As I began to tell her about the accident, she expressed concern if I were okay; I reassured her that I was fine. Then, she blurted out about a plane flying into the World Trade Center in New York. The news seemed so odd and bizarre that we were both having a difficult time understanding it. And just when we were about to conclude that it was probably an accident, she immediately blurted out again, in shock, "I don't believe it! Another plane just flew into the other tower!" Then, within the flash of a moment, our confusion turned into another emotion, one that was more chilling than the first. We both said it out loud, "Terrorists!"

Minutes later, Michelle drove up on the parking lot. Her face was a mixture of bewilderment and anguish.

"Mom! I saw your car when I drove up," she said while walking toward me, but as she got closer, she exclaimed, "Oh, my goodness! Your face!"

"I know, it's the only thing that is really hurting me. I'm just…"

She interrupted, "Should you be standing?"

"I'm okay."

"Mom, this was a really bad accident. Your car looks horrible. How did it happen? Your face?"

Her questions and comments were coming faster than my explanations, but she eventually calmed down as I recounted the story and shared the news of the planes hitting the World Trade Center.

"Wow, this morning has been crazy. First, I passed by a crime scene where someone discovered a dead body at a bus stop and now all of this news about New York. I can't believe it. You know, that's no accident. I mean, two planes just happened to fly into two skyscrapers in broad daylight. You know, that's got to be terrorists," she said.

"I know. Cheryle and I were saying the same thing."

At that moment, Todd drove up. I could see him glancing at the car as he made his way over to us. Staring at me in his approach, I could see him methodically scanning me.

"Mom, your face," he said while touching me lightly on the shoulder and examining me. "You were in a really bad accident. Maybe you should be sitting down somewhere. Where are you hurting?"

"Like I told Michelle. I feel fine. It's just starting to feel sore."

"Yeah, you also got some mild cuts and bruising on your face, probably from the airbag. And your left eye…it looks minor, but with all of this and looking at your car, you probably need to go to the emergency room."

"No, I'm okay."

"Well, how's your neck?"

"Fine."

"Any numbness or tingling in your hands or feet?"

"No."

"What about your vision?"

"It's fine."

"Do you have a headache?"

"No."

"Mom, are you sure?"

"Todd, I'm okay."

He took in a deep breath and looked at me. Then, he rubbed his fingers against the back of my neck and head, "Well, I guess, a brief neurological exam is out of the question."

"Todd, I've been in accidents before, and I'm telling you, I'm fine. Just this burning sensation on my face."

"Well, at least, let me give you some ibuprofen before you start to really stiffen up."

After I had finally convinced Todd that I was all right, the conversation turned back to the subject of the planes hitting the World Trade Center. It seemingly took a long stretch of time before the police and wreckers arrived. I just wanted to get home to lie down and relax, but that would not happen. Once home, I, along with the rest of the country was shocked by the images of smoke bellowing from the Towers. Sitting there, while Todd tended to the cuts on my face, I forgot about my pain and stared at the television screen in disbelief. Each time they replayed the video of the planes flying purposely into the twin skyscrapers, a terrible feeling grew inside me. It was so shocking, so far from anything I had ever witnessed or could even imagine that it seemed unreal. But the nightmare was real and then, we watched the horror. Right before my very eyes, the south tower filled with people, standing tall against the New York sky, collapsed straight down into something that I never again want to see. The building holding all of those lives disintegrated into a terrible roar and a cloud of smoke and ash. The downward wave of death hit the ground level, turned into a tsunami of thick soot and flooded all of the nearby Manhattan streets. We all stared at it in shocking disbelief. Then, we watched as it happened again – this time with the north tower. It was worse than a nightmare. The only sound that could be heard in my den as we watched the unfolding catastrophe was a collective gasp, followed by silence. I will never forget that day or where I was when it happened. It is ironic that my accident happened about the same time as the planes hit the World Trade Center towers.

With each passing hour the story expanded, and the numbness and shock of what I first felt increased as I learned of more facts: two more plane crashes – one at the Pentagon and the other in an open field in Pennsylvania. Starting with that day, everyone's attention in my home was glued to the television, which essentially remained on news stations. It was all that we and everyone else talked about. One day while watching CNN coverage of the area in and around "Ground Zero," Todd jumped up and exclaimed, "I don't believe it!"

"What?" I asked.

"That's the Millennium Hotel. I booked our reservations there. That's where we were supposed to stay during our concert."

My eyes darted from him back to the television screen. The images showed the interior of the hotel and its lobby blackened with smoke and some of its windows had been blown out. The scene captured through the lens of the camera looked eerie; it was hard to believe that the "bombed" location was in the middle of Manhattan. Looking at the devastation, I could not help but feel a connection with the tragedy. My concert was two months away, and naturally, when the conductor, Jonathan called me, we talked about the tragedy. He had long since moved from Oregon to New York City and was a conductor-in-residence at Carnegie Hall. Although he described the general mood of the city as anything but upbeat, he was still excited about our concert and tried to give a positive spin by saying that New Yorkers needed something positive like our concert. He was also delighted that the orchestra and the chorus, which consisted of choirs from around the country, as far away as California, were still committed to the Thanksgiving weekend event. There had not been a single cancellation.

During our conversation, we also discussed the orchestration of the music. We had hired someone recommended by Jonathan to accomplish this endeavor. Although the cost of it was a considerable sum for us, we were able to raise the money. However, at one point during the payment process, the orchestrator offered me a proposition of waiving his fee in exchange for giving him the copyright for two of my songs. Of course, I did not agree to this. But one of the choirs alerted me to some confusion about the sheet music sent to them. It seems that their copies had been printed with someone else sharing the copyright. Stunned by the revelation, I was quick to let Jonathan know that all the songs in "The Nativity" oratorio were previously copyrighted the year before and on file in the Library of Congress with me as the sole composer. He assured me that the mix up had been cleared up, and everything continued to run smoothly.

We worked toward our concert date even though our daily conversations were consumed with the news surrounding the 9/11 attacks. This time, my youngest son, Gaius, joined us in helping with preparations. He was involved with putting together press kits that had to be mailed to all of the top media outlets. We were especially interested in the major network affiliates: NBC, ABC and CBS in New York. But once again, the unimaginable happened.

Walking through the den, I glanced at the television. Charles was watching a breaking news report about a letter containing anthrax that was mailed to the NBC studio in New York. Initially, I did not fully understand what anthrax was, but it was not long before the airwaves exploded with information about it. Stories began to stream in of other letters containing anthrax and about people in Florida being exposed. It seemed like every day brought more deadly news and rumors of anthrax. Then, days later, it got worse. Another wave of letters containing a mysterious white powder found its way into the hands of more unsuspecting people. It was anthrax and this time the letters were sent to two Democratic U.S. senators. Although those intended targets were not harmed, anyone who had touched the tainted letters in its travels potentially ran the risk of exposure and death. Five people were already dead as the result of inhaling anthrax, two of them postal workers.

News of this particular type of threat had a chilling effect. The idea that something so deadly could appear in your mailbox in a harmless, innocent-looking letter was a scary scenario that really gripped the public. It definitely put people on edge, especially in the media industry, a point we soon discovered.

I remember when Gaius and I were calling some of the newspapers and television stations for a contact person; everyone we talked to seemed suspicious of us. Information that was common and readily released to anyone who asked for it just weeks earlier was now either not given or only provided after giving a convincingly detailed explanation of why we wanted the information in the first place. For years, I had done this sort of thing without any difficulty, but this was a whole new world.

Despite the changes, we were determined to continue our marketing task on schedule, and one morning Gaius left for the post office with a mailbag containing letters to the media in the New York area. However, he returned sooner than expected, carrying the same bag still stuffed with letters.

Upon seeing him walk through the door, I asked, "I thought you were going to the post office?"

"I did, but I couldn't mail the letters."

"Why not?"

"The man at the post office was tripping," he said while collapsing on the sofa and dropping the bag on the floor.

"What man?" I asked.

"The postal worker."

"What?" I said, completely puzzled.

He continued, "There was nobody else in there except me, and as soon as I walked into the place, the postal worker behind the counter started looking at me funny."

"Why was he doing that?" I inquired.

"Oh, wait; it gets even crazier. The man started staring at my mailbag and asked me, 'What's that and what are you mailing?' I couldn't believe it. So, I said, 'Man, this is a post office, right?' But he just kept on looking at me suspiciously. Anyway, I decided to shrug it off and do what I needed to do to get out of there. So, I told him that I wanted to mail some letters to New York. No sooner than the words, New York, came out of my mouth, that he looked like he was about to jump out of his skin."

"You're kidding!"

"No. You should have seen him. He started looking around like something was about to happen. I realized then that he was scared; so, I had to immediately start explaining that my mother was a composer and about your music being performed at Carnegie Hall. I even showed him a letter and told him that I was mailing out press releases. Man, I had to do some fast talking because the way he was looking, I didn't know what he was going to do."

"Oh, my goodness."

"I know it's crazy. Anyway, after he finally calmed down, he told me, 'Man, when you said New York, I didn't know what was going down.' After he said that, I just looked at him; I couldn't believe it."

"All of that just from walking into a post office?" I asked.

"Yup. You should have seen him. Anyway, I thought everything was cool. So, I started opening my mailbag, and I asked him how long it would take for it to get there. And you won't believe what he told me. First, he said that he didn't know. Then, he said that I was wasting my time mailing them."

"What?"

"Can you believe it? He said that nobody is going to deliver any mail going to New York. Then, he started talking about how he was a supervisor and how he normally didn't work the counter but had to fill in since so many of his mail clerks were calling in sick because they were scared of anthrax."

"Is it that bad?" I asked.

"It must be. And when I tried to push the issue, he told me, 'Man, don't you know what's going on? People are dying. All of that anthrax stuff is happening up there, and you are trying to mail something to New York. Nobody is going to want to touch your mail.' I just looked at him. And I could tell by the expression on his face that he was dead serious. So, I picked up my bag and walked out. I guess we won't be mailing any press releases."

"Unbelievable," I responded.

From watching the news, I was well aware of how the 9/11 attacks were having a rippling effect on the nation as well as the world, but the added threat of the anthrax letters was causing a worsening anxiety that now seemed to be attached to every small corner of America. Gaius' incident at the post office was my first direct encounter of how the terrorist attacks had impacted life close to home, but there would be others. The entire nation was guarded; suspicions were constantly fueled by an endless supply of daily information that spewed out of their television sets, and like the rest of the country we kept close watch on news reports. It was commonplace that our television was set to the national news channels, but at 5 o'clock, we routinely turned our television to the local news, instead, to watch Michelle. She was an evening anchor for one of the local news stations. One day at the height of the anthrax scare, Michelle called home to let us know about a live breaking story. There was an incident of something unusual at the main post office.

At the opening of the news program, Michelle's face appeared on the screen. Her words, matching her facial expression, were delivered in an urgent tone that was both sharp and direct. "Good evening, this is Michelle Robinson. We have a breaking news story that is developing at the main post office on Third Street. From our reports, that post office has been closed off as a HAZMAT team is investigating a suspicious substance. For an update, we go live to the scene."

The reporter, who seemed strangely excited, recounted the details of the story. With a rapid pace, he rambled on as he recited a list of eyewitnesses, involved officials and possible theories. However, the one thing he said that did stand out during his report was that anthrax had been ruled out. I was glad to hear that it was not anthrax, but watching the scene with scores of emergency officials moving about in the background did not allay my concerns. The flashing blue and red lights on the tops of the crowded vehicles gave a sense of high alert. The threat of anthrax had been eliminated, but the HAZMAT crew dressed in protective suits with helmets and oxygen tanks was still investigating. Something still seemed to be amiss. As Charles and I sat watching and wondering what was going on, Todd walked in the front door. He had just gotten off from work from one of the local emergency rooms.

"What's going on?" he asked, seeing our intense focus at the television.

"Something is happening at the main post office," Charles said.

"Oh yeah, I heard about it. A bunch of those guys who worked there came into the ER today, and it was something else."

"Really? From the post office?" I asked.

"Uh, huh. They were worried about having anthrax," Todd responded.

"On the news, they said it wasn't anthrax," Charles

remarked.

"It wasn't," Todd replied. "In fact, we haven't seen any anthrax, but that hasn't stopped people from coming in everyday, claiming that they've been exposed to it. And today was the worst. It started this morning with this one postal worker who was brought in by ambulance. When the paramedics rolled through the door, she was sobbing and crying and claiming that she couldn't breathe. She told everybody in the ER that she had been exposed to anthrax. Then, others started coming in. It was crazy."

"What was wrong with them?" Charles asked.

"Just scared, and you couldn't convince them that they didn't have anthrax. I've never seen anything like it. Talking about fear. I've had patients come in and tell me that they were afraid to even open their mailboxes."

As Todd continued to talk, we watched Michelle as she went off the air. While still engrossed in our discussion about anthrax, Michelle showed up later at the house on her dinner break and joined the conversation.

Charles was the first one to ask her about the post office event, "Did they find out what was causing the problem?"

"Oh, yeah. They found out," she started to chuckle. "Investigators have not released the official report yet, but it seems that somebody mailed some food from outside the country which had gone bad, resulting in an odor that caused everybody to freak out."

"Spoiled food! You got to be kidding?" Charles commented.

"No, that's what they said off the record."

"I told you, nothing but fear," Todd added.

Days were moving by swiftly. Time was running out and we had not contacted one media source. I was beginning to worry about our limited efforts in generating publicity about our concert. It did not ease my concerns when I heard on the news that a number of theater productions had been cancelled due to low turnout. The seemingly nonstop string of calamities was having an adverse effect on travel and tourism across the country. This was so prevalent that the mayor of New York City made a public plea to encourage people to visit New York. Ironically, I was not worried about our concert being cancelled; none of the choirs had backed out. Everything was on schedule, but I was worried about people not showing up for the concert. Since we could not afford paid advertisements, we were relying on increasing public awareness of our event through the local media. But this was New York, one of the top media markets in the world which also meant that it was one of the most difficult to crack – a task that was compounded by all of the city's recent troubles. Yet, the potential for media exposure was great. However, there was another problem; we were sitting in Memphis with a stack of concert notifications...collecting dust.

With our inability to mail traditional press releases in the usual manner, our advertising efforts had been severely hampered, but we could not just simply give up. As a result, Charles came up with an alternate plan of picking a couple of days to call every possible news and media outlet. We decided that a couple of weeks before the concert would be the perfect time slot to announce our event. It was early enough to allow any interested media, looking for a last-minute story, adequate time to gather their resources to cover the event but, hopefully, not too late when all available slots would have already been booked. The time that we chose was November 12, 2001, a calendar date which was approximately two weeks before our concert. It was also the same date that American Airline 587 would take off from JFK Airport en route to Santo Domingo in the Dominican Republic.

Gaius, who came over early to help me with the calls, joined Charles and me for breakfast before starting our telephone marathon the morning of November 12th. The television in the den, adjacent to our kitchen, was on a news channel, and its volume was easily within earshot of us at the dining table. Naturally, our conversation focused on the upcoming concert and of course, the events surrounding the 9/11 tragedy, but with the anticipation of our task for the day, our mood was light and upbeat. Then, we heard from the den the words that brought our chatter to an abrupt halt: BREAKING NEWS FROM NEW YORK. Jumping up from the table, I came face to face once again with ominous images on the television screen. The scene was chaotic, and among the confusion there was a plume of smoke rising up from a neighborhood and the words from a reporter gave brief details of the story. An American Airlines flight had taken off, but its journey ended moments later when it crashed in a nearby neighborhood in Queens. We sat there and watched in disbelief – another tragedy in New York. My heart ached as I learned more about the story and how the plane had crashed in the area populated by families of firefighters – some of whom had perished in the collapse of the World Trade Center.

After a period of time of being mesmerized by the news, Gaius and I slowly returned our attention to our previously planned objective. We had to make our media calls to New York, but that task was to be short-lived. After our first call was greeted with a busy signal, we moved to the next one on the list. But the second, third and fourth calls were also busy. I quickly realized what was going on, but Gaius was determined. Finally, he did reach someone at a TV station and before he could fully deliver his pitch, he was interrupted and told that every news agency in New York was busy with the plane crash and that his efforts would probably be a waste of time. Although she did offer a suggestion of faxing some information, we had reached a dead end. New York had seemingly been turned upside down, and on that day, it was closed to outside business. We hung the phone up, pushed aside our scripted notes and returned to the den to watch the news.

My sister, Doris, stopped by later to chat as she normally did, and of course, the conversation was about New York.

"What is going on in New York?" she loudly announced, stepping inside and moving past Gaius. It was her usual style of entrance in captivating everyone's attention in the room.

She continued as she walked into the den, "I can't believe it. Every time I turn on the TV, it seems like something terrible is happening there. Girl, I really feel sorry for them."

"I know," I commented.

"Those New Yorkers are really going through," she said while staring at the television and sitting down on the sofa. "So, are y'all still going to New York?" she asked.

"Yeah," I responded.

"You mean, the concert is still on?" she surprisingly asked.

"No one has backed out. Everything is still on."

"Really? Huh, I got to give it to you. Y'all don't quit," she said.

I could only smile. It was truly amazing that none of the choirs had cancelled and that everything was moving according to schedule. I could not help thinking of all the things that had happened over the past two months. We were just days away from leaving for New York and all the planning was done. The only thing that we had not been successful with was securing media coverage of the concert. It was a shortcoming that concerned me, but it was too late to do anything about it. There was only enough time to tie up loose ends and prepare to leave.

A couple of days later, I was at the grocery store doing some last-minute shopping. It was raining in a downpour, and to make matters worse someone inside the store had taken my umbrella out of my shopping cart. So, by the time I got back to my car, I was soaking wet and a little miffed. My cell phone rang; it was Cheryle.

Barely saying hello, she immediately blurted out, "Mom, you're going to be on NPR!"

The news was so shocking that I completely forgot about the damp chill on my skin and was eager to hear the details. Sitting in a parked car, I listened intently to her story. A couple of weeks earlier Cheryle had lunch with a friend who was visiting in Chicago on business for National Public Radio. Cheryle had only recently moved to Chicago with her husband, and prior to the relocation, she lived in Washington D.C, working as the Vice-president of Communications for NPR. She still had close ties with the news organization. It was during this luncheon that her friend mentioned that she was on her way to New York, and when Cheryle told her of my upcoming concert at Carnegie Hall, she wanted to know more. It was not until that day that she unexpectedly called Cheryle to deliver the wonderful news. NPR was going to be at my concert and I was going to be the featured story Christmas morning on "Morning Edition."

Everything was set, and on the Friday after Thanksgiving we arrived in New York. After checking in at the hotel, attending the rehearsals was my first order of business, but I also had to mentally prepare for the NPR interview. In the same hotel where the rehearsals were taking place, I took the elevator upstairs to a room where the reporter was staying. Cheryle and Todd accompanied me, and like me they were excited. It was not long before the three of us walked into a nicely appointed room and was greeted by an NPR correspondent. Her name was Cheryl Corley, a young woman who, in addition to her pleasant demeanor, had a calm and soothing voice. She exchanged pleasantries for a while but promptly turned to business as Cheryle and Todd left. Sitting at a table in her hotel room, the setting was casual until she turned on a recorder. I have had many interviews before, but this was the most thorough one to date. She took her time and questioned me for nearly two hours; at one point, she had me relaxed enough that I sang one of my songs. It was the first time since the "Sounds of a Miracle" album that I was recorded singing my music. After it was over, I went back to the rehearsal. It would be a month later before I would hear the results of the interview.

On the morning of the concert, there was one more thing left to do. It was the one place that had nothing to do with the concert, but the one place that everyone wanted to visit – Ground Zero. I did not know what to expect, but I had to see it. For the past two months our daily lives had become linked to the television and all the events that were related to this one spot. When we got there, the entire area surrounding Ground Zero was barricaded off from the general public. Yet, there were scores of people crowded alongside a chain-link fence, trying to capture a glimpse of the epicenter of the horrific tragedy. To say that the mood was solemn would be an understatement. But standing there and watching traces of smoke still rising up from the mound of rubble was an eerie reminder of what had taken place more than two months ago.

In the cab ride back to the hotel, all we could talk about were the images of the destruction, but by the time we reached our room, my spirit picked up. It was only hours away from my second Carnegie Hall premiere, and like the first concert, I was filled with anticipation. But as I looked out the window, it had started to rain. It continued to rain all afternoon. But I didn't have time to dwell on the weather. I had to get dressed for the evening and prepare to do one more interview before the concert. Soon, I headed to the hotel lobby to meet with Michelle for an interview. Her TV station had flown a cameraman to New York, so she could do a story on me for her special segment, "Phenomenal Woman." Michelle said that her news director wanted to share the success of a Memphian with local viewers. It was gratifying to not only have my daughter interview me but knowing that she also would grace the stage that evening at Carnegie Hall as the narrator of my oratorio, "The Nativity."

Later, standing in front of the hotel and waiting for the car service, it was still raining. I tried not to dwell on it, but the weather looked dismal. With the moisture and chill, it was difficult to look out the foggy back windows of the car. Our transit to Carnegie Hall would have normally been a short trip, but the combination of the wet streets and slowed traffic stretched out the time and added to my anxiety as to whether anyone would show up.

As the driver pulled up to the famed hall, I saw a long line of people standing in the rain on the sidewalk, waiting to get into my concert. I looked over at Charles and said, "Wow, can you believe this?" Then, with my eyes closed and my hands over my mouth, I whispered, Thank you, Lord." My greatest fear had been dispelled. The people were there. In fact, the crowd was larger than it was at my first Carnegie Hall premiere. The noise of the people moving into their seats was a welcomed sound, a sound that was soon replaced with a hush as the house lights dimmed. Soon, only the music of the choir and orchestra filled the hall, and I was filled with exhilarating joy as I listened to the dynamic performance of my oratorio. The audience was totally captivated by "The Holy Child," sung by the children's choir.

It was fascinating to watch Jonathan conduct, as he, too, seemed to be caught up with this song. It was a grand performance! This time, at the end of the performance, I was invited to the stage amidst a thunderous applause. Bowing to a standing ovation, it was a wonderful feeling to see how the people had enjoyed my music. After the concert, I stood in an area just off stage as members of the choir came to me to have their choir books autographed. Following this unexpected flurry of adoration, I was whisked out the back door of Carnegie Hall to my waiting family and friends for a post-concert celebration at the hotel.

For weeks after the concert, I eagerly waited to hear my story on National Public Radio. I had been told that the story would air three times on Christmas morning, beginning at 7:30. All during the night before, I tossed and turned until I woke up very early Christmas morning; it was still dark outside. Our house was completely quiet; the silence was comforting. Although I was a bit nervous, my heart was filled with joy. Not since I was a child had I experienced such excitement on Christmas morning. It would be more than an hour before my story would be broadcast, and I lay in bed reminiscing about my recent concert and my NPR interview. I tried to remember some of the questions that Cheryl Corley had asked and the answers I had given. Finally, with one last look, I glanced at the time and got out of bed. The hour of my moment of anticipation had arrived. I went over to the radio and with a click, the radio dial that was already set for the NPR station, illuminated. And before long, it blurted its salutation that I was waiting to hear, "This is Morning Edition with Bob Edwards." His distinctly baritone voice resonated and filled the stillness of the room. "At this time of the year, the sounds of Handel's 'Messiah' and Bach's 'Christmas

Oratorio' fill many concert halls," he continued. "A new oratorio is being added to the repertoire. "The Nativity," by black American composer Earnestine Rodgers Robinson, has had its premiere at Carnegie Hall...."

As Charles and I listened intently to the interview and the music, I marveled that the composer being interviewed was really me. It seemed surreal to hear myself talking about my music on National Public Radio; in fact, I could have easily ascribed the entire interview as an incredible dream, but the phone rang, reminding me that I was indeed living the moment. It was Michelle.

"Mom, I just heard you singing on NPR. Why didn't you tell me?

"Michelle, I didn't tell you because I didn't think that Cheryl Corley was going to use it in the story."

"But it was interesting how she had the baritone soloist come in after you and sing the same part," Michelle remarked.

"Yes, I thought that was uniquely interesting too. But, still, I would not have sung if I had known that she was going to use it in the story."

We both chuckled. Smiling and sensing the accomplishment of this moment, I was overwhelmed with joy.

Chapter 20

Triumph in Prague

After another success in New York, I set my sights on a new dream. I wanted to have my music performed in Europe. There was no single event that I could point to which sparked this idea, but something inside me was definitely propelling me toward this new goal. However, I did not have any viable contacts in Europe nor did I have any idea of how to proceed toward this dream. But the lack of details did not bother me. I was trusting God for the unbelievable, yet again.

It was a Wednesday morning, and everything was going well; just like the typical day in my house, it was busy. I was in my bedroom while Todd and Gaius were in the home office working on the computer. Charles was at his computer in the den, and although the television set was blasting the news, he was mostly ignoring it this morning. It was tax season, and as an accountant this was his busiest time of the year.

Everything was in order until it happened. CRASH! It was not the ordinary crash of something falling; instead, it was the bone-chilling thud of something much heavier hitting the floor. The sound ripped through the entire house. As I immediately took off for the den, my heart ached with a stabbing jolt; my initial startled reaction had been quickly replaced with a more dreadful emotion. And before I could reach the den, I already knew what had happened. It was Charles; he had fallen. Todd and Gaius, who were there mere seconds before me, were trying to assist him. Sprawled out on the floor, Charles attempted to protect his right leg, and although he was not yelling in agony, his facial expression told me of his excruciating pain. No one spoke it out loud, but everyone in the den knew that it was serious.

Later in the emergency room, our concerns were eventually confirmed when he was diagnosed with a fractured hip. It had been years since the first surgery on his opposite hip, and although he was told at that time that his chances of learning how to walk were dismal due to his balance problem, he stunned all the doctors with his amazing recovery. Just as incredible was the fact that Charles never allowed his neurological condition to hinder him. In fact, he never made any reference to his disability since he was first diagnosed. It had not been an issue – until now.

The next morning Charles was prepped for surgery.

Several hours later, he was wheeled back into his hospital room where we had been waiting. The nurse attending him from the operating room stated that everything had gone well and that he was still drowsy from the anesthesia. As soon as they had finished moving him into the bed and cleared the room, I touched Charles on his shoulder to do my assessment.

"Charles?" I softly whispered. He gave me no response. I tried again, this time more forcefully. "Charles?"

He partially opened his eyes to my voice but quickly went back to sleep. This was unusual for him, and I was a bit concerned. I tried shaking him gently, but he only mumbled something, not opening his eyes. The nurse came back into the room and saw me.

"It's going to take a while for the anesthesia to wear off," she said, trying to reassure me.

But after she left, I stared at Charles. I was well aware that this was not normal for him. After the previous surgeries, he had never responded like this. Though it nagged me, I accepted the nurse's explanation that everything was normal. However, as soon as he started his recovery, the change was apparent to everyone. Charles was more agitated than usual and less focused which extended and complicated his hospital stay, but finally, he was discharged home weeks later to start his physical therapy.

I was glad he was home because I thought that getting him back into familiar surroundings would be the answer to his returning to his usual self. The first thing that he did when he got home was to call one of his clients and tell him that his work was completed and could be picked up. I thought that this was a very good sign. Being surrounded by the sounds of familiar voices and the usual traffic of everyone flowing in and out of our home was the perfect antidote to hasten his recovery; and although he continued to improve, there was one thing that he had not recovered – his usual tenacity. He did not seem to be as motivated in doing his exercises, and neither the therapist nor I was successful in pushing him beyond the basics. It saddened me that he was not as aggressive in his rehabilitation as he had done in the past. But I was determined not to give up on his rehab; it was just going to take more time.

This new challenge had become such a priority to me that my music had been mostly pushed into the background, but that was about to change. One day while watching the therapist work with Charles, I received a call from Paul Freeman, who was the conductor for the Chicago Sinfonietta. Even though his call caught me by surprise, I knew who he was. Cheryle had a meeting with him a month earlier and had mentioned his name to me. At the time of their exchange, Cheryle was a vice-president at Amtrak, and Paul Freeman was trying to interest her in joining the Sinfonietta's board of directors. However, after she mentioned that her mother was a composer and that my music had recently premiered at Carnegie Hall, he immediately became interested in hearing more about my music. Eventually, he requested a score of my oratorio, "The Nativity," and even though I knew that he had received the materials, I was not expecting anything in particular. As a result, when he called me, I was caught off guard. My surprise was probably all the more magnified by his timing with the physical therapist being there. But the sound of his voice on the phone quickly shifted my attention.

"Earnestine, where did you study music?" he asked straightaway after a brief introduction. He sounded polite, but his tone showed that he was eager and very curious.

"I have no formal training in music," I responded.

"What instrument do you play?"

"I don't play a musical instrument."

Sounding a bit perplexed, he asked, "Well, how did you learn to write music like this?"

"It's a gift, a gift from God."

He paused. The few silent moments were so poignant that I could almost hear him thinking, processing my answers.

Finally, he spoke, "Well, you are definitely talented, and your music is beautiful."

He talked further about my music and asked more questions. The discussion was not an attempt by him to interrogate or intimidate me. He was simply curious and trying to understand my development as a composer. Then, he surprised me with an interesting proposal.

"As you may know, I'm also the conductor of the Czech National Symphony Orchestra, and every year we have a Christmas concert in Prague. And this year, I would love to present your oratorio, "The Nativity."

His words hung in the air, and my verbal gasp showed my obvious enthusiasm. I could not believe it – a European premiere of my music. My heart began to rejoice as he started to fill in the details. But my celebration came to an abrupt halt when I heard the price tag. The cost of the symphony's services would cost me $25,000, and that was the minimum. The figure rolled through my mind causing my words to go blank. The amount was staggering. We were just six months out from the Carnegie Hall concert, a venture that was costly in itself and had drained our resources. And to think, the $25,000 was a figure that did not include any of the other related costs such as travel or accommodations. The obvious revelation that we could not afford it quickly doused all of my earlier jubilation.

Finally, I broke my silence. "Oh, my goodness," I uttered out loud. Although I do not exactly remember what I said after that, my tone was a mixture of both gratitude and regret. While expressing thanks for offering such a spectacular opportunity, I also had to do the unthinkable; I had to say no. It was not easy, considering that having a European premiere was a dream of mine, but I explained to him the financial difficulty due to my recent concert and declined his offer. After hanging up the phone, my heart started to sink with regret until I heard something. It was a voice within me saying, "You are cutting off your blessing." No sooner than the words had registered within my mind, I picked up the phone again and called Cheryle. This time, my tone and decision were different. With an unshakeable assurance, I told her to contact Paul Freeman and accept his invitation. Of course, I had no solution to the problem at that time, but I decided to embrace faith and believe that God would bring about success.

Even after signing the contract, I still had no idea of how I was going to raise the money needed for this large-scale project. The amount was not the only concern; there was also the deadline. We only had three months to raise the entire sum, and the clock had already begun to wind down. The pressure was definitely on from day one, and I did not know where to start. But the task was set before us and there was no turning back. The only thing that I knew to do was what I had done before – I prayed for direction.

Up to this point, we had financed all of our projects with our own money. However, with such a short deadline staring us in the face, we did not have enough time to fund the venture entirely on our own. I had to look for assistance from within the Memphis community, but obtaining support from my hometown had been limited in the past. Fortunately, that was about to change. After having lunch with a longtime acquaintance, who was a prominent public figure in Memphis and also hailed from my old neighborhood of Douglass, ideas started to flow about funding possibilities in Memphis, and we generated a list of possible donors to contact. The meeting definitely started the momentum, and I was eager to begin my fundraising quest. The task was made much easier because of my daughter, Michelle, teaming up with me, which was ideal for a number of reasons. First, she was a familiar face in Memphis due to her years as a local reporter and news anchor, but the main reason was that she had a knack of coming alive when meeting people. As a result, her involvement in the project was an added advantage.

However, our time disadvantage was growing by the moment. We were just starting, and it was already summer. By autumn we had to raise the entire sum, and there was no time to lose. Every day that we scheduled a meeting, pitched our proposal and did not receive a positive response was a day lost and a day closer to our deadline. As we moved through our list of possible benefactors, the days turned to weeks. Everyone that we spoke with was pleasant and seemed interested in our concert, but no one was willing to commit money.

One suggestion that was given to us was the Memphis Arts Council. It was an obvious choice and the most logical option, but ironically, I did not approach them first. I knew that the organization was responsible for awarding grants to arts projects similar to mine, but I did not initially consider them as a resource for me. My hesitation was undoubtedly related to my past experiences. Locally, I had not been successful with the "establishment," and I could not help remembering my brush with the Memphis Symphony Orchestra and the way that rejection had occurred. As a result, I assumed that there was no way that the Memphis Arts Council would consider a grant for me. It was a mental block; so, when the idea of approaching them was first mentioned to me, I tried to rebuff the suggestion.

But despite my reservations, I knew that I had to at least try, and surprisingly, we were well received by the new president of the Arts Council.

After that preliminary meeting, Michelle and I sat in an upscale restaurant in an affluent section of Memphis, surrounded by several board members of the Memphis Arts Council. The atmosphere of that meeting was pleasant, very pleasant. For the first several minutes, they engaged us in lighthearted conversation that was enjoyable, but eventually, the talk and laughter turned into business as the questions began to focus on my music. However, unlike my encounter with the symphony, this group actually listened to everything that I had to say and seemed to be genuinely interested in my project. The lengthy meeting ended as well as it started, and as Michelle and I left, we both felt good about it. That was the last of our scheduled meetings. There were no more names on our list; we had explored all of our possibilities. Now, we had to wait – the hard part.

Our deadline was rapidly approaching, and the waiting felt drawn out. Usually, under regular circumstances, the suspense of waiting would have been a good reason for causing a rise in anxiety, but I felt a calmness. There was a peaceful feeling that God was going to work it out. All I had to do was stand still and believe. Therefore, in the midst of our waiting, it was a welcomed idea when Todd, who was working on the West Coast, suggested a timely break. He was flying back to Memphis to take Charles and me for a vacation on the East Coast. However, with the trip occurring only a few months after Charles had completed his rehabilitation, I was a little concerned that the travel would affect his recovery. Nevertheless, Charles was excited about the trip, and we were both looking forward to it. The past twelve months had been an emotional roller coaster that started with my accident and the Carnegie Hall concert and ended with Charles' hip fracture and our current struggle to finance an overseas concert. Therefore, the weeklong trip was much more than a vacation; it was a perfectly timed respite from a tumultuous year.

Flying into Washington, D.C., we rented a minivan with the plan of doing some sightseeing in the capital before driving north along the eastern seaboard into New England. Even with the traffic along the I-95 corridor being its usual hectic pace, the drive felt relaxing. After leaving D.C., our first stop was in Manhattan where we spent time shopping and reminiscing. It was a Sunday afternoon; the streets and sidewalks were unusually clear for New York, and we decided to go for a leisurely stroll. The relative scarcity of people was ideal since Charles required an electric scooter for any extended ambulation. Of course, there was the recent memory of the concert just months before, but as we made our way toward Times Square, we passed the New York Sheraton at which point Charles remarked about the last time he stayed there. It had been more than forty years since when we were first married, and he had been a hotel guest there as a junior executive with Mercury Records. Feeling as if we had stepped back in time, the three of us stopped in front of the hotel to embrace the nostalgia while Todd asked Charles questions pertaining to his life in the early 1960s. Listening to his answers brought a warm glow to my heart. I could feel the memories, and they made me smile.

The following day we left New York and continued our trek into New England where the reminiscing would continue. The short drive into Connecticut took us hours because of the traffic congestion. Despite this, I was especially excited about our next visit because I was going to see someone that would take me back to the frolic days of my youth of the 1950s. We finally arrived at a beautiful suburban home in West Hartford. After ringing the doorbell, the front door was opened by a small-framed, distinguished-looking woman. Although it had been nearly five decades since I had last seen her, time had been exceedingly kind to her. As soon as she saw me, both her eyes and arms opened wide with delight.

"Earnestine!" she exclaimed as she grabbed and hugged me.

It was Erness, my dear friend and music teacher from Douglass High School. The last time that I saw her was in 1956. We were both ecstatic with joy. The decades spent away from one another seemed to disappear in a flash as we fell into laughter and conversation. We fellowshipped and dined with Erness and her husband at their home as if a day had not been missed. Before we left the following day, we promised one another that we would never again lose touch. Todd continued our trip with Charles navigating our way through picturesque back roads, making stops in Newport, Rhode Island, and Martha's Vineyard before returning to Washington, D.C.

Throughout the trip I was constantly receiving updates from Michelle in Memphis. We were still waiting for a decision from the Memphis Arts Council, and in my absence, Michelle had become the contact person and my representative for any last-minute requests and additional meetings. One day, she called; her voice was bubbling with excitement when she told me that the Memphis Arts Council had agreed on sponsoring me. It was the news that we had been hoping to hear. The following morning, she called again, but her voice did not hold the same excitement. When she told me the amount of the donation, the reason for her deflated tone was readily clear; it was only a fraction of the amount that we needed. I hung up the phone, feeling dejected. I was so disappointed that I did not have the heart to tell Charles or Todd the crushing news. Instead, I just prayed quietly to myself.

That day as we drove past countless scenes of lush countryside, I was so consumed by my thoughts that my senses could not fully appreciate the beauty passing outside the window. My mind was being bombarded by questions of what had gone wrong with the Arts Council, but the mental exercise was a futile one because there were no obvious answers. Besides, the conclusion was the same. We had come up short despite doing everything that we could. But my disappointment did not stop my believing that God would deliver His promise; so, I continued to pray. The miles and hours flew past without my registering them until my phone rang again. It was Michelle. The excitement had returned to her voice, and before I could ask what happened, she blurted out, "We got the money! The Arts Council has increased the amount of the grant to $23,000."

I shouted, "Hallelujah! We're going to Prague!"

Todd sponsored the remaining amount, and we all shared the jubilation. The major hurdle had been successfully cleared, and we were on our way to Europe. The only thing left to do was to finish up the final preparations that included shipping the orchestral scores and obtaining everyone's passport. The passport issue turned out to be not as simple as I initially envisioned. For me, the process of obtaining a birth certificate, taking a photo, and filling out the paper work in a timely manner in order to meet our travel deadline was easy and straightforward. But I was only one person. There were sixteen others who had to do the same thing. That was the problem, and it took considerable effort making sure that everybody had their passport. Traveling to Prague with me was a relatively large group, which included my cousin, Asaline, my niece, Joyce, my grandchildren, my sons and daughters, and their spouses,

John and Maria. It was a delight to have my four young grandchildren with me; their ages ranged from 2 to 5 years old, and looking back, it was truly amazing how well they did on an international trip. After months of planning, everything was set, but there was one notable exception – Charles could not travel with us.

After the vacation to the East Coast, Charles informed me that he would not be making the trip to Prague. His news saddened me, but we both knew the reason why. Although he had enjoyed the vacation, it was physically taxing. Not at any time during the trip did he complain, but at the end of each day the fatigue on his face was noticeable. The vacation made it painfully clear that despite his resilience and desire, he did not have the stamina for the European trip. Although he had never mentioned it before, he was aware that he had not fully recovered from the surgery. We both knew it, but this was the first time that he had ever voiced his fragility to me. It was heartbreaking to hear his words, and I thought to myself, how could I make the trip without him? The person, who had pushed and encouraged me through the failures and was there when no one else was around, was now staying behind as I was making one of my greatest triumphs. First, I considered not going. The rest of my family could easily represent me at the event, but I knew that Charles wanted me to go. My heart warred with the conflict. I wanted to stay behind and care for him, but I prayed for direction. In the end, I decided to take the trip to Prague. My decision felt a little easier when Craig decided to stay back home and look after his Dad. Even my sister, Doris, volunteered to bring food over for the both of them – although I found out later that both Charles and Craig were looking forward to eating takeout every night. Nevertheless, I boarded the plane with a feeling that something was missing.

Two layovers and thirteen hours later we landed in Prague. Upon our exit from the plane, the changes were gradual at first. There were still the universal icons and English subtitles for "restrooms" and "baggage claim," but walking down the corridor toward Customs, I noticed that some of the usual colorful advertisements were in a language that was foreign to me. Of course, these visual changes were similar to our stop in Amsterdam, but we had very little time between flights. As a result, our time in the Holland airport was a blur with all of our energy spent running to find our terminal and make our connection. However, when we reached our final destination in the Czech Republic, I was more relaxed and better able to absorb my surroundings. After we had exchanged some of our money into Czech crown, hailed a shuttle and started our transit to the hotel, the transformation was complete. The billboards and street signs were all in Czech; even the houses and buildings had a different look to them. Our hotel, Hilton Prague, was adjacent to Congress Hall where my concert was being held. We had only a few hours before rehearsal, but we were eager to see the city. Despite the long trip, we forgot about getting any sleep and immediately set out to explore. Even though it was bitterly cold, we decided to walk, making our introduction into the surrounding culture all the more dramatic.

The aristocratic splendor of Prague was beyond my imagination. Walking the streets of Old Town and touring Prague Castle, I was mesmerized by the gothic architecture and the vast array of church spires, piercing the Czech sky. It was amusing to think that my footsteps had taken me from the gravel roads of my segregated neighborhood to the cobbled stones of the Charles Bridge built over 400 years ago. Just as captivating as the scenery of Prague was the idea of having a world-class symphony performing my work. Rushing back to the hotel, I was eager to hear the symphony practice my music.

During rehearsal the soprano soloist, Simona Prochazkova, delivered an electrifying performance of "Magnificat," which left us all spellbound. The sound of her voice lingered with me long after she had finished singing. Jiri Sulzenko, the baritone soloist, also gave a masterful performance. Sitting there, it was hard for me to believe that I was actually in Prague, listening to the Czech National Symphony Orchestra perform my oratorio, "The Nativity." My music was being played in a land known for its great composers. I knew that just 50 miles away was the place where Dvorak reigned. He had always been one of my favorite composers, and the more that I thought about his contributions and other master composers like him, the more glaring the contrast was of my work. Then, I questioned myself, "How are the people here going to accept my music?"

On the evening of the concert, I was still a bit nervous. It did not help matters much when I noticed that the orchestral hall was surrounded by bomb-sniffing dogs and several armed security personnel, some of them carrying automatic rifles. Todd had alerted me that there were a number of snipers perched on surrounding rooftops. Cars were being screened for explosives, and all hotel guests were being carefully asked to show identification. It was the most intense security that I had ever personally witnessed, and I did not know why until after the performance when I found out that there were so many dignitaries from several foreign countries.

Before the concert started, I was pleasantly surprised to read the program. The order of the program and my narration were written in both English and Czech. It was a memorable moment because it was the first time that my work had been translated into another language. Once the house lights dimmed, the concert began; it was incredible and judging from the audience they enjoyed my music. The Kuhn's Children's Choir singing "The Holy Child" and "A Savior Is Born," swept the audience off their feet.

I was told by one of the singers that the entire music community of Prague had come out to hear the concert. My joy could not be more complete. After the performance of my work, there was a brief intermission. Many had moved out of the auditorium and into the adjoining hall when I found myself being greeted by a distinguished gentleman. There was nothing out of the ordinary about him except he was surrounded by several very stern looking men that I later found out were his security detail. The gentleman extended his hand and introduced himself.

"Hello. I'm Arthur Avnon, the ambassador of Israel."

As I shook his hand, I smiled and said, "It's so nice to meet you."

Then he continued, "To be honest with you, when I left home this evening, I said to myself, 'I know that nothing will be said or done that will be uplifting to me.' But you mentioned my country several times. Your music is beautiful; you are very talented."

Again, I smiled and said, "Thank you."

As my son, Gaius and I stood talking with Ambassador Avnon, we were joined by Ambassador Christophoros Yiangou of the Republic of Cyprus, who came to tell me how he, too, had enjoyed my music. Before I could collect myself, the Ambassador of South Africa, Dr. Noel Lehoko and his wife came over and hugged me. When the concert ended, we were invited to the banquet hall for one of the most lavish receptions that I have ever seen. The setting was extravagant, the food was delicious and bountiful, and the people were so warm and wonderful. Throughout the evening they continually expressed to my family and me how they had enjoyed my music. I was greatly moved when a German opera director, unable to say in English what he felt about my music, began to pat his chest to let me know that my music had touched his heart.

At my premieres in New York people came from the surrounding states, but in Prague people came from the surrounding countries. It was a triumphant event and a marvelous experience. After the performance, I was invited to return to Prague to present my oratorio, "The Crucifixion." Unfortunately, my husband became very ill and I was unable to do so at that time. But I hope one day to return to Prague for a performance of my oratorio, "The Crucifixion."

Chapter 21

Dark before Daybreak

It was good to get back home, and I could hardly wait to tell Charles all that had happened in Prague. But Todd had a bolder plan of recounting our journey. My son-in-law, John, who is married to Michelle, had borrowed his parents' video camera in order to capture the memories of our trip, and Todd, who had become fascinated with the easy-to-use technology of Apple's iMovie, wanted to take John's video and make a home movie for Charles.

Days later, while Todd was working on his idea, Michelle and I were having a meeting with the director and staff of the Memphis Arts Council. They wanted to hear about the outcome of the concert. As we recounted how wonderful the trip and concert were, I was absolutely stunned when the chairperson turned to us and said, "Since you have visuals of your trip, if it's okay, I would like for you to show a five-minute video presentation for our annual donors' dinner next week." The request was so jarring that both Michelle and I automatically flinched before gathering our composure. We did have some footage of the rehearsal but not of the concert itself. But it was the words, "video presentation" and "next week," that shocked us the most, and we both instinctively knew that we could not turn down the request from the group that had sponsored our trip. For the next several minutes she gave us details about the dinner and that all of their top donors would be there. While Michelle gathered more information, I slipped out and called Todd to alert him regarding the change in plans. As soon as I got home, I joined Todd as our original idea of a home movie transformed into a full-fledged video presentation. That weekend, Todd and I spent day and night sitting in front of a computer with instructional manuals and video tapes, trying to put together a short video that would be suitable enough for the donors' dinner. On the night of the function, I gave a brief speech, thanked the Council and was warmly congratulated. We hired a soloist and harpist to perform, "Magnificat," the title song of my oratorio, "The Nativity," and, of course, there was the film clip. Much to the delight of the donors and the surprise of my family, the video was a huge success. And just mere days after showing the Prague clip at the Memphis Arts Council dinner, the idea of our next project was born – putting together a documentary.

Everyone in the family was bursting with a flurry of suggestions about our new project. Todd had already started an outline and had also decided to expand the scope of the project beyond Prague to include my entire journey. In addition to mapping out a detailed storyline, we began driving around the Memphis area and into nearby rural Arkansas, collecting content for the documentary. It was exciting traveling from place to place, hearing stories and reliving memories that were tagged to old family photographs that we came across and scanned into our laptop computer. We also took video footage of everything that we thought would pertain to our film. At one point, we found ourselves coasting slowly down a remote country road while we hung a camera out the window, shooting video. Nothing, no matter how seemingly insignificant, was ignored. Then, there were the interviews. In this area, Michelle was very helpful; she was instrumental in getting even the most anxious person relaxed enough to tell their story.

Everything was moving at a quick pace as the project took shape and grew. For months we spent every possible moment working on the documentary. Todd, who was working extra moonlighting jobs in order to buy new computers and audio equipment, spent all of his free time shooting footage and studying professional film software. When it came time to edit the film, the three of us, Todd, Michelle and I, joined forces while the rest of the family gave their critiques along the entire process. It was truly a collaborative effort, and by the time we had finished, we had surprisingly managed to create some buzz surrounding the project. It was remarkable that just within the span of six months, we had gone from an obscure idea to getting the attention of various film producers. All of our efforts were coming together, and everything was flowing smoothly. But there was something else rapidly approaching, an unexpected event that would be so pivotal that it would affect my entire family and especially me.

Though for the moment, we were all simply enjoying the excitement generated by the film project. Charles, who was especially enthralled by all of the rapid developments, waited every day to hear the latest updates. If I were too slow in delivering any news, he would start asking questions but only a few poignant ones, just enough to get me wound up to relay everything. This had always been his usual pattern whenever he wanted to hear me talk. Besides the obvious advantage of receiving information, I think that my talking also helped him to relax. Often, if I sensed that he was feeling a bit down or tense, I would strike up a one-sided conversation just to lift his spirits. Ever since I first met him, I always knew that Charles was not the overly talkative type. He rarely expressed his innermost feelings, but anybody, who had spent any amount of time around him, knew what he cared about most – his family. Outside of work, he spent all of his remaining time at home. He centered all of his extracurricular activities around his family. Whether it was family vacations, playing basketball with his sons, registering his children in classes or discussing business with me, he relished spending time with his family, and most of that time usually occurred within our home.

Therefore, it was not out of the ordinary that he was spending one particular evening, relaxing in his chair in the den. However, what he said next was out of the ordinary. It was just the two of us in the house, and when I first heard his voice, I thought that he was trying to get my attention.

"Earnestine. I have to exchange this house for a new

house, Earnestine." His words were precise and emphatic. I was stunned, but before I could think, he repeated his statement.

"Earnestine. I have to exchange this house for a new house, Earnestine."

The way he said my name at the beginning and the end really grabbed my attention. He kept repeating the same words over and over again. With each reiteration, the message sank deeper and deeper inside me. Not believing what I was hearing and not wanting to accept its ominous tone, I went into the den in hopes of uncovering a different explanation. Coming down the hallway, the words seem to echo off the walls and, in my head, but the message was still the same. Strangely, when I got to Charles, he was fast asleep not saying anything. Standing there, stunned and looking at him, my heart nervously pounded in my chest. I did not know what to do or say. I wanted to wake him and ask questions. But I knew the meaning of what he had said, and the mysterious nature of how it occurred would not let me forget that it happened. I never did ask him about it. There was not much time; Charles ended up back in the hospital, and this time, things would be different.

The admitting doctor diagnosed him with congestive heart failure. It was the same diagnosis as my mother, but Charles' course was totally different from hers. Unlike my mother, his symptoms did not follow a slow pattern of deterioration; with him everything started the very day after his last hip surgery. With that single incident, everything changed. Prior to that operation, with the exception of his balance problem, he was doing well. He had no complaints and was only taking one tablet for his blood pressure and one for his cholesterol, but after the hip surgery, his health turned upside down. The problems first started with his slow and difficult physical therapy, but then came the complications. Medicine that he had been taking for years was now causing problems and adverse reactions. His heart, which had only required minimal attention, had now suddenly become his greatest concern.

Sitting in a hospital room was becoming a familiar occurrence, and watching a nurse place an intravenous line, or as it is commonly called, an "IV," in Charles' arm was a routine that I never gave a second thought. But this time, it was not routine. 1 will never forget what unfolded. In fact, months later, I would reflect back to the very moment in time when this particular IV nurse did her routine duty. When she started, everything seemed normal, but very quickly everything became a bloody mess. At one point the nurse turned and asked me, "Did he have a blood thinner?" Not being a medical person, I was surprised at her question. As she fumbled through her ineptness of dropping items on the floor, her hands seemed to be all over the place, grabbing and picking up things, and all the while blood poured out of his arm.

"May I help you," a harsh voice blurted out of the bed's intercom. The voice startled the IV nurse who was unaware that Charles, using his other hand, had pushed the help button to make the call.

"Yeah. You guys need to send somebody in here. This nurse needs help," he replied in a matter-of-fact manner.

That horrible bloody scene was the first unforgettable memory of that hospitalization; my second one was far worse. According to the doctors, Charles was improving and close to being released, but to me he seemed more sleepy than usual which concerned me. There was nothing specific or alarming that I could pinpoint about his condition, just a feeling of something being wrong that I could not shake. I sat in a chair at the foot of his bed, and I looked at him.

"Charles?"

His eyes stared at me, and his breathing had started to become more labored.

"Charles, what's wrong?"

He said nothing, and immediately I called for help. Within minutes the room was swarming with medical personnel, and I was escorted out. More medical staff ran past me down the hallway toward Charles' room. It felt as if my heart was being squeezed. During the chaos I called Todd and the rest of my children, and soon thereafter Charles was transferred to the intensive care unit. That was my second unforgettable memory of that hospitalization.

After being in the intensive care unit, the primary cause for his decline was soon discovered. He had developed a hospital-acquired infection that was in his blood, and my mind immediately flashed back to that dreaded day of the bloody IV placement. Now Charles was in septic shock, lying in the ICU hooked to a ventilator with multiple bags of antibiotics and medicines flowing into his body. The hours turned into days as my family and I staked out a constant presence at the hospital. Charles slipped in and out of consciousness as the infection took its toll, but he fought back. Even the doctors, who were amazed by his resilience, commented to me on several occasions that they could not understand how Charles could sometimes be so alert and follow simple commands despite his teetering on the brink of death.

It was almost two weeks later when the ICU specialist decided to move the breathing tube from Charles' mouth to his neck. The doctor explained to me all of the medical reasons why this was being done, but for me, I was glad to see the change because I knew that he would be more comfortable with the tube out of his mouth and it would allow me to see his face more naturally and to communicate with him. After the procedure was done, there was a noticeable improvement in Charles' mood. Whenever I spoke to him, he would now open his eyes with the sense of a greeting that would always make me smile. On one occasion, he looked straight at me as if to get my attention and mouthed the word, "talk." My heart skipped with joy. I was still believing in his recovery despite all the bad news that I was being told every day. Gradually, he did improve, and his status was eventually upgraded so that he was moved out of the ICU and into a monitored room. I was relieved, and even though his condition was still considered to be guarded, I was not giving up.

The children and I spent around-the-clock shifts with him. I would arrive early in the morning and stay late into the evening, sometimes spending the night. Todd even hired a private nurse to be with him during the night when a family member could not stay, not wanting him to have a single moment without a familiar face. When he was having a good day, Charles would beckon me to talk about what was going on with the film project. I thought that maybe this was a sign that he was getting better, signaling his complete recovery. However, it was not long before he relapsed and was back in the intensive care unit, again struggling for his life. The time allowed for ICU visitation was very restrictive, only six slots per day and each session was only thirty minutes. But the children and I would spend every minute talking around his bed as if we were sitting in the family den; it was something that we all knew he liked. Sometimes at the end of the visit he would wake up briefly and at other times he would not. Regardless, if he opened his eyes or not, before leaving, I would always touch him on the shoulder and whisper a scriptural prayer that I had heard so much as a little girl:

The Lord bless thee, and keep thee:
The Lord make his face shine upon thee, and be
  gracious unto thee:
The Lord lift up his countenance upon thee, and
  give thee peace.
                              Numbers 6:24-26

    Day and night, I prayed. Although I was aware of his grave prognosis, I prayed that God would just give me a little more time with Charles. After leaving the ICU one night I was determined to pray all night for his recovery, but I heard a voice saying, "Yea, though I walk through the valley of the shadow of death. I will fear no evil: for thou art with me." Of course, I knew the popular scripture, and as soon as I heard the words, I knew that God would be comforting me through what I was about to face. But I also knew what it meant for Charles.

    For almost two months Charles fought a tenacious battle to overcome the hospital infection, but he was slowly becoming weaker. Despite my unyielding hope for his recovery, I could feel the end drawing closer. And the time with Charles was becoming even more precious. All of our children in Memphis were spending every possible moment with him at the hospital, and Cheryle would frequently fly into town from Chicago. When the situation became extremely grave, Cheryle spent the week in Memphis. Her arrival was a fresh addition and a relieving buffer between me and the doctors who were incessant in bringing me constant dire updates. It was great having her with me to answer calls from the hospital. As Cheryle stood at his bedside, it reminded me of a time a year ago when she was visiting, and his condition was not as serious. Lying in a hospital bed, he turned his attention to her and asked a startling question, "Cheryle, what do you want out of life?"

We all knew that Charles was a man of deep thought and he always had a way of surprising you at the least expected moment, but this question really stunned everyone in the room. Cheryle, faced with an age-old and life-defining question, was taken off guard and stumbled to give an answer. She was not the only one. I could tell from the faces of our other children in the room that they were all stunned by the question. So, in an attempt to rescue her, I turned the question back to Charles, asking, "What do you want out of life?"

Without hesitation, he answered firmly, "I have everything." The room went completely silent. Imagine a man that sick saying that he had everything. It melted my heart.

Now, a year later, Cheryle, Michelle and I flanked each side of Charles' bed again, talking, but deep in our own thoughts. It was Saturday, and Cheryle was having her last visit with her Dad before she left for the airport. Craig and Gaius were in the adjoining area, waiting for their chance to swap out with my daughters. The hospital would only allow three people at a time to visit inside the ICU room.

Eventually, Cheryle and I left the hospital and made our way to the car to head to the airport. I opened the car door and got in. But before I could close the door, a dove flew over and landed on my outside rearview mirror. It was so peaceful the way it perched within arm's length. We both sat silently, staring at it. After about ten-seconds, it flew away. Neither of us could bear to say what we were thinking. But quietly within, we knew that the end was near.

Early the next day, Todd and I arrived for the first ICU visit of the day. It was 6:30, Sunday morning, October 26, 2003. As I entered Charles' intensive care room, the images of that visit crystalized in my mind. As he lay there, I went over and whispered a prayer in his ear, assuring him that God was with him. The television in the room was on a sports channel and its volume was turned up which was a bit unusual. But Charles had a new nurse that morning who was obviously a football fan. It only took me a few moments to realize that it was an old game between Ohio State and Michigan and I smiled. Being born and raised in Columbus and attending Ohio State himself, Charles was an intense Buckeye fan and football was his favorite sport. My mind flashed to the images of him at our home, sitting and occasionally jumping out of his chair to yell, "Hot dog!" at the Ohio State football players when they made a touchdown. It was a weekend ritual that I had witnessed for 43 years; in fact, I remember the first time he took me to a homecoming game at Ohio State when we were first married. There was such a look of joy and excitement on his face as we sat in the football stadium on that wonderful autumn day. That moment seemed so far away but yet so close. Oblivious to the heart monitor beeping in the background, I smiled again and touched his hand. The familiar touch made me reminisce about a recent time only months ago when Charles had kissed my hand. It was so unexpected, but one day, he reached out, grabbed my hand and said, "There are very few things in this world that are precious, but you are precious." Then, he kissed the back of my hand and turned away. I didn't know what provoked the sentiment, but I was so moved that I did not ask. Now, I stood by his bed, holding his hand and sensing the end. It was only hours later that Charles passed away.

The loss was suffocating. I felt like a part of me had been cut off, and the pain was far worse than I could have imagined. It was good that my children planned all the funeral arrangements because everything seemed like a blur as if I was lost in a fog. Most of my memory of that time immediately following his death consisted of only images of the many visitors to the house, a seemingly endless delivery of gifts, flowers and food and a glowing article about Charles in the local newspaper. Even though I tried to make myself eat, the pounds disappeared off of me, and things did not get much better after the burial. I did not know how I was going to make it; each hour of the day seemed like a struggle and sleep provided no relief. Some days were easier to get through than others, and then there were days where it was hard just to get out of the bed.

Even though I was trying to keep up a strong outwardly appearance, I was still just going through the motions. It was difficult. There were constant reminders of Charles – the way our grandson sat in his chair or the sounds of a football game that appeared on the television. Everything reminded me of Charles. But, in February, there was one startling incident that really grabbed my attention. It occurred while I was shopping in a grocery store that was nearly empty. I moved around the store, slowly pushing my shopping cart with my mind only partially engaged in the activity. The other part was preoccupied with Charles' passing as I kept thinking if only I had a little more time with him. It was a recurring thought that kept rolling through my mind as I shopped, and even though I was only picking up a few items, my time in the store was drawn out. Then, standing next to my cart, I stopped at one spot and spent several minutes studying the nutritional label of various fruit juices. There was no one in my aisle except a store employee who was busily stocking food. After finally making my decision and placing the item in my basket, I discovered a Valentine Day's card that was mysteriously lying on top of my groceries. Perplexed and looking around to see who else was near me, I paused before reading the front of the Hallmark card – "For My Wife." My first impulse was that somebody was playing a cruel joke on me, but as I looked around there was no one except the stocker who was very involved in his own duties. Now, I was startled and a little frightened. Finally, I opened it and read:

> *It's an uncertain world that we live in*
> *where so much keeps changing so fast,*
> *And things that we thought we could count on,*
> *too soon become things of the past.*
> *So with all of my heart I feel grateful*
> *for the one precious part of my life...*

The message was so shocking that I just stood there mesmerized. The unexplained way the card appeared in the shopping cart was miraculous, but the very choice of the words themselves were also so remarkable as if Charles himself wrote them for me and placed it in my basket. For several moments, I stood in amazement. Finally, I decided that I wanted to find the envelope that matched the card. I was so dazed that I had trouble finding the greeting card section in the store. It was such an incredible occurrence that I purchased the card and mounted it in a frame, and to this day, it still warms my heart whenever I read those words.

My period of mourning had other welcomed moments of soothing relief. Our documentary and the subsequent promise of a movie with all of its energy, meetings and travel was a welcome distraction. But the distraction was only short-lived. My healing and the fanfare of the movie project unexpectedly came to a halt due to a string of catastrophic events. It first started with a call that my sister, Betty, who lived in Los Angeles, had been injured in a house fire. After flying to California, four and a half months after Charles passed, I was again sitting in the familiar territory of an ICU waiting room, and my emotional wounds started to reopen as I watched my sister die. Then, a year later, I lost another sister, Odesser, but the shock would continue as nine months after her passing I sat at the bedside of my third and last remaining sister, Doris, while she took her final breath. With each funeral, a little piece of me was buried along with each loss, and the part of me that remained was now numb.

Even though I felt like I was walking in a daze, in the back of my mind I knew that I had to make steps to improve, but the grief was so extensive. One day Michelle came over and with a burst of excitement in her voice, she said to me, "Mom, I know what your next oratorio should be about The Ten Commandments. Although I thought that she was probably trying to lift my spirits, I wondered what had brought this on. Then, she told me. She had watched a news segment where the reporter randomly interviewed people, asking each to name one or more of the Ten Commandments. And after interviewing a dozen or more people, only a few could provide one or two of the Ten Commandments. I looked at her in disbelief, and then I said, "Most definitely, I accept the challenge."

Over the next several weeks, I searched the Holy Scripture, ordered books and read day and night as I began the journey of composing, "Exodus." As I began the first song, "Cry of the People," I was also crying for the loss of my loved ones, and I suddenly realized that I was too heavy with grief to allow the music to flow out of me. All of my suffering had choked my spirit to such an extent that any creative aspirations had been nullified, allowing only my despair to thrive. I needed more time to heal, and God provided the path of my recovery.

My rehabilitation occurred in the most sublime manner. Whenever I would feel a surge of grief rising uncontrollably within me, I would quickly shift my focus away from the pain of the loss and reflect only on the wonderful times that we had shared. Then, I would thank God for giving me time with them. Remarkably, this provided relief, but it was only transient. As a result, I learned to frequently repeat this ritual of redirection and positive thinking, and over time the relief became more permanent. The use of this approach was especially poignant with the passing of my last sister, Doris. Every time that I came into the den and would see a picture of her, I would immediately feel the familiar knife of grief as if someone was stabbing my heart. My first impulse was to simply remove her picture so as to not be reminded. But instead, I decided to leave the photograph where it was and deal with the grief. I had resolved within myself that I would not move it until I was able to walk past it without feeling the pain.

It was an epic internal struggle—the darkest period of my life. Each day I was greeted with constant reminders of my sorrow and each day I repeatedly redirected my thoughts to memories of joy or some other subject matter. The battle waged on as days turned into weeks and the weeks into months. But I refused to succumb to the dark clouds, to be boxed in by gloom; I fought back during every waking moment by focusing only on the light. Finally, the darkness retreated, and a lasting peace came to rest over me—a peace that could only be obtained from being victorious. After enduring the loss of my husband and three sisters in rapid succession, there was no permanent scar of anguish, only the calm of understanding.

Chapter 22

Secret of My Success

The veil of my sorrow had lifted, and with the change I began to feel like myself again. Walking through my house, melodies began to flow into my heart and out of my mouth as I started composing, "Exodus." My sadness had miraculously been replaced with a budding joy, and the smoldering fog of grief that had blanketed my children also began to dissipate as the entire family started to swing back into their normal rhythm. Todd revisited the film project and decided to do a major overhaul of the documentary which also meant my being heavily involved in the project. Back to our usual weekly brainstorming sessions at the coffee shop, we also resumed our schedule of video shooting and interviewing; and once again, Michelle joined the project along with the rest of my children adding their input. The final film actually consisted of two versions: a short film entitled, "Sounds of a Miracle," and the longer feature length called, "Hidden Treasure." Along with the completion of the film, I also had finished my newest oratorio, "Exodus," and before long, I had an offer for my third world premiere at Carnegie Hall.

The tempo of my daily life had been turned up, and everything was coming together. Our original idea of a home movie was now a biographical film; all of the past triumphs and struggles had been chronicled and merged with my music into a documentary that Todd was now submitting to film festivals. Prior to the start of this project, none of us knew much about the logistics of film festivals, but like everything else that we had embarked upon, we learned quickly as we entered one festival after another. The whole ordeal of submitting our film, waiting for a decision and the ability of tracking our progress through the selection process fueled our excitement. There was one particular website that provided festival updates and acceptance notifications in addition to a blog where filmmakers could post their joys and grievances. Of course, Todd followed it closely which added to the allurement of our quest. Every day when we talked, the discussion was often filled with the promise of being selected. Any rejection that we received caused the usual disappointment, but after receiving a declining notification, we would immediately redirect our attention to the deadline of our next festival entry. Finally, we hit success with the Hoboken

International Film Festival. It was our first festival and "Hidden Treasure" was selected for their screening. But the short film, "Sounds of a Miracle" proved to be more successful in the long run. It was selected for several prestigious festivals: LA Shorts Fest, Rhode Island International Film Festival, Nashville Film Festival, Charlotte Film Festival, Palm Beach International Film Festival, and Indie Memphis, a hometown festival. My family and I were crisscrossing the country, screening our film and talking to festivalgoers. It was all so exciting.

There was one festival that was especially memorable for the most surprising reason. It had been raining all day, but the auditorium was packed with a crowd that was a colorful menagerie of America. Yet, despite their varied backgrounds, they had all assembled with a common interest of watching a documentary about my story of becoming a composer. As the final credits rolled off the screen behind me, the house lights were turned up and I nervously stood, front and center on the stage, and watched a host of hands being raised. At the end of a film festival screening, it is customary for the audience members to ask questions of the filmmakers and those connected to the film. Noticing a nicely dressed woman near the front, I picked her first. She appeared closer to my age and perhaps that is why I connected with her. She stood and asked, "How do you pray?"

I was stunned; my mind momentarily froze. Why would someone ask me a question like that at a film festival? Despite the awkwardness, I somehow managed to give her an answer, but that question stuck with me and lingered in my mind. It was not long afterwards that I began to realize that most of the inquiries at those festivals were begging the same type of question. This was not just the curiosity of someone seeking a piece of trivia or a simple factoid. These questions were deeper; they were philosophical queries related to "how" and "why." And I often struggled to give an answer; but it was not because of a lack of understanding. I knew what they sought. I could feel all of their answers inside me, but the challenge was verbalizing the response in a succinct manner.

Probing over my entire past, I searched for the one thing to explain it all—the secret of my success. And every search for this truth led me repeatedly to one incident— one bitter disappointment that became the turning point for my music and for me. Several years after I began composing music, I was presented with the opportunity of speaking to the internationally acclaimed opera singer, Leontyne Price. A friend of mine, Emily Adams, heard my song, "The Crucifixion," and loved it and thought it was the perfect song for Leontyne Price to perform. Emily, who grew up in Laurel, Mississippi, the birthplace of Ms. Price, knew relatives of hers in their hometown and was able to get her phone number in Manhattan.

One Sunday afternoon, I gathered the courage to call Ms. Price. After introducing myself and briefly sharing my story, I asked if I could send her a score of "The Crucifixion." I told her that I hoped she would like it and would be interested in performing it. The first words out of her mouth were, "How did you get my number?"

I simply said, "A friend."

She was livid. It was shocking to hear the level of rage in her voice. It was as though she were saying, "How dare a peon with no significance in her world, have the audacity to call and ask her to perform an unknown work." She became irate with me and ended our very brief conversation. What bothered me most was not that she didn't want to perform my music, but it was her harsh and demeaning manner in which she spoke to me. I was crushed to tears, and asked

God, "Am I ever going to get my music out?" He whispered, "If you persevere."

At that point, I realized that it was not going to be easy, but if I were to get my music out, I had to have faith and persevere against all odds. That was the secret.

Now, film audiences were asking, "How?" How was I able to wade through all of the obstacles, despair and hardships, through the dark corners of life, and come out shining on the other end? Beyond the images and sounds of the movie, they were trying to make sense of the unexplainable. They understood my story – that I was a woman, Black, from the South and that I had started with nothing. It was simple enough to understand that the idea of my having dreams and disappointments was nothing more than just the normal fabric of human nature, and there was nothing mystical about my getting married or the birth of my children. Those milestones, while special to any individual, are only normal events in the timeline of life. However, after viewing the documentary, the audience members started to assemble the pieces of my life, and a new realization was taking form in their minds. My existence was not just a list of random events; there was a pattern – a hidden, embedded code directing my path that could not be explained away by mere chance. Even without my knowledge, my life was a well-sculpted plan – a purposeful roadmap with each seemingly insignificant detail being an essential step toward my destination. Everything had fallen into alignment.

Looking at my story as it flowed across the movie screen, it had become apparent that each random part of my life, both good and bad, was actually a string of synchronized events that led to my standing at that film festival. Now, the main question on the minds of the people was, how did this happen? They all saw a woman who had spent years searching; yet, throughout my bewilderment, there was a paradoxical serenity. In the midst of the unknown, I had unknowingly moved step by step to my destiny, and all of this was done without wealth, advanced degrees, or even a plan. While I had failed and struggled on many accounts, I had accomplished the unthinkable; all of the dark times were actually blessings in disguise, and as that audience pondered this contradiction and searched for the secret of my success, they discovered one prevailing thread – a woman who prayed every day for guidance. And each day God provided direction. Sometimes it was a voice, a dream, or scripture and sometimes it was simply an emotion. But it was always God.

In the film there was the joy and inspiration of my music, and there was also the discovery of purpose that was born out of my faith and struggle. It was during the struggle that I was driven by faith and learned to fight to overcome every obstacle. As I reflect back on it now, faith became my guiding force along with perseverance and positive thinking. So, it is my hope that my music will uplift for generations to come and that my story will inspire others, young and old, to pursue their dreams. I thank God for a purposeful life. It is a resounding joy and a never-ending melody!

www.ingramcontent.com/pod-product-compliance
Lightning Source LLC
Chambersburg PA
CBHW031430160426
43195CB00010BB/676